INFORMATION
PROCESSING
concepts, principles, and procedures

James F. Clark

Fulton County Schools
Atlanta, Georgia

Judith J. Lambrecht

University of Minnesota
Minneapolis, Minnesota

Published by

J54 **SOUTH-WESTERN PUBLISHING CO.**

CINCINNATI   WEST CHICAGO, IL   DALLAS   PELHAM MANOR, NY   PALO ALTO, CA

Copyright © 1985

by

South-Western Publishing Co.

Cincinnati, Ohio

ISBN: 0-538-10540-2

Library of Congress Catalog Card Number: 84-50782

1 2 3 4 5 6 7 8 9 10 D 3 2 1 0 9 8 7 6 5 4

Printed in the United States of America

Preface

The effects of computer use have become an everyday part of your life. Whether you use a computer yourself or just interact with the output of computers used by others, it is important to understand this machine that is having such an impact on all of us. The principal goals of this book, therefore, are to introduce you to the many uses of computers and to help you learn the way in which computers process information. You will learn to speak and read several languages used with computers. Not only are these languages used in business, but they are popular in everyday life. In addition to learning how to communicate with computers, you will also learn how to write directions for computers in order to solve many kinds of problems.

Computers can be used in so many ways that only a small number of their applications can be covered in this book. Still, you should be able to understand the ways in which computers are being used in today's world to make this journey into the Information Age worthwhile.

To help you develop a deeper understanding of the concepts presented in the text, each chapter concludes with review questions. All new terms introduced and defined in a chapter are listed at the end of that chapter. These aids should be used to help you check your understanding of the material covered. If the questions and problems seem difficult, reread the material covering them.

A workbook is available for the text. The workbook contains various types of study guides and exercises designed to reinforce your understanding of the principles and procedures introduced in each chapter. Also available is a set of applications for the computer. These applications, available on diskette for the Apple® II[1], IBM[2], and TRS-80®[3] microcomputers, will help reinforce your understanding.

If your goal is computer literacy, you will find that this text and its accompanying materials are all you need. If your goal is a career in information systems, these materials will develop the foundation upon which to base advanced studies.

---

[1]Apple® II Plus, Apple® IIe, and Applesoft® are registered trademarks of Apple Computer, Inc. Any reference to Apple II Plus, Apple IIe, or Applesoft refers to this footnote.

[2]IBM is a registered trademark of International Business Machines. Any reference to the IBM or the IBM Personal Computer refers to this footnote.

[3]TRS-80® is a trademark of the Radio Shack Division of Tandy Corporation. Any reference to the TRS-80 or to the Radio Shack Microcomputer refers to this footnote.

COBOL ACKNOWLEDGMENT

The following acknowledgment is reprinted from *American National Standard Programming Language COBOL, X3.23-1974* published by the American National Standards Institute, Inc.

Any organization interested in reproducing the COBOL standard and specifications in whole or in part, using ideas from this document as the basis for an instruction manual or for any other purpose, is free to do so. However, all such organizations are requested to reproduce the following acknowledgment paragraphs in their entirety as part of the preface to any such publication (any organization using a short passage from this document, such as in a book review, is requested to mention "COBOL" in acknowledgment of the source, but need not quote the acknowledgment):

COBOL is an industry language and is not the property of any company or group of companies, or of any organization or group of organizations.

No warranty, expressed or implied, is made by any contributor or by the CODASYL Programming Language Committee as to the accuracy and functioning of the programming system and language. Moreover, no responsibility is assumed by any contributor, or by the committee, in connection therewith.

The authors and copyright holders of the copyrighted material used herein

FLOW-MATIC (trademark of Sperry Rand Corporation), Programming for the UNIVAC® I and II, Data Automation Systems copyrighted 1958, 1959, by Sperry Rand Corporation; IBM Commercial Translator Form No. F 28-8013, copyrighted 1959 by IBM; FACT, DSI 27 A5260-2760, copyrighted 1960 by Minneapolis-Honeywell

have specifically authorized the use of this material in whole or in part, in the COBOL specifications. Such authorization extends to the reproduction and use of COBOL specifications in programming manuals or similar publications.

REVIEWER ACKNOWLEDGMENT

The authors would like to acknowledge the contributions of the following people in reviewing the manuscript and recommending excellent changes for revisions.

Dr. James E. LaBarre
University of Wisconsin-Eau Claire
Eau Claire, Wisconsin

Mrs. Emma Jo Spiegelberg
Laramie High School
Laramie, Wyoming

Dr. Kathy Brittain White
University of North Carolina at Greensboro
Greensboro, North Carolina

Contents

PART ONE – Impacts of the
                  Computer on Society

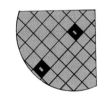

PART TWO – The Electronic
                 Computer System

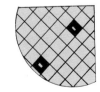

PART THREE – Information Processing

PART FOUR – Software Concepts

PART FIVE – Applications Programming Languages

PHOTO ACKNOWLEDGMENTS

For permission to reproduce the photographs on the pages indicated, acknowledgment is made to the following:

PART OPENER PHOTO ACKNOWLEDGMENTS

For permission to reproduce the photographs on the pages indicated, acknowledgment is made to the following:

PART ONE
Impacts of the
Computer on Society

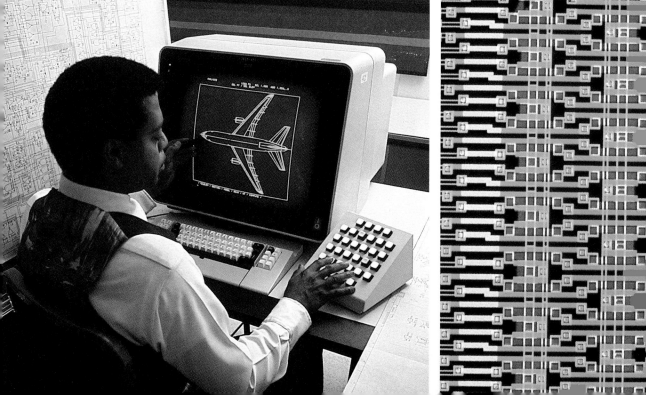

1 Social Impact of the Computer

Objectives:

1. Describe the benefits of the computer to individuals.

2. Describe the advantages of the computer to businesses and their employees.

3. Describe the negative aspects of computer use.

Some people compare it to the discovery of the wheel or the invention of the printing press. Others say its effects on society are more important than those of the Industrial Revolution. Some say that the very survival of the human race depends on it. A totally different opinion is that this device ignores human values, that individual differences and rights are not recognized, and that our way of life is threatened.

The device, of course, is the computer—the electronic device that does computations and makes logical decisions according to instructions that have been given to it. It is apparent that the computer's impact on society is great, whether good or bad. Why do these different opinions exist? The computer is a tool, a complex and powerful tool, but still a tool to do tasks that might also be done without it. These tasks might not be done as well without the computer. They might not be done as fast. As with any tool, however, people make the choice to use its power to help or to harm themselves or others.

BENEFITS OF THE COMPUTER TO INDIVIDUALS IN THEIR DAILY LIVES

You are probably aware of many ways in which the computer affects your daily life. There are other ways of which you are probably not aware. Let's take a look at some of the benefits of the computer to you as an individual.

Information Sources

Businesses known as **information utilities** have large computers that store huge groups of information about many different things. These groups of information are known as **data bases** and are available for your use. You can then obtain information on many topics, read the daily news, play games, make your own airline reservations, obtain the latest stock market quotations, or perform other activities. The range of services provided by information utilities is continually increasing.

To get information from an information utility you can use a small computer. A device known as a **modem** attaches the small computer to a phone line. Communication can then be set up between your computer and the large computer. You pay a fee to the utility for the amount of time your computer is hooked up to theirs. Some services available from the utility also require payment of additional fees.

Electronic Banking and Shopping

Banks have used computers for years. Nearly every bank offers an electronic teller, such as the one shown in Figure 1.1, that is in service 24 hours a day. Many customers prefer the machine to a human teller, even during hours when the bank is open. Growing numbers of banks are offering bill-payment-by-phone services. To use one of these services, you tell the bank the name and address of each business that you pay on a regular basis, along with your account number at each business. Payments that are the same every month, such as rent or mortgage payments, can be scheduled for automatic payment. Items that vary in amount, such as the phone bill or electric bill, are paid when you instruct the computer to do so. To tell the bank's computer to pay your bill, you simply dial the

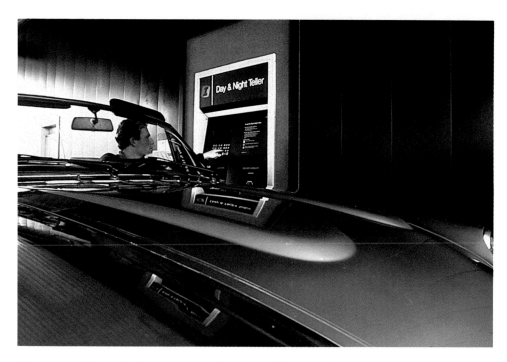

Figure 1.1 *Many bank customers find 24-hour tellers useful.*

computer's phone number. Then, using your phone's keypad, enter your bank card number and secret password, the codes for the transfer of payment to the business from either your checking or savings account, the business' code number (bank provides this), the amount of money to be paid, and the date on which the payment should be made.

Many banks have started issuing identification cards that allow their customers to use other banks' 24-hour tellers nationwide. **Debit cards** have also been introduced. These cards look just like credit cards, but cause the amounts of purchases to be immediately deducted from the checking account rather than appearing on a bill days or weeks later. Since items must be paid for immediately, persons who use debit cards to purchase items will be inclined to buy fewer items on impulse than those who use credit cards.

In addition to the use of debit cards, computers are changing shopping in many other ways. Many stores have joined forces with the information utilities discussed earlier. After "browsing" with your computer, and perhaps watching animated demonstrations of products, you may immediately place your order with a business' computer. Figure 1.2 shows a person shopping by computer.

Figure 1.2   *Use of the computer can make shopping easier.*

Household Control

Most likely, you or your friends don't yet live in a fully computer-controlled house. However, you may be surprised by the number of household devices that may be computer controlled. Refrigerators, ranges, microwave ovens, washers and dryers, stereos, televisions, video disk players, and thermostats, for example, may contain small computers. Figure 1.3 shows some of these devices. Some houses, however, have all aspects of their operation under the supervision of computers. The air-conditioning system is under computer control to produce the most comfort at the lowest cost. Lawn sprinklers are turned on automatically whenever needed. Fire alarms and burglar alarms keep constant watch. The control unit (Figure 1.4) can automatically call the fire department or police department if an emergency develops.

Figure 1.3   *Typical computer-controlled household devices*

Figure 1.4
*This computerized
control unit can
automatically call for
help.*

Household tasks such as grocery shopping and cooking may be computerized. At least one major appliance manufacturer has built a computer-coordinated kitchen in which a computer always knows what groceries are stored in the kitchen. The system uses the **Universal Product Code**, which is the series of bars of varying widths that are printed on grocery items by their manufacturers to identify the items. As you unpack groceries to store them, you move a **scanner** across the bar codes. The scanner is a device that reads the coded numbers represented by the bars and feeds the numbers into the computer. In addition, all of your recipes may be stored in the computer. You tell the computer what recipe you are using and it deducts from its records all the ingredients you will need. As you plan the next week's meals, the computer checks to see what items you need to purchase. It will prepare your grocery list and transmit your order to a grocery store computer, where the order will be prepared for immediate pickup or delivery. If you have some leftover meat loaf, onion soup, and green beans, the computer can show you the recipes for several food dishes you can make using those particular leftovers. The computer can even weigh ingredients for you and watch over the cooking process.

Learning Aids

Computerized learning aids come in many varieties. Perhaps the most common are learning toys such as the one shown in Figure 1.5. There are all kinds of computer-assisted learning programs for use on home computers. Data bases, such as those discussed in the first part of this section, can make research for school projects much easier. There are computer programs to provide all kinds of personal improvement, such as one that analyzes your writing style and helps develop your writing skill.

Figure 1.5
Many learning toys contain computers.

Weather and Environment

Probably every commercial television station in the country uses some form of computerized presentation equipment on its weather show. This equipment may show temperature ranges, precipitation, and wind flow. What is not obvious in watching a television weather report, such as shown in Figure 1.6, however, is the great amount of computing that goes into the forecasts. Even though weather forecasting is still nowhere close to being 100 percent accurate, forecasts are much more accurate than ever before.

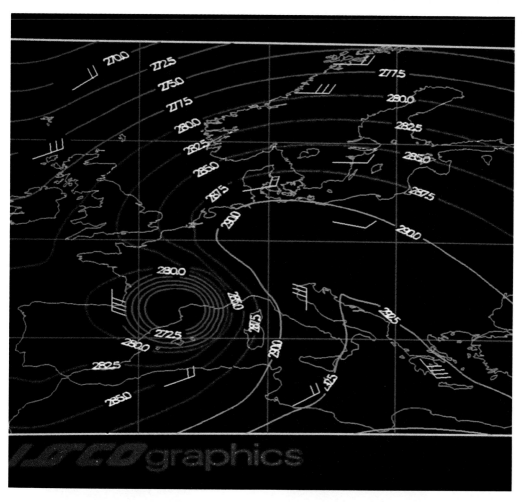

Figure 1.6   *Weather displays are the result of many computations.*

In addition to weather forecasting, various other environmental successes are possible due to computers. Tracking of oil spills and the flow of other pollutants in streams, for example, has helped overcome environmental hazards. The path that water currents will take, changes in the wind, and changes in water temperature affect the direction in which pollutants will travel. When computers predict the direction of travel, action can be quickly taken to clean up the mess.

Transportation

Almost every kind of transportation has been affected by computers. Rapid-transit trains operate with no crew members. Many airliners (including the 767 in Figure 1.7) can fly to their destinations and land under the control of the computer, making flight safer and more efficient. The captain serves as a manager, telling the computer what to do. For a number of years, computers have provided functional controls in your car, such as spark control and fuel control. Each new car introduced seems to add more computerization. Systems are already developed that keep cars from running into each other, as well as systems that always "know" where a particular car is and show its location on an instrument panel map. Another system reduces the car's wind resistance by changing its height and attitude toward the wind. It does this by inflating or deflating air bags at each corner of the car.

Figure 1.7
Computers make flight safer and more efficient.

Community Service

Fire fighting and the saving of lives are aided by the computer. Computerized mapping systems can quickly point out the location of a problem and identify the emergency crew closest to the scene. Computers can help decide where to place equipment and personnel to ensure the shortest response time. In some communities, computers can keep fire fighters updated with floor plans of buildings in which they may need to fight a fire.

Crime Control

Crime control is another area in which computers help to organize much information. States have agreed, for example, to share drivers' license records for persons whose licenses have been taken away. These people cannot go to a neighboring state for a license. Other records of crimes committed are kept by the FBI's National Crime Information Center. For example, this information has been used to find stolen cars driven across state lines. In other cases, computers have been used to analyze the details of a series of homicides that seemed to be committed by the same person, eventually leading to the arrest of the criminal. Officers may have **terminals** (keyboards and screens) in their cars for immediate access to information stored in the computer. Figure 1.8 shows such a terminal. Society as a whole is protected when the computer helps in the arrest of persons involved in crimes.

Figure 1.8
Information stored in the computer is available to the officer through this terminal.

Health Promotion

Computers have long been used for routine record keeping by hospitals. However, today many people owe their lives to the computer. A modern hospital is a showplace of computerized equipment. **Sensors** (devices that detect changes) can be attached to patients to tell when there are changes in temperature, heart rate, blood pressure, or other vital signs. If there is a negative change, the hospital staff is alerted immediately, in many cases saving lives. Medical tests that were once very time-consuming or impossible are now completed quickly by computer. A machine such as the one shown in Figure 1.9 can scan the body and provide three-dimensional views never before thought possible. New technology is providing computers with the ability to help doctors diagnose illnesses.

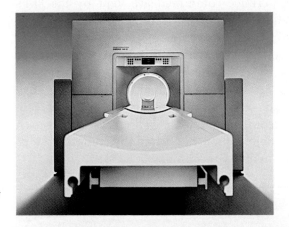

Figure 1.9
This scanner provides three-dimensional views of the body.

All the medical uses of computers discussed thus far have dealt with diagnosis and emergency lifesaving. An equally exciting area in the medical use of computers, however, is the direct use of computers in the treatment of a patient. Computer-controlled pumps can already inject drugs into the blood stream. Technology is being developed that not only injects the drug, but also performs the full-time measurement of chemicals within the body, with the computer making second-by-second decisions on how much of the drug is required. Such uses of the computer should provide much better treatment for diabetes, for example.

Persons who have lost the use of their legs through spinal cord injuries are now walking through computer stimulation of their leg muscles. Important beginnings have been made toward artificial vision for the blind. Computer-controlled wheelchairs and robot arms that respond to the spoken word are proving to be of tremendous value to the disabled.

ADVANTAGES TO BUSINESS EMPLOYEES

Computers are needed to perform business operations requiring the handling of much data. Computers have made it possible for businesses to serve more customers and to earn profits by doing so. Meanwhile, how have employees benefitted from the use of the computer?

Routine and Dangerous Tasks Eliminated

A major impact on employees has been the removal of routine record-keeping tasks. When the computer does the calculations, employees who previously performed routine tasks, such as large amounts of adding and multiplying, can now do more interesting work. The tasks may be handled by the computer in such routine jobs as payroll clerk, invoice clerk, accounts payable clerk, and accounts receivable clerk. In the production end of a business, humans have been relieved of many dangerous jobs, such as the welding of auto bodies. Figure 1.10 shows robots busily welding automobile bodies.

Figure 1.10
Robots can perform many dangerous and dirty jobs.

New Jobs Created

The computer has allowed many businesses to operate better and to grow. New jobs have been created. In the computer field, there is a demand for computer operators (persons to operate computers), for programmers (persons who write instructions for computers), and for **systems analysts** (planners who design company procedures for using computers). You will learn more about these jobs as you progress through this text.

The jobs just mentioned are required to efficiently use the computer within a business. Many other computer-related jobs have also been created because of the computer. Engineers make and repair the equipment. Salespersons sell computers to increasingly more businesses, schools, and individuals. Teachers train persons to fill the new computer-related jobs. Researchers and scientists seek answers to questions which require complex calculations that could not be made without the computer. Entire new areas of technology such as robotics and biotechnology (combination of biology and engineering) are developing.

BENEFITS TO BUSINESS

Many people believe that business in developed countries could not operate today without the computer. The services and goods needed by the public require many companies to supply them. Millions of people living in our communities are served by many companies that produce or sell cars, food, and other merchandise. Goods and services, such as banking, telephones, gas, and electricity, are supplied by many other companies. These items could not be provided to so many people without the use of the computer. The following paragraphs present many of the benefits of computers to business.

Speed and Availability of Information

Information can be quickly obtained on the status of business operations. How many payments are due from customers? How much money is owed to other businesses? Is inventory low? What is the current profit or loss of the company? These are important questions to any business, with or without a computer to help obtain the answers. A computer makes information about what is happening in the business available immediately, allowing timely response to both problems and opportunities.

Projections and Forecasts

One of the most important benefits of the computer for businesses is that it enables them to accomplish tasks that were previously impossible. With its tremendous computation speed, the computer can perform analyses and projections in time for them to be of value in making decisions. The computer can enable the manager to do a lot of "what if" experimentation. For example: What should happen to the company's profits if it could produce 300 products an hour instead of 290, or what would be the effect on labor cost and company profits of one proposed labor settlement versus a different settlement?

Better Control of Expenses

The computer can help control expenses in many ways. One way is in the control of inventory, the merchandise on hand. To serve its customers, a business needs to have on hand the merchandise a customer wants to purchase. On the other hand, tying money up in items that people aren't buying generally reduces profit. The computer can be of great value in keeping up-to-date records of all stock purchased, tracking all completed sales, and indicating when reorders should be made. The small computer in Figure 1.11 is located in a warehouse for keeping up with inventory; it can "talk to" a larger computer at company headquarters. The computer can help produce savings in many other areas as well. For example, manufactured items can be made to meet higher quality standards, resulting in less waste.

Figure 1.11
Many warehouses have computerized inventory control.

Improved Image

Computers can help a business provide much better service to its customers. In such cases, the customer thinks more highly of the business and is likely to speak of it favorably to friends. Keep in mind, however, that this can also work the other way. A business can, through poor management, use computers in such a way that customers become upset and take their business elsewhere.

CAD/CAM

CAD/CAM stands for computer-aided design/computer-aided manufacturing. Although CAD/CAM is fairly new, it is having a tremendous impact in manufacturing businesses. Engineers using computers are able to design new products more easily than ever before. Computers can do all the necessary mathematical computations, such as the computations to determine the size and material required in order for a particular part to be strong enough to perform its function. The computer can produce a drawing of the product and even simulate the operation of the product. Changes in design desired by the engineer can be immediately displayed on the computer, complete with new drawings and analyses of operation.

The operations described in the above paragraph are the CAD part of CAD/CAM. The ideal is that CAD is used to design parts, then tools under the control of CAM actually produce the parts as designed. For the most part, this ideal has not yet seen widespread use, but progress is being made.

NEGATIVE ASPECTS OF COMPUTER USE

You would probably not want to return to a lifestyle in which computers were not used in your everyday life. However, there are some very real problems that have resulted from computer use.

Computer Crime

No one really knows the extent of computer crime. However, you only need to examine the newspapers (Figure 1.12) to read about the persons who get caught. Computer crime may involve changing computer records for personal gain, such as a student changing a course grade. Other criminals may use the computer to commit theft. For example, they may have merchandise shipped to a phony business at no charge, or they may enrich a bank account by transferring a few cents into it from each of thousands of other accounts. Then there are persons who purposely damage computer systems or data. For instance, a programmer who gets mad at an employer may cause the computer to erase vital records from the system. There are cases of what might be called "spying" by computer, where a criminal will "listen in" on data being transmitted from one business location to another. Fortunately, computer users have become more aware of the dangers from computer-related crimes and are beginning to take more steps to protect their computer systems and data from misuse.

Figure 1.12   Many criminals use computers.

Loss of Privacy

Many persons have a concern about the possible loss of privacy caused by computers. Information on millions of people is stored in thousands of computers across the country. Personal privacy begins to disappear when the first charge account is opened, when the first checking account at a bank is opened, or with the first filing of an income tax return. Personal privacy is lost when businesses collect too much information about a person. Privacy is lost when that information is obtained by people who do not have the right or the need to have it.

The problem of privacy is even greater when misinformation is passed on. Charge account billing errors, for example, can give persons poor credit ratings. Even after the billing errors have been corrected, the credit ratings may not be changed due to oversight.

Restructuring of Jobs

The great growth in the number of computers has definitely caused changes within the employment market. Many blue-collar jobs are eliminated as businesses replace manual labor with highly automated production lines using robots. White-collar jobs, including some in mid-management, are also being affected as computers with a greater degree of decision-making ability begin to appear. Some persons fear that in the future there will be two classes of jobs. There will be those in highly paid positions, such as top managers and a few computer experts, and there will be large numbers of persons in low-paying, low-skill service jobs. These persons think that the midrange of employment opportunities will be eliminated.

What the future holds cannot be accurately predicted. It is obvious, however, that a lot of retraining (Figure 1.13) will be necessary. Most persons are probably already resigned to going through several different, but related, careers as technology progresses. It may help keep things in perspective, however, to consider the outcry that took place when the dial telephone was invented, thereby putting large numbers of telephone operators into temporary unemployment. If telephone calls today were still connected by hand, a major portion of the country's population would probably need to be employed as telephone operators. As has happened many times before in our history, as old jobs are eliminated, new jobs are being created. Also, as automation has improved productivity and lessened the need for manual labor, workweeks have decreased from around 70 hours to around 40 hours. It is doubtful many persons would argue for the good old days before automation and the reduction of the workweek. Most likely, the problems caused by computer displacement of jobs will be resolved by taking a lesson from history.

Figure 1.13
Many workers must
be retrained.

SUMMARY

The computer is a powerful tool. Used properly, it can vastly improve the quality of life. Such diverse areas as information utilities, banking, household operation, learning, public safety, transportation, and the environment benefit from the use of computers. Businesses use computers to make information available more rapidly, to do forecasting, and to control expenses. Engineers use computers to design products.

Used improperly, the computer can cause many problems. Criminals have discovered that it is an excellent tool for committing a wide variety of crimes. Many persons think that the storing of large quantities of information about individuals threatens their privacy. In summary, the computer—good or bad—is what we make it.

REVIEW QUESTIONS

1. What is an information utility? A data base? (Obj. 1)

2. Describe how computers can provide better service for bank customers. (Obj. 1)

3. How may computers be used in the home? (Obj. 1)

4. Name some ways the computer is used in dealing with the weather and environment. (Obj. 1)

5. How have computers affected transportation? (Obj. 1)

6. How have computers improved community services? (Obj. 1)

7. Describe ways in which computers improve health care and the quality of life for those who are ill or disabled. (Obj. 1)

8. What are the advantages of computers for business employees? (Obj. 2)

9. Name some jobs that have been eliminated and some that have been created due to the increased use of computers. (Obj. 2)

10. How does the speed of the computer help businesses? (Obj. 2)

11. Name a way in which the computer can help control expenses for a business. (Obj. 2)

12. What is CAD/CAM? (Obj. 2)

13. What are some of the ways in which criminals have used computers? (Obj. 3)

14. How can computers cause loss of privacy? (Obj. 3)

15. What changes are computers causing in the employment market? (Obj. 3)

VOCABULARY WORDS

The following terms were introduced in this chapter:

information utility	scanner
data base	terminal
modem	sensor
debit card	systems analyst
Universal Product Code	CAD/CAM

WORKBOOK EXERCISES

Chapter 1 in the workbook is divided into three exercises: True/False, Matching, and Completion. Complete all three exercises in Chapter 1 of the workbook before proceeding to Chapter 2 in this text.

DISKETTE EXERCISE

Complete the diskette exercise for Chapter 1 before proceeding to Chapter 2 in this text.

PART TWO
The Electronic
Computer System

COMPUTER AIDED
DESIGN

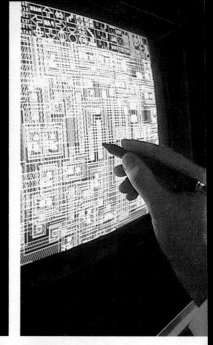

2 Functions and Components of Computer Information Systems

Objectives:

1. Define an information system and identify its functions.

2. Describe the roles of input, processing, and output in an information system.

3. Identify the components of a typical computer system.

4. Explain the function of each of the components of a computer system.

Whether a computer is flying an airplane or preparing paychecks, it is still a computer, and its basic function as part of an information system is the same. The definition of an information system, the role the computer plays in it, and the components of the computer are the subjects of this chapter.

FUNCTIONS OF AN INFORMATION SYSTEM

Data consists of facts in the form of numbers, characters, or words. The job of putting data into usable form is called **informa-**

tion processing. A **system** is simply a group of devices and procedures for performing a task. Therefore, a system that processes data is called an **information system**. In an information system, data is created or collected and fed into the system. Data that enters the system is known as **input**. Useful information leaves the system as **output**; that is, processed information. In between the input and output, the data is processed. **Processing** consists of steps set up to make sure everything that should be done to the data is done. Refer to Figure 2.1 for an illustration of this basic cycle of input, processing, and output. Then study the following paragraphs for more details.

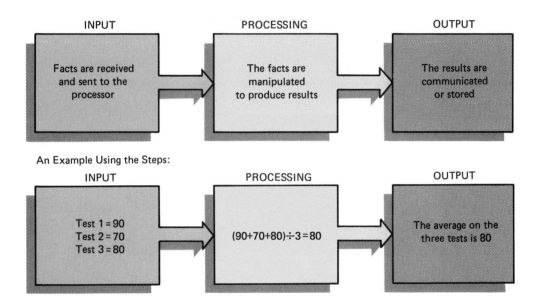

Figure 2.1   *The basic information processing cycle*

Input

What is the origin of the data that is input into information systems? It comes from many sources. Information about students in a school, for example, comes from registration, grade reports, and similar sources. Data regarding hours worked by an employee is taken from forms or a time clock. Information on test scores is obtained from scored tests. The data to be processed is referred to as **raw data** or **original data**. If raw data is first written on forms, the forms are known as **source documents**. Many applications don't use source documents, however; the data is fed directly to the computer as it is originated. Frequently part of the input is data that has been collected and processed in an earlier period. Figure 2.2 shows an example of an application of this type.

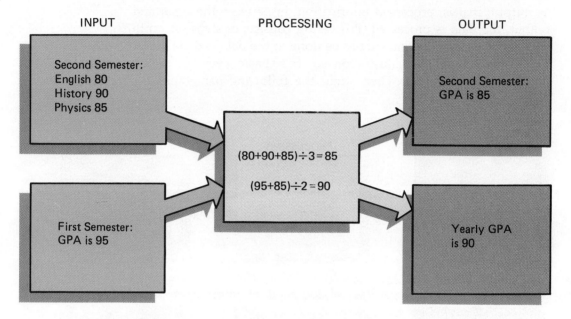

INPUT **PROCESSING** **OUTPUT**

Second Semester:
English 80
History 90
Physics 85

First Semester:
GPA is 95

$(80+90+85) \div 3 = 85$

$(95+85) \div 2 = 90$

Second Semester:
GPA is 85

Yearly GPA
is 90

Figure 2.2 *Previously processed data may serve as input to a system.*

Processing

In any case, data goes to the computer for processing. Processing includes such things as doing arithmetic, making comparisons, and putting data into the desired order. Computers follow processing steps in much the same way that the human mind does. For both, each step leading to the desired result must be included in the processing plan, and these steps must be in logical order. When steps are left out, when steps are out of order, or when logic is not followed in laying out the solution to a problem, the computer won't produce the desired result. When the same is true of people, wrong answers and wrong decisions are also given.

Output

Once the processing of data is finished, output takes place. Output is the process of storing the processed information or communicating it to a user. If stored, the information is available whenever needed. In either case, the information will eventually reach the user. The user may be a human; on the other hand, the user may be the same, or another, information system.

There is nothing unusual about the cycle of input, processing, and output. You have used it many times in making purchasing decisions or writing term papers. In making a purchasing decision, you collect information about a product and its prices in various stores. This is the input stage, which passes the data along to your brain. Your brain processes the data and decides at which store you should make your purchase. You then go to the store and purchase the item, thereby completing the output phase of the cycle. In writing a paper, you first decide on the subject and consider an outline of the kinds of things you want to say about the subject. You collect many facts from reading, from interviews, and from expert opinions. These facts are the input. Then you put the facts in the order you want them in your paper, which is the start of processing. The processing plan also includes writing a first draft, checking the first draft for accuracy and good English skills, and making corrections. The finished paper is the output of the system.

The steps of input, processing, and output are essential in an information system. Regardless of the kind of information being produced, or whether the system is manual or computerized, the processing of data uses these three functions. Data enters the processing system, various operations are done on the data to convert it to useful information, and the useful information leaves the system. Names of students are facts. Arranging the names in alphabetic order so a certain name can be found quickly is a form of information processing. Recording test scores made by students, preparing bills for customers, and classifying the kinds of jobs obtained by high school graduates are other examples of information processing. Another example is using a computer to design a new automobile or control a steel mill.

COMPONENTS OF COMPUTER SYSTEMS

A **computer** can be defined as a device in which data and the instructions for processing it are represented as electronic codes or impulses. Now let's look at the components (parts) that make up the computer that may be used in an information processing system. The components can be divided into two large groups known as hardware and software. **Hardware** is a term used to describe all the physical equipment, or components, in a computer system. The instructions the computer uses to process data are known as **software**. Software consists of individual sets of instructions known as **programs**.

Computers come in a wide range of capabilities and speeds. Years ago, all computers were large in size and were called **mainframes**. Smaller, less powerful computers were invented and were called **minicomputers**. Then the "computer on a chip" was invented and called the **microcomputer**. The problem with these names, all based on the physical size of the computer, is that microcomputers have become more powerful than minicomputers used to be, and minicomputers have become more powerful than many mainframes used to be. All three categories of machines have become increasingly smaller in size. To add to the confusion, incredibly fast and powerful computers known as **supercomputers** were created. Computers range all the way from very small to very powerful. A computer system may range in size from the hand-held unit in Figure 2.3 to supercomputers, such as the one in Figure 2.4.

Figure 2.3
Hand-held computer

Figure 2.4 *The CRAY X-MP Computer System*

In the remainder of this chapter, we will take a detailed look at the hardware of computer systems. Software will be examined in detail in Chapter 9. Remembering the names of the different pieces of hardware is easy; three of the names are based on the names of the functions of an information system. These three are the input device, the processor, and the output device. To this list we add memory and auxiliary storage. See Figure 2.5 for an illustration of the way the components interact.

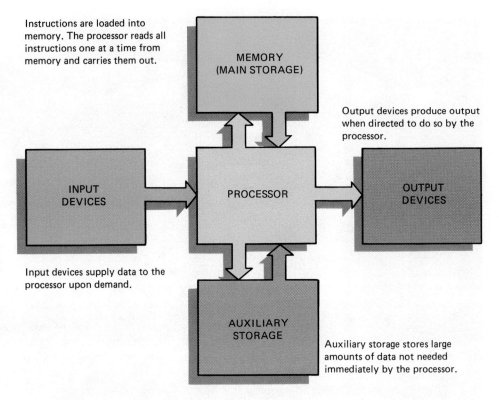

Instructions are loaded into memory. The processor reads all instructions one at a time from memory and carries them out.

MEMORY (MAIN STORAGE)

Output devices produce output when directed to do so by the processor.

INPUT DEVICES

PROCESSOR

OUTPUT DEVICES

Input devices supply data to the processor upon demand.

AUXILIARY STORAGE

Auxiliary storage stores large amounts of data not needed immediately by the processor.

Figure 2.5   Components of a computer system

Input Devices

All computers have one or more input devices. An **input device** receives data and feeds it to the processor. Commonly used input devices include keyboards, such as the one in Figure 2.6, and optical scanners. A **keyboard** sends data to the processor each time a key is struck. An **optical scanner** sends data to the processor as it "looks at" data in printed or written form. Numerous input devices will be considered in detail in Chapter 4.

Processors

All computers do processing by following detailed instructions in a program. The computer system unit that receives and carries out these instructions is the **processor**. All computer systems, regardless of size or make, have processors (also referred to as CPUs or central processing units). The processor performs many different functions. It receives and temporarily stores instructions as well as the data to be processed. It moves and edits stored data. It

Figure 2.6
The keyboard is a popular input device.

makes arithmetic computations. It makes decisions of logic, such as determining if two numbers are equal. It directs the action of the input and output devices. Therefore, the processor may be defined as that part of a computer system that receives and stores instructions and data, performs arithmetic and logic operations, and directs the action of the input and output devices.

The processors shown in Figures 2.7 and 2.8 are **microprocessors**; that is, all of their processing circuits are contained in one piece known as an integrated circuit. (The term **integrated circuit (IC)** refers to any electronic "chip" that contains large numbers of electronic components; ICs are also used for memory and other applications in a computer.) All small computers and many larger computers use microprocessors. Some supercomputers are made from many microprocessors working together.

Figure 2.7
Uncovered microprocessor

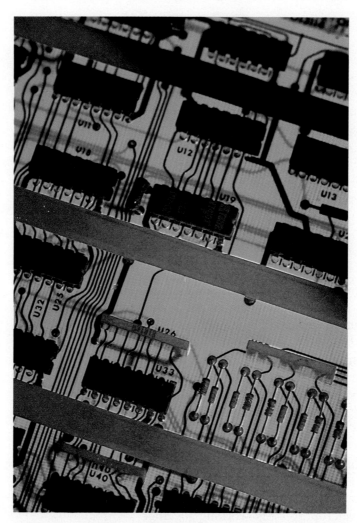

Figure 2.8
Microprocessor

The different functions of the processor are regulated by a clock that delivers regular impulses. The idea of the clock is somewhat similar to installing a pacemaker in a human; pulses from the pacemaker keep the heart beating in the proper rhythm. Likewise, the clock pulses keep the processor functioning in the proper rhythm. Typical clock speeds for microprocessors are 5 megahertz and 8 megahertz. A **megahertz** is a million cycles, or pulses, per second. The fact that a particular processor may be running at a clock speed of five million cycles per second does not mean it can do five million arithmetic computations per second. Many processing operations require more than one clock cycle to be performed.

Main Storage

The instructions being followed by a computer do not all reside in the processor at once. Most of the time, they are stored in locations known as **memory**. Memory may also be referred to as **main storage**. From there, each instruction is copied into the processor and executed (carried out). Likewise, the data being processed is not loaded into the processor all at once. It, too, spends most of its time in memory, being moved into the processor when necessary for processing. The processed data is then returned to memory for further use or output.

The memory of a computer is made from electronic circuits that, like the processor, are contained on integrated circuit chips. Figure 2.9 shows such a chip. Memory can accept, hold, and release data, as well as the instructions for processing the data. Data and instructions are stored as electronic impulses in specified locations in memory. You can imagine memory as being like a large number of mailboxes, each box being labeled with a number. This number is known as a **numeric address**. Any desired "mail" (data) may be placed in specified locations. Generally, the first storage location in memory is given an address of 0; the second, an address of 1; and this process continues up to the number of memory locations required. The amount of data that can be stored in one memory location varies. However, with small computers, each location is

Figure 2.9
A typical memory chip surrounded by salt crystals

generally capable of holding one byte. A **byte** is equal to one character (you will learn a more formal definition of byte in Chapter 3). For example, the letter *M* can be stored in one memory location. The word *computer* requires eight locations, one for each letter. Figure 2.10 shows how this word might look if stored in memory beginning at location 100. The processor can look at the data stored in a memory location without actually removing the data. Whenever a new item of data is placed in a memory location, however, it replaces the data that was previously there.

NUMERIC ADDRESSES

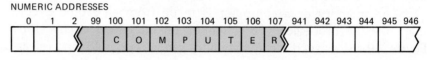

Figure 2.10   *Data stored in memory*

The number of memory locations in a computer system is generally stated in terms such as 128K or 768K. The K is short for kilo, which means 1,000. However, due to the different numbering system used inside the computer, one K of memory is really 1,024 memory locations. Therefore, 128K of memory is really 131,072 (128 times 1,024) memory locations. There is a physical limit on the largest address number a given processor can use. For example, the processors in many less powerful microcomputers can address up to 64K of memory; that is, they cannot physically refer to a memory address larger than 65,536. Many microprocessors can address one **megabyte** (one million bytes). More powerful microprocessors and larger computers can address many megabytes of memory.

It requires only a tiny fraction of a second for the processor to place data in memory or to look at data already there. The processor simply "addresses" the desired memory location and gives a write or read command. The concept is similar to placing a number of persons in a room and asking one of them a question. Only the person to whom the question is addressed answers. For example, you may ask, "Sue Jones, how much money do you have?" Sue, not William or Henry, will answer the question. Remember that in the computer, however, each memory location is identified by a numeric address rather than a name. This concept will be further developed in later chapters.

There are many kinds of memory chips, and new ones are constantly being developed. However, memory chips can generally be classified as either volatile memory or nonvolatile memory. Most computers contain both volatile and nonvolatile memory.

Volatile Memory   Volatile means "prone to evaporate." What that has to do with computer memory is that characters stored in **volatile memory** "evaporate" when the computer is powered down (turned off). That is, the memory locations lose their data when the power is turned off. Volatile memory is generally known as **RAM** (random-access memory). It is called random access because the processor can jump directly from one location to another in random order as data is stored and retrieved. This is where data is stored while it is not being processed. Rapid progress has been made in packing increasingly more storage locations onto one RAM circuit chip. Chips that can hold the equivalent of over 32,000 characters were introduced in 1983. The first chip capable of holding the equivalent of over 125,000 characters may soon be introduced.

Nonvolatile Memory   **Nonvolatile memory** does not lose its data when the power is turned off. Therefore, it is frequently used to store instructions necessary for getting the computer started when it is powered up (turned on). Nonvolatile memory is frequently referred to as **ROM**, or read-only memory. This term is appropriate since the computer can only read data from a ROM chip; it cannot write or store data in the chip. Though many persons refer to all nonvolatile memory as ROM, there are really several subdivisions of nonvolatile memory based on the method by which data is stored in the chips. Storing data in a nonvolatile memory chip is frequently referred to as programming the chip, since the process is so different from storing data in RAM. With true ROM, the data or instructions contained in a memory chip are placed there (programmed) during the manufacturing process. A memory chip known as a **PROM** (programmable ROM) is not programmed at the factory. Instead, a special device is used to place data in it. Once the data is in, it cannot be changed. **EPROMs** (erasable PROMs) can be erased by use of ultraviolet (black) light, then reprogrammed. **EEPROMs** (electronically erasable PROMs) can be erased and reprogrammed by electrical pulses instead of ultraviolet light. The newest member of the ROM family is something of a cross between an EEPROM and RAM. The computer can write and read the memory, but the data does not disappear when power is lost. The amount of data that can be stored in one nonvolatile memory chip varies depending on the type of chip.

Auxiliary Storage

Virtually all general-purpose computers include supplementary storage devices that hold data outside the memory of the computer. These supplementary storage devices are known as **auxiliary storage**. Auxiliary storage devices are **on-line** to the computer; that is, they are connected directly to the computer. They are, therefore, under the control of the processor and accessible to it at all times. Figure 2.11 shows a **disk drive**, the most common form of auxiliary storage. The disk drive records data in a method similar to that used by a cassette tape recorder.

Figure 2.11 Magnetic disk drives

Auxiliary storage is used to hold computer programs so they may be read into the computer's memory when they are needed. Large amounts of data may also be stored on auxiliary storage. Remember from an earlier section that data stored in RAM is volatile. Therefore, any data that needs to be kept for future use is usually recorded on a magnetic disk before the computer is powered down. Chapter 6 will explain in detail the operation and use of auxiliary storage.

Output Devices

Just as a computer system must have at least one input device, it must also have at least one output device. An output device records, prints, or displays information in usable form. The most common output devices are **cathode-ray tubes**, commonly known as **CRTs**, and **printers**. CRTs display output on televisionlike screens; printers produce output, in the form of written characters, on paper. Figure 2.12 shows a CRT, while Figure 2.13 shows a printer. Output devices will be discussed in detail in Chapter 5.

Figure 2.12
CRT used for computer output

Figure 2.13
Printer used for computer output

SUMMARY

The purpose of an information system is to process raw data, converting it into useful information. The information processing cycle includes the steps of input, processing, and output. These steps are the same regardless of whether the processing is being done manually or with the aid of a computer.

A computer system used to process data consists of hardware (the physical parts) and software (the programs). The hardware is made up of input units, the processor, main memory, auxiliary storage, and output devices. These parts are common to all computers, from tiny hand-held units to extra-fast supercomputers.

REVIEW QUESTIONS

1. What is an information system? (Obj. 1)
2. List the three functions (steps) in the information processing cycle. (Obj. 1)

3. What is the role of each of the steps in the information processing cycle? (Obj. 2)

4. What is the difference between hardware and software? (Obj. 3)

5. What is the function of an input device? Describe two commonly used input devices. (Objs. 3, 4)

6. What is the function of the processor? (Obj. 4)

7. What is the function of memory? (Obj. 4)

8. What is the function of auxiliary storage? Describe a commonly used auxiliary storage device. (Objs. 3, 4)

9. What is the function of an output device? Describe two commonly used output devices. (Objs. 3, 4)

10. What is the difference between volatile and nonvolatile memory? (Obj. 4)

VOCABULARY WORDS

The following terms were introduced in this chapter:

data	microprocessor
information processing	integrated circuit
system	megahertz
information system	memory
input	main storage
output	numeric address
processing	byte
raw data	megabyte
original data	volatile memory
source documents	RAM
computer	nonvolatile memory
hardware	ROM
software	PROM
programs	EPROM
mainframe	EEPROM
minicomputer	auxiliary storage
microcomputer	on-line
supercomputer	disk drive
input device	cathode-ray tube
keyboard	CRT
optical scanner	printer
processor	

WORKBOOK EXERCISES

Chapter 2 in the workbook is divided into three exercises: True/False, Completion, and Crossword Puzzle. Complete all three exercises in Chapter 2 of the workbook before proceeding to Chapter 3 in this text.

DISKETTE EXERCISE

Complete the diskette exercise for Chapter 2 before proceeding to Chapter 3 in this text.

3 Representation of Information in the Computer

Objectives:

1. Describe the functions of character codes.

2. Distinguish between the ASCII code and the EBCDIC code.

3. Explain how the binary number system is used in the computer.

4. Describe the use of the hexadecimal number system.

5. Define parity check and explain how it is implemented.

Each character is represented inside the computer by a number. In other words, inside the computer, the letter *A* is not stored as an *A*; it may be stored as the number 65.

INTERNAL CODING OF INFORMATION IN THE COMPUTER

Two different codes are commonly used for representing data inside the computer. In each of the codes, a number is assigned to each character, digit, and punctuation mark. Each time a key on a keyboard is struck (Figure 3.1), the code number for that key is generated and input into the computer. Inside the computer, the code number is stored in memory chips (Figure 3.2). When output is to be produced, the code number of each character is sent to the output device, such as the printer in Figure 3.3. In addition to code numbers for all the visible characters, there are also numbers for various control functions, such as tabulating, backspacing, and positioning the cursor.

Figure 3.1
*Each character
produces a unique
code number.*

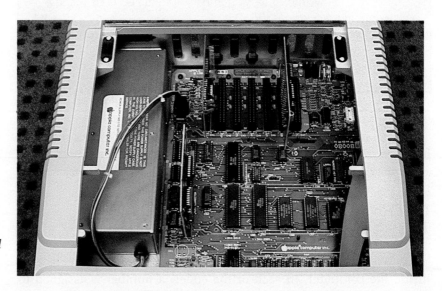

Figure 3.2
*Character code
numbers are stored
in the computer's
memory.*

Figure 3.3
Outputting a
character's code
number will print
that character.

ASCII Code

Most small computers, such as the one shown in Figure 3.4, use a code known as ASCII. **ASCII**, which stands for the American Standard Code for Information Interchange, uses the numbers 0-127, for a total of 128 possible characters. Many manufacturers have expanded the code to the numbers 0-255, for a total of 256 possible characters. Different manufacturers assign different characters, such as graphics, to the extra numbers. In standard ASCII, code numbers 0-31 are nonprinting characters known as **control characters**. Control characters are designed to control the communication between a computer and another device, such as a terminal or printer. Therefore, when sent to an output device, the control-character code numbers normally do not produce a display that can be seen. Some manufacturers, however, have chosen to use various control-character code numbers for shapes that can be displayed.

Figure 3.4 *Most small computers use the ASCII code.*

Figure 3.5 (the ASCII code chart) shows the standard 128-character ASCII code. For the control characters (code numbers 0-31), the assignments that are fairly standard among most manufacturers are defined in the chart. Code numbers that are used for differing purposes by different manufacturers are not defined in the chart. In addition to being used internally by most small computers, ASCII is also widely used in **data communications**; that is, for sending data from one computer system or device to another.

ASCII CONTROL CHARACTERS

Code	Name	Control Key	Description
0		@	
1		A	
2		B	
3		C	
4		D	
5		E	
6		F	
7	BEL	G	*Bell.* On computers that can "beep," printing ASCII Code 7 will produce the sound.
8	BS	H	*Backspace.* In addition to being produced by striking the H key while holding down the CTRL key, Code 8 is produced by the backspace key.
9	HT	I	*Horizontal tab.* On computers with a tab function, the printing of this code moves the cursor to the next tab stop. This is produced also by the TAB key, if present.
10	LF	J	*Line feed.* When the line feed is printed, it causes the cursor to move to the next line on the screen. It does not cause the cursor to return to the left side of the screen.
11		K	
12	FF	L	*Form feed.* With many printers, printing of this code causes the paper to move to the top of the next page.
13	CR	M	*Carriage return.* Printing of the carriage return code causes the cursor to move to the left side of the screen.
14		N	
15		O	
16		P	
17		Q	
18		R	
19		S	
20		T	
21		U	
22		V	
23		W	
24		X	
25		Y	
26		Z	
27	ESC	Varies	*Escape.* On computers with an escape key (ESC), this code is produced when that key is struck. The response of the computer to this key depends on the software being used.
28			
29			
30			
31			

Figure 3.5a *Standard ASCII code chart: control characters*

ASCII CHARACTER CODES

Code	Character	Code	Character	Code	Character
32	Space	69	E	106	j
33	!	70	F	107	k
34	"	71	G	108	l
35	#	72	H	109	m
36	$	73	I	110	n
37	%	74	J	111	o
38	&	75	K	112	p
39	'	76	L	113	q
40	(	77	M	114	r
41	)	78	N	115	s
42	*	79	O	116	t
43	+	80	P	117	u
44	,	81	Q	118	v
45	- (hyphen)	82	R	119	w
46	.	83	S	120	x
47	/	84	T	121	y
48	0	85	U	122	z
49	1	86	V	123	{
50	2	87	W	124		
51	3	88	X	125	}
52	4	89	Y	126	~
53	5	90	Z	127	Delete
54	6	91	[		
55	7	92	/		
56	8	93	]		
57	9	94			
58	:	95	__ (underscore)		
59	;	96	'		
60	<	97	a		
61	=	98	b		
62	>	99	c		
63	?	100	d		
64	@	101	e		
65	A	102	f		
66	B	103	g		
67	C	104	h		
68	D	105	i		

Figure 3.5b   Standard ASCII code chart: character codes

EBCDIC Code

EBCDIC stands for Extended Binary Coded Decimal Interchange Code. It is used by many larger computers, such as the one in Figure 3.6. EBCDIC uses code numbers 0-255, for a total of 256 possible characters. The code number representing each character is different from ASCII, but the idea is the same. Even though some computers and devices use the ASCII code and some use the EBCDIC code, communication can easily be set up between devices using different codes. It just takes a simple translation step by one of the systems to communicate between the two codes.

Figure 3.6 *Many large computers use the EBCDIC code.*

ELECTRONIC REPRESENTATION OF CODED INFORMATION

The circuits inside the computer can be thought of as using electronic switches that are either turned on or off. Since on and off represent only two conditions, it is impossible to directly store code numbers, such as 65 and 117; that is, the ASCII or EBCDIC codes cannot be directly stored inside the computer. Instead, they are converted into a series of *on's* and *off's*. In effect, imagine eight on/off switches grouped inside the computer. These eight switches can store one character code. By turning various switches on and off, there are 256 different combinations possible. These combinations represent the 256 different characters of the codes.

Binary Number System

To get the proper combination for each character, the code is converted to a binary number. **Binary** means two, so a binary number is made using only two digits, 0 and 1. There can be as many 1's and 0's as required within the eight switches to represent a particular number. Each 0 can be thought of as representing a switch that is turned off, while each 1 represents a switch that is turned on. Each 1 or 0 is known as a binary digit, usually referred to as a **bit** (BInary digiT).

Before we figure out how to represent numbers in the binary number system, let's review the decimal number system you use every day. In the decimal system, a digit's value becomes ten times larger each time it is moved left. There are ten digits, 0-9. Since each column represents a value ten times as large as the one to the right of it, we say the number system has a base of 10. The **base** is the number you multiply a digit by when you move it one column to the left. For example, the digit 1 has a value of 1 when placed in the right-hand column. When the 1 is moved to the left, with a zero taking its place in the right-hand column, its value becomes 10. With another move to the left, the digit 1 takes on a value of 100:

100	10	1	← **Column Values**
		1	In the right-hand column, 1 has a value of 1.
	1	0	Move the digit one column to the left and its value becomes 10 times as large.
1	0	0	Move the digit one more column to the left and its value again becomes 10 times as large; that is, 100 times as large as the digit in the right-hand column.

When there are digits in more than one column, just add their column values. For example, the number 201 can be considered as follows:

100	10	1	← **Column Values**
		1	The 1 in the right-hand column has a value of 1.
2			The 2 in the third column is worth 100 times 2, or 200.
2	0	1	Add the values in the columns to get a total of 201.

Now let's see what happens when we apply this same concept to the binary system. Each column has a value twice as large as the previous column, so the binary system has a base of 2. As you know, there are only two digits, 0 and 1. The following table shows this:

4	2	1	← **Column Values Given as Decimal Numbers**
		1	In the right-hand column, 1 has a value of 1.
	1	0	Move the digit one column to the left and its value becomes twice as large.
1	0	0	Move the digit one more column to the left and its value again becomes twice as large; that is, four times as large as the digit in the right-hand column.

Again, with digits in more than one column, just add their column values. For example, the number 101 in binary can be considered as shown in the first table on page 50.

The code numbers used to represent characters inside the computer each consume eight columns consisting of 1's and 0's. The eight 1's and 0's make up a unit known as a **byte**. Since each 1 or 0 is known as a bit, you can say that eight bits make a byte. Since each column is twice as large as the one before, 1's in the various positions within the byte have the values shown in the second table on page 50.

4	2	1	← Column Values Given as Decimal Numbers
		1	The 1 in the right-hand column has a value of 1.
1			The 1 in the third column is worth 4 times 1, or 4.
1	0	1	Add the values in the columns to get a total of 101 in binary. To convert to decimal, add the decimal column values (4 + 1), for a total of 5. In other words, 101 binary and 5 decimal are the same value.

128	64	32	16	8	4	2	1	← Column Values
1	1	1	1	1	1	1	1	

128	64	32	16	8	4	2	1

Values of the various positions in a byte

Now look at how several characters may be stored. The letter *A* has an ASCII code of 65. Therefore, it is stored in binary by placing a 1 in the column worth 64 and a 1 in the column worth 1, for a total value of 65:

128	64	32	16	8	4	2	1
0	1	0	0	0	0	0	1

The letter *A* stored in binary.

The underline character (__) has an ASCII code of 95. To store it in binary, place 1's in the columns worth 64, 16, 8, 4, 2, and 1. Note that these column values added together make 95, which is the ASCII code number:

128	64	32	16	8	4	2	1
0	1	0	1	1	1	1	1

The underline (__) stored in binary.

Digits may also be stored in character format. For example, the ASCII code for the digit 4 is 52. Therefore, represent the 4 in binary by placing 1's in the columns that add up to 52:

128	64	32	16	8	4	2	1
0	0	1	1	0	1	0	0

The digit 4 stored in ASCII Code.

When numbers are to be used for mathematical computations, they are frequently stored in a way other than ASCII or EBCDIC. The easiest to understand of these methods is pure binary. **Pure binary** is a method in which a number is stored directly in binary, rather than coding it first in some other manner. This means that a number is represented simply by placing 1's in the columns whose values add up to that number. For example, the number 14 is represented by placing 1's in the columns with values of 8, 4, and 2:

128	64	32	16	8	4	2	1
0	0	0	0	1	1	1	0

14 stored in pure binary.

If necessary, the length of the number can be increased. Storing the number 521, for example, requires 10 bits:

512	256	128	64	32	16	8	4	2	1
1	0	0	0	0	0	1	0	0	1

521 stored in pure binary.

Hexadecimal Number System

The **hexadecimal** number system is frequently used when referring to data stored in the computer or data being transmitted from one unit to another. The hexadecimal system has a base of 16. That is, each column's value is 16 times the column to the right. The table below illustrates this:

4096	256	16	1	← Hexadecimal Column Values
		2	3	The number 23 in hexadecimal converts to 35 in decimal. The 2 in the second column is worth 2 times 16, or 32. Adding the 3 in the right-hand column gives 35.

You already know that a number system has the same number of digits as its base. Therefore, the decimal system has 10 digits and the binary system has 2 digits. Likewise, the hexadecimal system has 16 digits. The digits are 0-9 plus A, B, C, D, E, and F. The digit *A* is equivalent to the decimal 10, *B* is equivalent to 11, and so on. The largest digit, *F*, is equivalent to a decimal 15.

Hexadecimal numbers cannot be used inside the computer; only binary works there. Hexadecimal numbers, however, form a convenient "shorthand" notation for referring to the contents of a byte. Let's take a look at the letter *N*, which has an ASCII code of 78. The letter is stored in a byte as follows:

128	64	32	16	8	4	2	1	Binary column values.
0	1	0	0	1	1	1	0	Digits for ASCII code 78 (*N*).
8	4	2	1	8	4	2	1	Binary column values with byte divided into two units.

With the byte divided into two units, each half may be referred to as a **nibble**. Here is the way hexadecimal may be used. First, look at the left-hand nibble, 0100. Add the values of the columns containing 1's. In this case there is just one, in the 4 column. This gives a total of 4. Now look at the right-hand nibble. Add together the column values where there are 1's. That is, add 8, 4, and 2, for a total of 14. You now have a total of 4 from the first four bits and a total of 14 from the last four bits. In hexadecimal terms, this gives the number 4E. (Remember that the value 14 is known as the digit *E* in hexadecimal.)

Now let's prove that ASCII code 78 (stated in decimal) is exactly the same thing as ASCII code 4E (stated in hexadecimal):

4096	256	16	1	← **Hexadecimal Column Values**
		4	E	The E in the right-hand column is the same as decimal 14. Now remember that the second column in hexadecimal is worth 16 times as much as the first column. Therefore, the 4 in the second column is really worth 4 times 16, or 64. Add the 64 to the 14 from the first column, and you get 78.

Parity Checking

When data is being transmitted from one device to another, especially over long distances, it is possible for various kinds of interference to cause errors in the character codes. That is, the code received may have a 1 where a 0 was transmitted, or a 0 where a 1 was transmitted. By counting the number of 1's in each code received, many errors can be caught. For example, if all code numbers should contain an even number of 1's, a code with an odd number of 1's would be in error. This would work well, except that some correct character codes contain an even number of 1's, while others contain an odd number. To get around this problem, an extra bit, known as a **parity bit**, is added. Therefore, with eight bits used to represent a character, the parity bit becomes the ninth bit. Parity means equality; therefore, the parity bit may be recorded by the transmitting device as either a 1 or a 0, whichever is required to equal an odd or even number of 1's.

Counting the number of 1's in each character code to make sure they are all even or all odd is known as a **parity check**. The use of odd numbers is known as odd parity. The use of even numbers is known as even parity. Let's look at an example using even parity. The letter *A*, as stored in binary, contains two 1's (an even number of 1's). Therefore, if you are using even parity, you record a 0 as the parity bit. That's because you already have an even number of 1's:

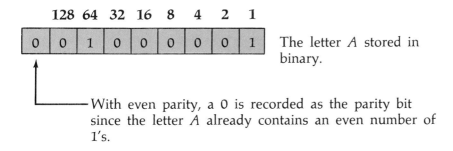

128 64 32 16 8 4 2 1

| 0 | 0 | 1 | 0 | 0 | 0 | 0 | 0 | 1 |

The letter *A* stored in binary.

With even parity, a 0 is recorded as the parity bit since the letter *A* already contains an even number of 1's.

The letter *X*, as stored in binary, contains three 1's (an odd number). Therefore, if using even parity, a 1 is recorded as the parity bit to make a total of four 1's (an even number):

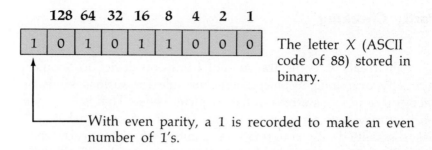

The letter X (ASCII code of 88) stored in binary.

With even parity, a 1 is recorded to make an even number of 1's.

Any time data is stored, retrieved, transmitted, or received, the number of 1's in each character can be counted. If the quantity is not properly even or odd, it is obvious that either a 1 accidentally changed to a 0 or a 0 accidentally changed to a 1 during the operation. The response of the system to a parity error depends on how it has been programmed. It may ignore the error, retransmit the data, or just stop.

All the work of handling a parity check is normally done by software supplied with the computer. The user or programmer is usually not concerned with adding parity bits, checking parity bits, or handling parity errors. Frequently, however, the user setting up a system for data communications will be required to specify whether parity is to be checked, and whether it should be odd or even.

To review, even parity is the state of parity in which a 1 is added in the parity bit position as necessary to maintain an even number of 1's for each character. Odd parity, on the other hand, is the reverse of even parity. A 1 is added in the parity bit position as necessary to maintain an odd number of 1's for each character. The parity bit does not change the character that is coded. The bit is automatically added as a check on the accuracy of the computer equipment. Note that a parity check does not check for mistakes in the actual data.

SUMMARY

Inside the computer, each character is represented as a numeric code rather than the character itself. The two most commonly used codes are the American Standard Code for Information Interchange (ASCII) and the Extended Binary Coded Decimal Interchange Code (EBCDIC). The codes serve the same purpose, but the numbers that represent each character are different.

Regardless of the coding system being used, numbers inside the computer are stored in binary format. Hexadecimal numbers are sometimes used by humans in referring to the contents of binary storage locations in the computer. Frequently, parity checking is done to help ensure that a character code being transmitted from one place to another is not accidentally changed during transmission.

REVIEW QUESTIONS

1. Do all computers use the same coding system for representing characters? (Obj. 1)

2. How are the ASCII and EBCDIC codes alike? How are they different? (Obj. 2)

3. For what purposes are character codes used? (Obj. 1)

4. On what size computers are the two codes likely to be used? (Obj. 2)

5. How are letters, numbers, and symbols represented in the ASCII code? (Obj. 2)

6. Which of the two codes allows the greatest number of characters? Is this always true? (Obj. 2)

7. Can communication be set up between computers using different codes? Explain. (Obj. 1)

8. In what number system are character codes stored inside the computer? (Obj. 3)

9. Describe the relationships among a bit, a nibble, and a byte. (Obj. 3)

10. Of what value are hexadecimal numbers, since they cannot be stored directly in the computer? (Obj. 4)

11. Explain the relationships among decimal, binary, and hexadecimal numbers. (Objs. 3, 4)

12. What is the purpose of a parity check? (Obj. 5)

13. What is the procedure for performing a parity check? (Obj. 5)

14. What is the difference between even parity and odd parity? (Obj. 5)

VOCABULARY WORDS

The following terms were introduced in this chapter:

ASCII	byte
control character	pure binary
data communications	hexadecimal
EBCDIC	nibble
binary	parity bit
bit	parity check
base	

WORKBOOK EXERCISES

Chapter 3 in the workbook entails three exercises: True/False, Completion, and Crossword Puzzle. Complete all three exercises in Chapter 3 of the workbook before proceeding to Chapter 4 in this text.

DISKETTE EXERCISE

Complete the diskette exercise for Chapter 3 before proceeding to Chapter 4 in this text.

4 Input Devices and Media

> **Objectives:**
>
> **1.** Name various input devices and describe their characteristics.
>
> **2.** Describe applications for which each input device is appropriate.

Earlier, you learned that a computer system is made up of several basic units: input devices, the processor, output devices, main memory, and auxiliary storage. All the units can take several forms. However, there are numerous types of input and output devices. This chapter goes into detail about the input devices; the next chapter covers output devices.

You know that an input device receives data and communicates it to the processor. Input begins with a command from the processor to the input unit. The command is given because an instruction in a program tells the processor to do so. Once the command is given, the input device transmits data coded in the binary format learned in Chapter 3. As the data is received, the processor generally stores it in main memory so it will be available for use. Some input devices use media; others do not. **Media** refers to the materials upon which data is recorded prior to being sent to the computer. For example, characters may be written on paper, in which case paper is the **medium** (the singular form of media). As another example, data may be recorded on a strip of magnetic tape, in which case the tape is the medium.

VIDEO DISPLAY TERMINALS

A **video display terminal** (VDT) consists of a keyboard and a display device. Most frequently the display device is a CRT. Both an input device and an output device, the VDT remains the most popular method of "holding a conversation" with a computer. However, its popularity as a method for entering huge batches of data into the computer has declined. When any system is set up for two-way communication between the user and the computer, it is said to be **interactive**. Due to its interactive abilities, the VDT is frequently used in information retrieval systems and reservation systems.

Following the lead of some European countries, there is much interest in the **ergonomic** design of devices such as video display terminals and the desks with which they are used. This means that use of the devices should be comfortable and nontiring, allowing the operator to produce more work. Note that the keyboard in Figure 4.1 has been placed in an easy-to-use position, while the CRT is some distance away from the operator and can be turned and tilted to reduce glare and make reading easier.

Figure 4.1
An ergonomically designed VDT work station

SPEECH RECOGNITION DEVICES

For many applications, the ability to instruct a computer by voice command is valuable. This can be done by use of a **speech recognition device**. For example, a laboratory technician (Figure 4.2) may verbally give test results to the computer. By doing so, the technician bypasses the steps of having to write the results on paper, converting them to computer codes, and then keying them into the computer. In addition, both hands are left free to work. A computer technician may speak over the phone to a computer in the parts warehouse to determine the availability of a part. You may command your voice-controlled telephone to make a call for you. Handicapped persons can command wheelchairs or robot arms through the spoken word.

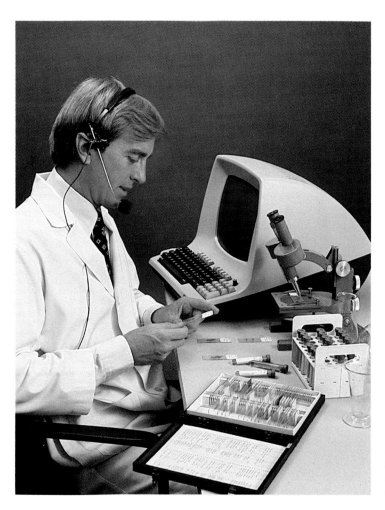

Figure 4.2
Speech recognition devices allow hands-off data entry.

As valuable as these applications are, the ideal would be a computer input device that could recognize what might be called free-form speech; that is, ordinary conversational speech. Present systems, as impressive as some of their performances may be, can only recognize several hundred words. They must be trained to recognize one or, at most, a few different voices. There is so much variation in speech from one person to another that it is very difficult for a computer to accurately recognize words. Humans use thousands of different words in everyday speech. Many words sound similar, and the meanings of many words vary depending on the sentences in which they are used. For the large-scale use of computer voice recognition to become possible, a system that can accurately recognize all those words in different situations will have to exist. Research in advanced voice recognition is under way in many labs, but experts in the field think it will be a while yet before large-scale speech recognition becomes feasible.

OPTICAL-CHARACTER READERS

An **optical-character reader** (OCR) is one type of scanner, or input device. It works like the reading method that humans use. When light is placed on a printed form, the human reader scans the form. Images of the letters, numbers, or marks are reflected to the eye. The images are transformed into nerve impulses and sent to the brain. The brain has been programmed through learning and experience to recognize the images. In a similar fashion, a character reader, like the one in Figure 4.3, can read numbers, letters of the

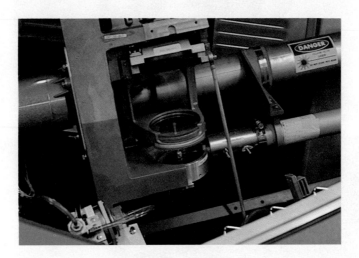

Figure 4.3
Optical-character reader

alphabet, and symbols directly from a typed, printed, or handwritten page. Electronic elements placed in a **matrix** (row and column arrangement) inside the device react to light reflected from the page. The pattern of a letter falls on the matrix (as it would on a human retina), thereby generating electronic impulses. The impulses being received are mathematically compared to stored records of what the impulses from various characters should look like. When a character is identified, its code is transmitted to the processor. Figure 4.4 shows the process. The concept of a matrix will be discussed in greater detail in Chapter 10.

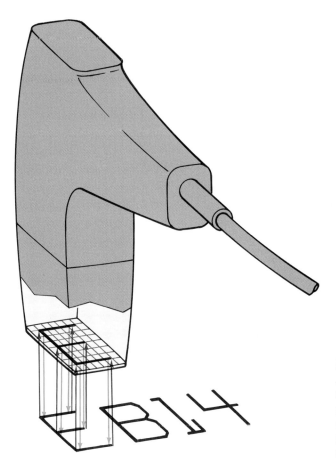

Figure 4.4
An optical-character reader compares the pattern of a character with patterns stored in memory.

An optical-character reader requires only one marking position per digit or character. It is, therefore, very suitable for handling a large quantity of data or wide variation in possible responses. Figure 4.5 shows a piecework ticket for a payroll and also an invoice. These forms are used for recording optical characters in pencil. Note that the directions show the worker the proper way to print numbers so that the computer will accept them. The numbers scanned must be a close match to the model characters stored by the scanner, otherwise reading errors will occur. Note that only the specially printed characters on the ticket are intended for reading by a scanner. There is far too much variation in normal handwriting to allow present scanners to read it with an acceptable degree of accuracy.

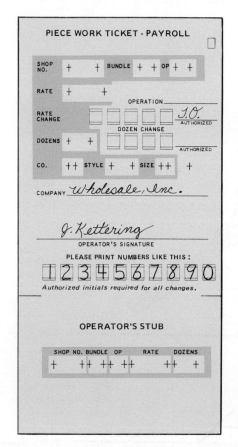

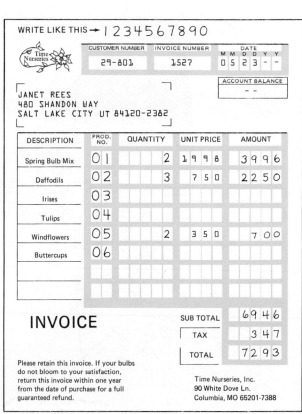

Figure 4.5 *Handwritten characters for OCR must be written in a defined style.*

The use of OCR forms makes it possible to have on-the-spot data recording at low cost. A worker can record the amount of time it takes to complete a job. A customer's purchases can be recorded, and so on. The only equipment needed for this kind of recording is a pencil and an OCR form.

Some optical-character readers read only data recorded in special styles of type and printing, such as those shown in Figure 4.6. However, many readers can accept almost any type style. Regardless of the needs of a business, there is probably a scanner on the market to meet those needs.

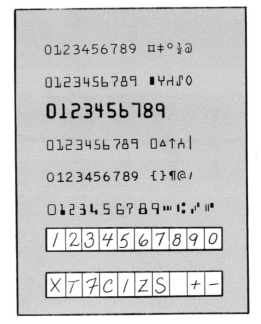

Figure 4.6
Special type styles designed for optical-character recognition

OCR equipment is frequently used in department stores. Figure 4.7 shows an optical scanner being used to read the price ticket on an item. Usually the scanner reads a stock number rather than the price; the computer to which the scanner is attached then looks up the stock number in a price table to determine the amount to charge for the item. This makes it easy to ensure that customers receive the sale prices on items that are specially priced, or to change the prices when necessary.

The OCR has also become an important tool in the business office. Text that has been created on one typewriter or printer can very easily be input into another system through use of a character reader such as the one in Figure 4.8. This use of character readers will become less necessary, however, as more and more office equipment is linked together electronically.

Figure 4.7
Wand scanners are used for entering transaction information into a computer system.

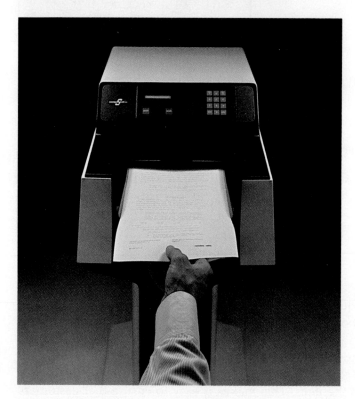

Figure 4.8
Some word processing systems use page scanners for input.

OPTICAL-MARK READERS

The **optical-mark reader**, shown in Figure 4.9, is a scanner that senses the presence or absence of marks made by regular pencil or pen on specially designed forms. This is the simplest form of optical reader since it does not require the "intelligence" of a character reader. The form is predefined into a matrix of marking positions. All the mark reader has to do is determine whether or not there is a mark (usually a rectangle or circle) at each of the positions. It is up to a computer program to determine what the presence or absence of a mark at a particular location means. Optical-mark recognition is frequently used for test scoring, data collection, inventory control, and other applications where the number of different responses and volume of data are somewhat limited. The range of possible responses must be limited because each possible response must have a designated marking spot on the medium. Figure 4.10 shows one input medium that may be used. Note that the locations for recording each kind of data are predefined on the form.

Figure 4.9 *An optical-mark reader senses marks instead of characters.*

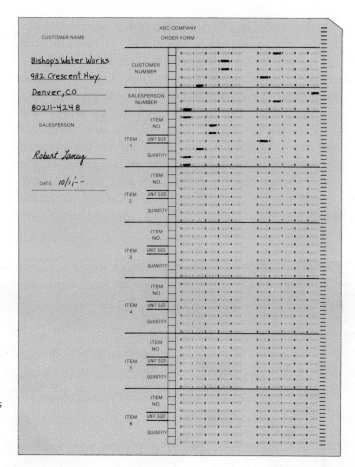

Figure 4.10
Optical-mark readers use forms (media) with predefined marking locations.

BAR-CODE SCANNERS

A **bar-code scanner** can read bars, or lines, that are printed on a product. These bars, which represent data, are generally printed in a code known as the **Universal Product Code** (UPC). The code is printed on a product by the product's manufacturer and is made up of a series of vertical bars of varying widths that reflect a laser beam from a scanner. The bars are a coded form of numbers, as shown in Figure 4.11. The first five digits at the bottom stand for the manufacturer or processor of the item. The second five digits identify the particular product of that manufacturer or processor. Note that the bar-code scanner does not read the actual digits; it reads the coded bar representation of the digits. Because of the design of the bars and the scanners, the codes can be read from almost any direction or angle, as shown in Figure 4.12.

Figure 4.11
A Universal Product Code imprint

Figure 4.12 *A bar-code scanner in operation*

Retail stores (especially grocery stores) use bar-code scanners to automate the check-out process. Bar-code scanners transmit the product identification characters directly to a computer. The computer then looks up the correct price and description in data which it has previously stored in a table. The customer gets a sales slip listing the names of the items purchased, and the items are automatically deducted from the store's inventory. Store managers thus have a system of instant inventory control. In addition, the store doesn't need to prepare price tags. Also, since the cashiers do not need to key in prices, time is saved and errors are reduced.

Bar-code scanners are also used in industries other than the retail business. For example, the U.S. Postal Service places bar codes on certain letters for automatic routing of mail.

MICR READERS

Banks in the United States use **magnetic ink character recognition** (MICR) for much of their data input. An MICR reader is an input device that is used to process data printed in magnetic ink with specially designed numbers and symbols. A check written on a depositor's account in one bank is often deposited in another bank. Eventually the check must be returned to the bank on which it was drawn. Then, in cancelled form, the check is returned to the maker along with a statement. A bank must keep accurate records of deposits and withdrawals for its depositors. It must also assist in keeping balances straight between banks. The extremely large volume of data required for this much record keeping requires a nonmanual method of data input such as MICR. Without a data input system such as MICR, it would be extremely difficult for banks to process the many millions of checks written.

In MICR, checks and deposit slips have all essential data printed on them in magnetic ink. The numbers and special symbols (there are no alphabet letters) appear in an unusual-looking style. This style gives each character a different magnetic area, creating differing electronic impulses when the documents go through a reader. The reader can transmit the data directly to a computer system for immediate processing or store it on disk or tape for later processing.

Note that the check in Figure 4.13 has characters printed in magnetic ink at the bottom in several different fields. A **field** is a space or group of spaces needed to record a single fact. Starting at the far left of the check is data to identify the bank on which the check is drawn. The first four numbers, 1232, stand for the Federal Reserve number; the next four, 0523, are the unique identification numbers of the particular bank. The 2 in this field is known as a **check digit**. That is, it is used to check the accuracy of the reading of the other digits. The check digit is calculated from the preceding digits by using a mathematical formula. When the number is read, the formula is applied to the first eight digits and the result is compared to the check digit printed on the check. If the two digits are not the same, it means an error was made in the reading of the number. The numbers in the account number field, 6854509, are those given by the bank to the particular depositor's account. All these numbers are printed on the checks and deposit slips in magnetic ink before they are issued to the account holder. The special symbols at the beginning and end of the two sets of numbers are punctuation marks. Just as a capital letter is used at the beginning of a sentence and a period at the end, these symbols alert the MICR reader to the beginning and end of a group of numbers.

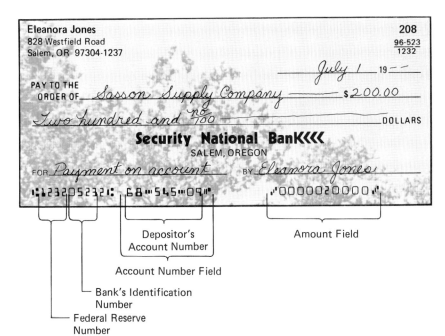

Figure 4.13
Magnetic ink characters are used on checks.

The figures in the amount field, 200.00, are the amount for which the check is written. These figures are imprinted in magnetic ink at the bottom right of the check. They are imprinted by the receiving bank after the check has been written, delivered to the person or business to whom it was written, and cashed or deposited in the bank. Deposit slips use magnetically encoded numbers in a similar fashion. In addition to entering data into banks' computer systems, the MICR numbers are used to control machines that sort checks for return to the correct bank and depositor. See Figure 4.14 for an illustration of such a sorter.

Figure 4.14
Checks being sorted for return to banks

MAGNETIC SCANNERS

A **magnetic scanner** operates on the same principle as a tape recorder. The tape it reads, however, is usually only a short piece no more than a few inches long. Some retail stores use price tags on which short strips of magnetic tape contain the stock numbers of the products. The largest use of magnetic scanners, however, is to read encoded information on the back of credit cards and 24-hour teller machine cards used by banks. For the latter, a magnetic strip on the back of each depositor's identification card contains the person's account number and other information. When the card is inserted into the teller machine (Figure 4.15), the magnetic scanner reads the tape on the back of the card and transmits the depositor's account number to the processor.

Figure 4.15
The magnetic strip is read by the teller machine.

REAL-TIME SENSORS

Real-time sensors are one of the newest developments in computer input. Real time means "while it is happening." Therefore, a real-time sensor is like a sentry. It constantly monitors a process or event and transmits its findings to the processor without the need of human assistance. There are many applications for real-time sensors, so we'll look at just a few. The computer that controls the ignition and fuel systems in your car uses several real-time sensors for input. Sensors are constantly measuring such things as engine speed, vehicle speed, and the level of carbon monoxide in the exhaust. This data is constantly input to the computer. After processing the information, the computer produces output in the form of commands to the ignition and fuel systems. These commands will keep efficiency as high as possible while, at the same time, keeping air pollution produced by the engine within an acceptable range.

In a control room in a large hotel (Figure 4.16), sensors are constantly measuring important variables, such as temperatures. The computer checks to see if temperatures are within the normal ranges. If not, the computer can take corrective action by making adjustments to the equipment or by alerting a human operator to make adjustments.

Figure 4.16   *The controlling procedures in this hotel are constantly monitored by computer.*

When a computer-controlled burglar alarm is activated, several real-time sensors will actively monitor the area and feed the computer information as to whether or not an intruder is present. Energy costs in large buildings can also be cut dramatically by computer systems equipped with real-time sensors. The sensors constantly transmit data to the computer telling it how much electricity is being used, which appliances are in operation, what the temperature is, and other information. The computer is then able to control the appliances to achieve the desired level of comfort and operation, while at the same time keeping peak usage of electricity as low as possible. Real-time sensors are also used in fire alarms and in the control of transport vehicles such as airplanes and rapid-transit cars.

One of the most exciting developments in real-time sensors is the creation of robots with senses of vision and touch. This development makes it possible to use robots in applications not previously possible. The robot in Figure 4.17 is inputting what it "sees" to the computer that is controlling its operation.

Figure 4.17
A robot with vision

OTHER INPUT DEVICES

There are several kinds of input devices that have not yet been discussed in this chapter. The following paragraphs describe some of them.

Light Pen

A **light pen** is one of several types of input devices that may be used to point out locations on a CRT. For example, if there are four items to choose from on the screen, the user might be requested to press the light pen against a dot printed on the screen in front of the desired item. The image on a CRT is made by a beam that constantly repaints or refreshes the picture; without the constant repainting, the image would quickly fade away. The end of the light pen contains a part that reacts when the dot over which it is positioned is refreshed. The computer then calculates the position against which the light pen is pressed (Figure 4.18). Depending on the computer program with which a light pen is used, the operator may draw shapes, move images from one part of the screen to another, and so on.

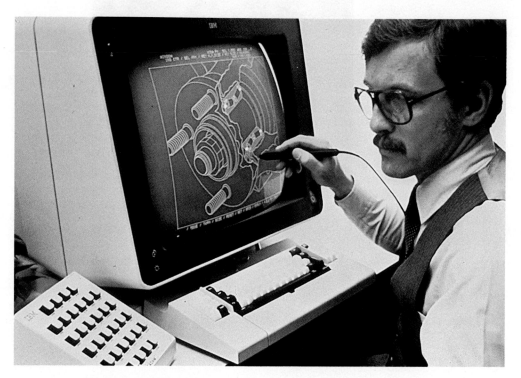

Figure 4.18   *An engineer uses a light pen in designing a part.*

Mouse

The **mouse** is a pointing device used with a video display. Like its living counterpart, a computer mouse has a body and a tail. The tail is a wire connecting the body to the computer. The body contains one or more push buttons. As the body of the mouse is moved, a marker known as a **cursor** moves on the CRT. When the mouse is moved up, the cursor moves up; when the mouse moves left, the cursor moves left; and so on. Once the cursor is in the desired location, pressing a button on the mouse causes an action to be taken. The type of action depends on the computer program in use at the time. For example, suppose the computer is part of an electronic-mail system. The cursor is moved to an image of an in-basket on the screen. When the button on the mouse is pressed, the waiting mail, such as letters for the day, is presented on the screen. The mouse is also frequently used to make selections from several options available, as the person in Figure 4.19 is doing.

Figure 4.19
A mouse controls computer input by placing the cursor in the desired location.

Digitizer

The **digitizer** converts shapes into numbers for storage by computers. For example, if you have a favorite cartoon picture you would like to transfer to a computer for display, you can trace the picture with a digitizer. The digitizer transmits the proper numbers to reproduce the picture on the CRT. The picture you trace is **two-dimensional**. That is, it is flat and has a length and a width. All digitizers can handle two-dimensional objects. Some can also handle three-dimensional objects. **Three-dimensional** objects have depth as well as length and width. With a digitizer, such as the one shown in Figure 4.20, an engineer can trace an outline of an existing part. The size and shape of the part are thus input into the computer for analysis or further work on the design.

Figure 4.20
A digitizer
represents the shape
of an object in
numbers.

SUMMARY

Many kinds of input devices exist. Each type has capabilities that make it appropriate for particular applications. Video display terminals are useful for just about any application that requires interactive communication between the user and the computer. Speech recognition devices allow a worker to do other things with the hands while inputting data into the computer. Various kinds of scanners are appropriate for applications that require the reading of data written on products, price labels, checks, identification cards, and so on. Real-time sensors allow efficient control of manufacturing processes, home appliances, and airplanes, just to name a few. The mouse is becoming more popular as an input device. Also, there are many input devices designed for special uses.

REVIEW QUESTIONS

1. Which type of input device is commonly used for interactive applications? Describe its characteristics. (Objs. 1, 2)

2. What is a medium? (Obj. 1)

3. What are three applications for speech recognition devices? What is a limitation of such devices? (Objs. 1, 2)

4. Compare optical-character readers and optical-mark readers. (Obj. 1)

5. Under what conditions would an optical-mark reader be an appropriate input device? When would an optical-character reader be preferable? (Obj. 2)

6. How are bar-code scanners used in grocery stores? (Objs. 1, 2)

7. Describe how banks use MICR for data input. (Objs. 1, 2)

8. How does magnetic scanning work? What are some applications of magnetic scanning? (Objs. 1, 2)

9. What is the primary difference between real-time sensors and the other input devices you are familiar with? (Objs. 1, 2)

10. Compare the primary functions of a light pen, mouse, and digitizer. (Objs. 1, 2)

VOCABULARY WORDS

The following terms were introduced in this chapter:

media	field
medium	check digit
video display terminal	magnetic scanner
interactive	real-time sensor
ergonomic	light pen
speech recognition device	mouse
optical-character reader	cursor
matrix	digitizer
optical-mark reader	two-dimensional
bar-code scanner	three-dimensional
Universal Product Code	
magnetic ink character	
recognition	

WORKBOOK EXERCISES

Chapter 4 in the workbook consists of four exercises: True/False, Matching, Completion, and Crossword Puzzle. Complete all four exercises in Chapter 4 of the workbook before proceeding to Chapter 5 in this text.

DISKETTE EXERCISE

Complete the diskette exercise for Chapter 4 before proceeding to Chapter 5 in this text.

5 Output Devices and Media

Objectives:

1. Name commonly used output devices and describe their characteristics.

2. Describe applications for which each output device is appropriate.

In this chapter you will learn about the most commonly used types of output devices. You will learn their characteristics and the kinds of applications for which they are best suited.

VIDEO DISPLAYS

The **video display** is one of the most common devices used for computer output. It is especially well suited for interactive applications requiring both input and output, such as reservation systems or word processing. Most video displays use a CRT, although other methods of displaying the data are becoming more common. As you learned in Chapter 4, a video display is frequently combined with a keyboard in a unit known as a video display terminal.

Some computers may be attached to a standard television set, which then serves as a video display. Home televisions, however, are totally unsuitable for use with many computer systems. Due to the way they are made, television sets can display only a limited number of characters on the screen. That number is too limited for business information processing. Video displays used in business information processing usually contain either 24 or 25 lines of 80 characters each. Displays with 132 columns are becoming more common, as are those that can display up to 60 lines. A few can display the equivalent of several printed pages of text at the same time.

Video displays may be either monochrome or color. **Monochrome** means only one color. Common display colors are green, amber, and white. Full-color displays are coming into much greater use. They can do an excellent job of presenting information in an easy-to-understand form. A **graphic** (a chart, drawing, or picture) looks much better in color. For applications involving words and numbers, however, color displays may be harder to read. For that reason, some displays can easily switch between monochrome and color. In Figure 5.1, note the different appearances of the graphics and text on the different displays.

Figure 5.1 *Appearance of output on different video displays*

There are two primary methods of moving output from the computer to a video display. In one method, the character codes are transmitted one after another from the processor to the display. The display stores the character codes in its own memory and performs the necessary electronic functions to display the characters on the screen. In this method, the processor sends the data to the display and forgets about it. When using a video display terminal, this is almost certainly the method that is being used. The second method is referred to as a **memory-mapped** display. In this case, the display actually serves as a "window" into the memory of the computer; that is, a group of locations in main memory is dedicated to holding information for the display. To change a character in a screen location, the computer just places the code of the character in the corresponding location in main memory. For displays that can show **high-resolution graphics** (very detailed graphics), as much as 64K or more of storage may be used just to remember what is to be displayed on the screen. The greater the number of individual **pixels** (points of color) that can be displayed on the screen and the greater the number of colors, the greater the memory required to hold the image.

PRINTERS

Printers are commonly used devices that place output on paper. Placing output on paper is generally called making a hard copy of the information. With the exception of video displays, printers are the most common output device. Nearly every computer application uses a printer in some way. Just a few uses are printing bills, letters, and accounting records. When examining available printers, you find tremendous differences: differences in speed, print quality, price, and special features. Some printers can only produce characters; others can print detailed graphics. Some printers can use only one color, while others can print in several colors. Figure 5.2 shows the kind of multicolored graphic output that is possible.

Figure 5.2
Color graphic output from a printer

There are several methods used to place characters on a sheet of paper. In some printers, the paper is struck to form the images; these printers are known as **impact printers**. Impact printers are best used when multiple copies of the same document are needed. **Nonimpact printers**, on the other hand, form the characters without actually striking the paper. Regardless of the method of printing, a character code is received from the computer. The printer then converts the code into the proper mechanical and electronic action to print the character.

Daisy Wheel Printers

A **daisy wheel printer**, such as the one shown in Figure 5.3, is an impact printer. It gets its name from the fact that it uses a print wheel that resembles a daisy. Figure 5.4 shows the actual printing mechanism. The print wheel rotates until the desired character is in position in front of the paper. Then a hammer strikes the petal of the daisy. An inked ribbon between the daisy wheel and the paper causes an image to be printed.

Figure 5.3
*A daisy wheel
printer produces
letter-quality output.*

Daisy wheel printers produce what is known as letter-quality print; that is, the characters are made from unbroken lines and look as if they were produced by a good typewriter. This is important when printing letters and other documents that must be of high quality. In exchange for such fine-quality printing, however, the user pays a price in the form of low speed. In fact, some daisy wheel printers are extremely slow, around ten characters per second.

Figure 5.4
The daisy mechanism

Dot-Matrix Printers

A **dot matrix** is simply a row and column arrangement of dots. Therefore, a dot-matrix printer (the impact printer shown in Figure 5.5) produces a character by forming it from rows and columns of dots. The part of the printer that does the printing is known as the **printhead**. As it moves across the paper, tiny pins or wires in the printhead tap the paper through a ribbon to form the image. There is wide variation in the number and arrangement of the pins or wires used to do the printing. The most common arrangement is a simple vertical stack of pins as shown in Figure 5.6.

Figure 5.5
Typical dot-matrix printer

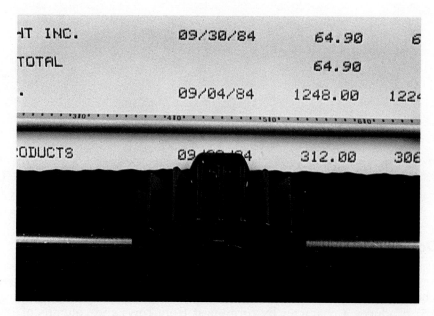

Figure 5.6
*Dot-matrix print
mechanism*

The print quality of a dot-matrix printer varies depending on the number of dots used to form a letter. If many dots are used, the character will look better than if it is made of only a few dots. That is, characters that are formed in a 5 x 7 (five columns, seven rows) matrix will not look as nice as ones formed in a 16 x 35 matrix. Some manufacturers of dot-matrix printers claim letter-quality print for their machines, but the print is not as impressive as that produced by daisy wheel printers.

The print speed of dot-matrix printers ranges from around forty characters per second to several hundred characters per second, which is quite adequate for most small computer systems. A few dot-matrix printers use more than one printhead to achieve even higher speeds. Compared with other types of printers, most dot-matrix printers are fairly inexpensive.

Ink-Jet Printers

The **ink-jet printer** is a nonimpact printer which is growing in popularity. As the name implies, liquid or dry ink is squirted onto the paper. The exact technology used varies from one manufacturer to another. Ink-jet printers produce nice-looking print, and many of them can produce different sizes and styles of characters on the same line. Some can print in several colors. A typical ink-jet printer is shown in Figure 5.7.

Figure 5.7
An ink-jet printer shoots ink onto the paper.

Band Printers and Chain Printers

Band printers and chain printers are impact printers that operate on the same general principle. A **band printer** uses a rotating band or belt containing characters; a **chain printer** uses a rotating chain containing the characters. The printers contain hammers to strike the characters against the paper. A ribbon between the characters and the paper produces the images. Figure 5.8 shows a band printer.

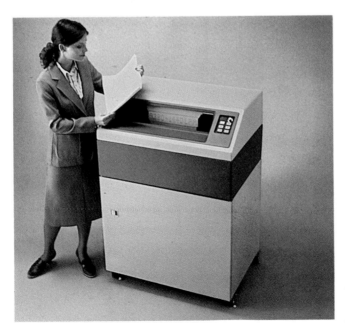

Figure 5.8
Band printers are fast and reliable.

Band printers and chain printers are much faster than the daisy wheel and dot-matrix printers described earlier and can print as fast as 2,000 to 3,000 lines per minute. They are also much more expensive.

Laser Printers

The **laser printer** is the fastest (and most expensive) printer available. The fastest ones can print over 20,000 lines per minute. When printing 12 lines per inch, for example, the printer shown in Figure 5.9 can print around 167 11-inch pages per minute. Another advantage of the laser printer is that a business form can be printed on blank paper at the same time the output data is being printed. The laser printer can also produce different sizes and styles of printing.

Figure 5.9 *Laser printers are the fastest printers available.*

A laser printer is a nonimpact printer that works somewhat like a copying machine. In a copying machine, light shines on an original copy. The light is reflected onto a light-sensitive drum which transfers toner (ink) to the copy. In a laser printer, the character codes that are output by the computer control a laser beam that literally "writes" the output onto a drum sensitive to photographic impressions. The drum then transfers the characters to paper. Figure 5.10 shows a laser in operation.

Figure 5.10
Laser in operation

The printers that have been discussed here are ones that are commonly used. There are other types, and manufacturers are constantly introducing new printer models, some of which utilize different technology.

Regardless of the kind of printer being used, it is probably connected to the computer by one of two commonly used **interface** (connection) methods. If the interface is **serial** (one after the other), the codes for the various characters to be printed leave the computer and travel to the printer one bit at a time. That is, the bits of each character are transmitted to the printer in single file. If the interface is **parallel** (side by side), all the bits of a character travel at the same time. That is, the bits are transmitted all at once over several wires. There are several variations of these two basic methods. If the printer is to function properly, however, the computer and the printer must be compatible.

SPEECH SYNTHESIZERS

Speech synthesizers, output devices which imitate the human voice, are available for nearly every application. There are so many "talking" machines—talking games, talking cars, talking appliances, talking calculators, and music-reading singing computers—that it sometimes looks as if manufacturers want each item to have a voice, whether it needs one or not.

Seriously, however, synthesized voices are very appropriately used in many situations. Talking machines are giving phone numbers to persons who dial directory assistance. They perform electronic banking by using the phone as a terminal. Talking typewriters, calculators, and reading machines are a tremendous aid for the blind. In addition, computer-assisted learning in such areas as foreign languages can be much more effective when the computer can speak.

COMPUTER OUTPUT MICROFILM

Computer output microfilm, commonly referred to as COM, is used when large amounts of data must be printed and stored for future use. Under such conditions, output printed on paper may require too much storage space. Also, too much time may be needed to search through the paper output to find a given item.

Computer output microfilm uses a photographic process. Computer output is recorded directly on photographic film by a unit like the one shown in Figure 5.11. The unit converts computer signals to written characters and exposes the film, which is similar to taking a picture. The image of each character is reduced greatly in size, making dense storage (many characters in a small space) possible. The microfilm may be developed in the unit or removed for development.

Figure 5.11
Computer output can be recorded on microfilm.

The microfilm produced may be in long rolls. It may also be in small rectangular sheets called **microfiche**. To read either type, a person must use a special reader. The reader (Figure 5.12) is a machine that magnifies the image to a size that can be read by the human eye. Many of the readers can produce a paper print of any required information. Many of the machines also have automated search mechanisms to help locate desired data.

Figure 5.12
A microfilm reader magnifies images from microfilm.

COM provides a very fast way of recording human-readable output from a computer. The film itself is inexpensive and compact. However, complete COM systems can be very expensive. Government agencies, insurance companies, banks, utility companies, and other businesses that must store a large volume of computer-generated data are the most likely users of COM.

PLOTTERS

A **plotter** is generally used to print graphic output. That is, it can draw maps, produce art work, draw any shape line, and so on. A plotter draws output using one or more pens that are controlled by instructions from the processor. Since the pens can contain various colors of ink, multicolored output is easy to achieve. Some plotters are limited to printing on standard-sized sheets of paper; others can work on paper of almost unlimited size. Mapping, weather forecasting, drafting, and engineering are just some of the areas in which plotters are used. In addition to producing graphic output, the plotter can also perform some printing functions. Figure 5.13 shows a plotter producing a graphic display.

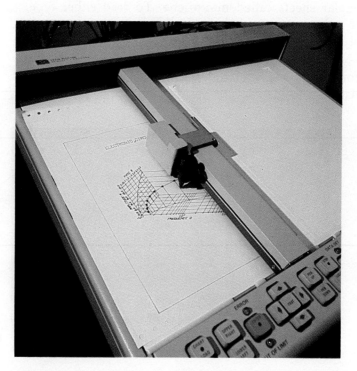

Figure 5.13
A plotter produces graphic output.

REAL-TIME CONTROLLERS

A **real-time controller** is an output device that converts computer output to some kind of action that controls a process. Often, the action consists of turning a valve on or off. In an automobile (Figure 5.14), the computer gives commands to controllers on the ignition and fuel systems. In an aircraft, computer commands go to controllers for the various flight-control commands as well as to the engines. When commanded by a computer, a real-time controller performs the function for which it was designed.

Figure 5.14
The Datsun 280-ZX has real-time controllers combined with voice recordings that monitor the car's processes.

ROBOTS

Robots can serve as output devices. Under control of a computer, the robot produces output in the form of motion to perform work. If the instructions being given to the computer are changed, the robot's motions can change and it can do a different kind of work. Newer robots can also provide input to the computer through the use of television cameras and other devices. The processor uses this input along with the programmed task instructions to produce output.

SUMMARY

Whatever the computer application, an appropriate output device is available; video displays and printers are the most commonly used devices. Video displays are especially helpful for interactive applications and for showing graphic information. Full-color displays are especially good for graphics. Many different kinds of printers are available. Some of them can print graphics or print in different colors.

Speech synthesizers may be used in any application where voice output is appropriate. Plotters quickly draw elaborate designs, such as building plans. Real-time controllers enable computers to operate various kinds of machinery. Robots under computer control can produce useful work through their movement capabilities.

REVIEW QUESTIONS

1. What output device is commonly used for interactive applications? Describe its characteristics. (Objs. 1, 2)

2. Name and describe the features of six different kinds of printers. (Obj. 1)

3. Which kind of printer would you select to print very impressive letters? huge numbers of telephone bills? Explain your reasoning. (Obj. 2)

4. Under what circumstances would you consider using COM rather than a printer? Why? (Obj. 2)

5. What characteristics of a plotter make it an appropriate output device for outputting the plans of a large building? (Objs. 1, 2)

6. What is the difference between a real-time controller and a robot? How are they alike? Can they be used for the same applications? (Objs. 1, 2)

VOCABULARY WORDS

The following terms were introduced in this chapter:

video display	band printer
monochrome	chain printer

graphic	laser printer
memory mapped	interface
high-resolution graphics	serial
pixel	parallel
impact printer	speech synthesizer
nonimpact printer	computer output microfilm
daisy wheel printer	microfiche
dot matrix	plotter
printhead	real-time controller
ink-jet printer	

WORKBOOK EXERCISES

Chapter 5 in the workbook consists of three exercises: True/False, Matching, and Completion. Complete all three exercises in Chapter 5 of the workbook before proceeding to Chapter 6 in this text.

DISKETTE EXERCISE

Complete the diskette exercise for Chapter 5 before proceeding to Chapter 6 in this text.

6

Auxiliary Storage Devices and Media

Objectives:

1. Describe commonly used auxiliary storage devices and media.

2. Identify applications for which each of the commonly used auxiliary storage devices is suitable.

As you learned in Chapter 2, auxiliary storage is storage that is not part of memory (main storage), but is on-line or available to the processor. Auxiliary storage is under control of the processor. Thus, the device will store or record data whenever instructed to do so by the processor. When instructed, it will also read or play back data to the processor.

All auxiliary storage devices are either sequential-access or random-access devices. **Sequential access** is a term used to describe a device that records and reads back data only in a one-after-the-other sequence. **Random access** is a term used to describe a device that can go directly to the location of particular data without having to read through all the data in front of it. A sequential-access storage device is somewhat like a cassette tape player. The tape player cannot get to the fourth selection, for example, without actually winding the tape through the first three. It doesn't matter whether the tape is on play or fast forward, you still have to wait for it to move past the unwanted selections. A random-access storage device, on the other hand, is somewhat like a stereo record; you can set the needle down exactly on the desired selection. It is not necessary for the needle to play through the unwanted selections.

MAGNETIC DISKS

Data to be processed by a computer is often recorded on a magnetic disk. Disks are especially useful for applications in which data must be accessed in random order. A good example of such an application is an airline reservation system. In an airline reservation system, one caller may be interested in a flight to Los Angeles on February 4, the next may want to fly to London on January 5. The system must be able to read quickly from auxiliary storage, in any order, information about the flights. The use of a disk is the easiest way to accomplish this.

Principles of Magnetic Disks

A **magnetic disk** is an input, output, and storage medium similar in appearance to a stereo record with a smooth surface. It is coated on both sides with microscopic bars of a substance that can be magnetized. Recording is done magnetically by a method similar to that used by a tape recorder. The magnetic surface, however, is a rotating disk of grooveless tracks rather than a long strip. A **track** is a path on which data is recorded, usually on a magnetic medium. The tracks are arranged as shown in Figure 6.1. As the disk is rotated beneath a read/write head, the tiny bars are magnetized in the proper code pattern for each character. Figure 6.2 shows an imaginary section of one track on a disk.

Each side of a disk is a surface. Therefore, data on a disk may be recorded on either one or two surfaces. The disk drive uses a movable read/write head for each surface on which recording may be done. Thus, if recording is to be done on one side of a disk, there is one head. If recording is to be done on both sides of a disk, there are two heads. The heads travel in or out to position themselves over the disk track that is to be used. When new data is recorded on a disk, any data previously recorded on the same area of the disk is erased. When data is read, on the other hand, there is no change; the data remains on the disk.

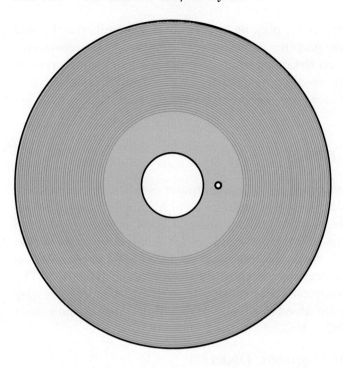

Figure 6.1
*The tracks of a disk
are arranged inside
one another.*

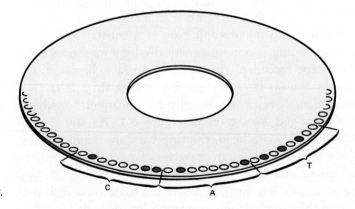

Figure 6.2
*Coded magnetized
spots represent
characters on a disk.*

As mentioned earlier, data stored on a magnetic disk can be accessed randomly. Random access is sometimes referred to as **direct access**. That is, the head can move directly to the desired track rather than sequentially moving through all other tracks before it. If you wish, however, a disk drive can also access data sequentially. The ability to act as either a sequential-access or a random-access device has made the disk drive the most popular auxiliary storage device. It can be used for virtually all applications.

Disks can be divided into two categories: flexible disks and hard disks. Flexible disks and their drives cost much less than hard disks and their drives. However, flexible disks can't hold as much data and are much slower.

Flexible Disks

A **flexible disk**, frequently referred to as a **floppy disk**, is a small, pliable magnetic disk. The first floppy disks were 8 inches in diameter. However, disks 5¼ inches in diameter and 3½ inches in diameter are now commonly used. See Figure 6.3 for an illustration of a 5¼ inch disk and the drive into which it is inserted for writing and reading.

Figure 6.3
A 5¼ inch floppy disk and its drive

To make reading and writing easier, floppy disks are divided into segments known as **sectors**. Imagine that a disk is marked into slices as if it were a pie already cut into servings. This cuts each track on the disk into small pieces, as shown in Figure 6.4. Each of these small pieces is a sector. One sector full of data is the smallest amount of data that can be written or read at one time. The number of characters stored in one sector depends on decisions made by the hardware manufacturer. With many computer systems, a disk sector holds 256 characters. Floppy disks are rotated inside their drives at about 300 revolutions per minute. The read/write heads actually contact the disks as the drives operate.

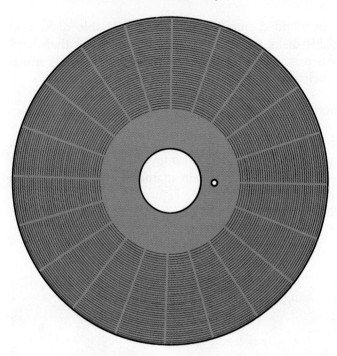

Figure 6.4
Each track is divided into sectors.

The amount of data that can be stored on one disk varies tremendously depending upon the way the particular drive and disk are made. Capacities from about 320K to 2 megabytes are common, and 10 megabytes of storage is possible.

Hard Disks

A **hard disk** gets its name from the fact that it is made of rigid material; it does not bend like a floppy disk. While the read/write head on a floppy disk actually contacts the disk surface, the head of a hard disk floats a tiny distance above the disk surface (often less than a millionth of an inch). Since there is no physical contact, there is no wear of the disk surface. Rotating at about 3600 revolutions per minute, hard disks can transfer data to and from the computer at a much faster rate than floppy disks.

Hard disks are generally 5 inches, 8 inches, or 14 inches in diameter, although other sizes are available. In a hard disk drive, there may be one disk, or there may be several disks stacked on top of one another on a common vertical shaft, or a **spindle**. When there are several disks, you may refer to the group of disks as a **disk pack**. There is just enough space between the disk surfaces to allow movement of the read/write heads (see Figure 6.5). Many hard disk drives use disks that are sealed against dust and dirt; these drives are called Winchester drives, a nickname for the particular technology they use.

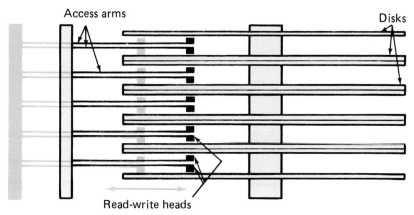

Access arms

Disks

Read-write heads

The heads move in and out to position themselves over the desired tracks.

Figure 6.5
Read/write heads move between the disks.

The use of multiple disks can increase the speed of reading and writing by reducing the amount of head travel time. For example, suppose the words of a rather long document are to be recorded on disk. If the entire document is recorded on one disk surface, the write head moves into position over a track and uses all available space on that track. The head then moves to another track and uses all space available on that one, and so on. This may require several moves from one track to another. Suppose, however, that the data to be written is divided among several disk surfaces. In this case, all the write heads can move into position over the different surfaces and the entire document can be written with no further head movement. This can greatly increase the speed of data reading and writing. You may refer to all the tracks of the same number on different disk surfaces as a **cylinder**. For example, all the third tracks put together make up a cylinder. See Figure 6.6 for an illustration of this.

Hard disks may be either fixed or removable. If a disk is removable, it may be taken out of the disk drive for storage and replaced by a different disk. A fixed disk cannot be removed from the disk drive; it is permanently mounted.

Because a hard disk does not bend, data can be packed much closer together than it can be on a floppy disk. Since many disk drives can be attached to the same computer system, the total amount of storage that can be on-line to the computer at any one time is almost unlimited. Figure 6.7 shows several hard disk drives.

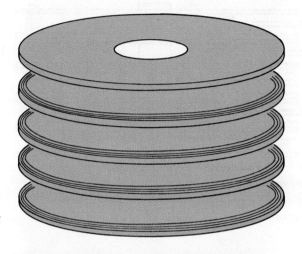

Figure 6.6
A cylinder on a disk pack

Figure 6.7
Representative hard disk drives

MAGNETIC TAPE

Magnetic tape is a long strip of flexible plastic like the tape used in an ordinary cassette tape recorder. The tape is coated with microscopic bars of a material that can be magnetized. Magnetic tape may be on reels or contained in one of several kinds of cartridges.

Tape drives like the one in Figure 6.8 record data on the tape as magnetized spots in the proper pattern for each character. When the tape is read, the spots produce electronic impulses as they are moved past the read head of the tape drive. Figure 6.9 shows how the magnetic spots might appear if they were visible. Note that each character code is recorded across the tape, with one bit in each channel. A **channel** is a recording path along the tape. A read/write head is positioned over each channel on the tape. Tapes generally have nine channels, even though seven-channel tapes are available. The heads either read the data that is already on the tape and transfer it to the computer for processing, or they write the processed data coming from the computer onto the tape.

Figure 6.8 A typical tape drive

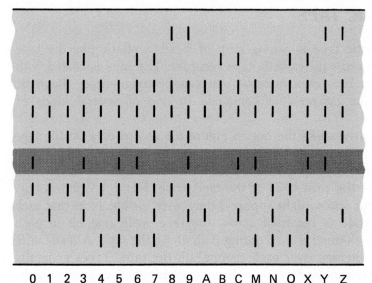

Figure 6.9
Characters coded on a tape

0 1 2 3 4 5 6 7 8 9 A B C M N O X Y Z

Many very inexpensive home computers use ordinary cassette tape recorders for data storage. Such a tape contains only one channel; bits are recorded one after the other. In other words, a character that is written crosswise on a seven-channel or nine-channel tape is written lengthwise on a cassette tape.

As with a disk, writing on tape erases data previously recorded on it. The new data erases the old data as the new data is recorded. However, reading data on tape does not erase the data. (You can erase a tape on a tape recorder by recording over it. But you can play a tape many times without ever erasing it. The idea is the same.)

A tape drive is a sequential-access device. When a certain item of data is to be found on a tape, the computer reads all the items one after the other until it locates the desired one. The contents of the **record** (related data treated as a unit) can then be displayed on a CRT, printed, or otherwise processed. For many applications where data needs to be stored or retrieved in random order, the use of tape is not practical. For some jobs, however, it is very appropriate. For example, suppose pay amounts are to be computed and paychecks prepared. A tape contains the name and other information about each employee. The tape can simply be read from start to finish, processing the information about each employee in order. Tapes are also good for making backups. A **backup** is simply a copy of all the data on an auxiliary storage device. The copy is made so that the data will still exist if the medium on which the data was originally stored is damaged.

BUBBLE MEMORY

Bubble memory consists of small magnetic "bubbles" that move on an endless "notched track" through the chip containing them. A partial chip is shown in Figure 6.10. Figure 6.11 shows how the bubbles can be visualized. They are arranged according to the binary code used by the computer; the presence of a bubble represents a 1, while the absence of a bubble represents a 0. For access, the bubbles move through the chip. Therefore, bubble memory is a sequential-access device. It is, however, very fast for a sequential-access device. Bubble memory is particularly valuable for applications where data needs to be recorded away from an office or plant; the data remains in the chips even when power is removed.

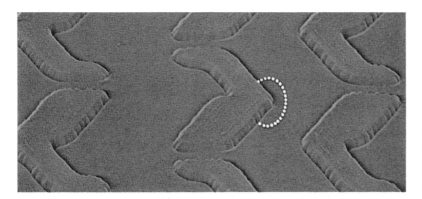

Figure 6.10
A bubble memory chip retains its data even with the power removed.

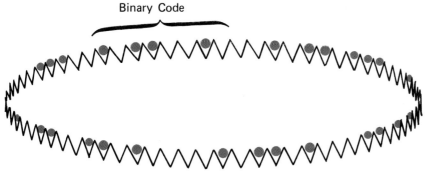

One Character in
Binary Code

Figure 6.11
Magnetic bubbles move across a surface.

LASER DISKS

A **laser disk** (Figure 6.12) is one of the most exciting storage methods that has been developed. Using disks similar to those of video disk players and audio disk players, laser disks record data by the presence or absence of holes. The microscopic holes are burned in the disk by a laser beam and they are read back by a beam. The holes represent the codes for the recorded characters. Laser disks are random-access devices. Most laser disks are not erasable and reusable, though a few are. Storage capacities for laser disks begin at about one billion characters per disk. This makes them very valuable for applications where huge quantities of data must be stored. For example, insurance companies with tremendously large files of customer data would find laser disks very attractive.

Figure 6.12
The holes in a laser disk represent characters.

SUMMARY

Almost all computers intended for general use have some form of auxiliary storage. The storage may be either random access or sequential access. If it is random access, the device can read or write a particular group of data without reading or writing everything that physically comes before it on the medium used. If it is sequential access, the device can read or write a particular group of data only by going through everything recorded before it on the medium.

The most commonly used random-access device is a disk drive. Some disk drives are designed to use floppy disks, while others use hard disks. Storage capacities and access speeds are higher with hard disk drives. The most commonly used sequential-access device is a tape drive. Bubble memory (which is sequential access) and laser disks (which are random access) are newer methods that are becoming more widely used.

REVIEW QUESTIONS

1. What is the purpose of auxiliary storage? (Obj. 1)

2. What is the difference between a random-access storage device and a sequential-access storage device? (Obj. 1)

3. Which commonly used storage devices are random-access devices? (Obj. 1)

4. Which commonly used storage devices are sequential-access devices? (Obj. 1)

5. Describe how data is recorded on a disk. (Obj. 1)

6. What are the main differences between floppy disks and hard disks? (Obj. 1)

7. Describe how data is recorded on a tape. (Obj. 1)

8. What is the most important thing to consider in deciding whether to use random-access storage or sequential-access storage? (Obj. 2)

9. Name an application for which random-access storage is appropriate. (Obj. 2)

10. What are some applications for which sequential-access storage is appropriate? (Obj. 2)

11. How is data recorded with bubble memory? (Obj. 1)

12. How is data recorded with a laser disk? (Obj. 1)

VOCABULARY WORDS

The following terms were introduced in this chapter:

sequential access	spindle
random access	disk pack
magnetic disk	cylinder
track	magnetic tape
direct access	channel
flexible disk	record
floppy disk	backup
sector	bubble memory
hard disk	laser disk

WORKBOOK EXERCISES

Chapter 6 in the workbook consists of three exercises: True/False, Matching, and Completion. Complete all three exercises in Chapter 6 of the workbook before proceeding to Chapter 7 in this text.

DISKETTE EXERCISE

Complete the diskette exercise for Chapter 6 before proceeding to Chapter 7 in this text.

PART THREE

Information Processing

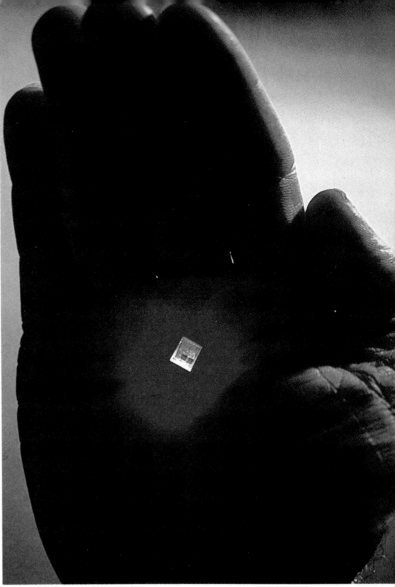

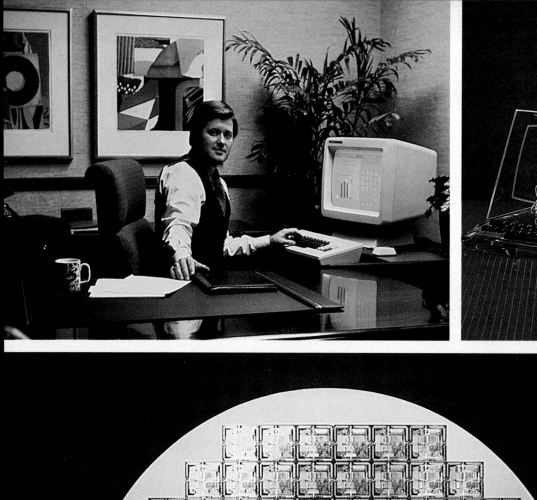
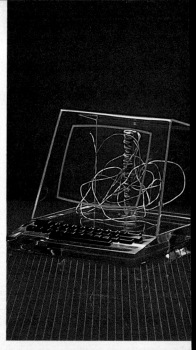
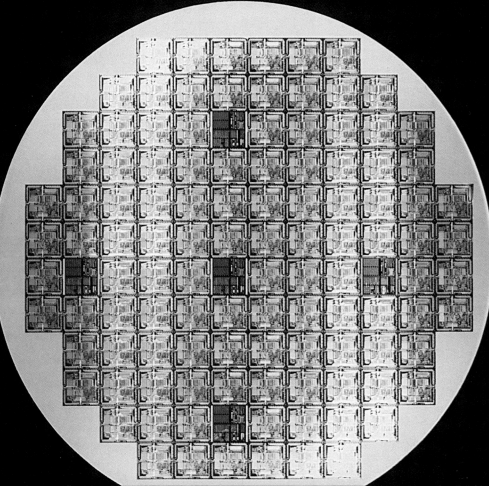

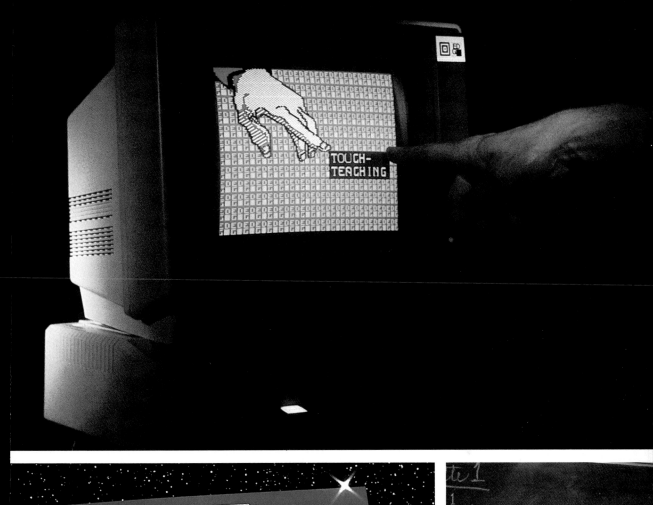

7 Information Processing Functions

Objectives:

1. Define data processing and word processing. Describe the similarities and differences in data processing and word processing.

2. Describe the data processing functions.

3. Describe the word processing functions.

4. List benefits of the integration of data processing and word processing into information processing.

In previous chapters you have taken a fairly detailed look at the hardware used in information systems. Now let's take a detailed look at some of the functions of information systems.

INTEGRATION OF DATA PROCESSING AND WORD PROCESSING

Originally computers in business were used primarily for data processing. **Data processing** is the converting of facts into usable form. Most computer applications involved arithmetic computations or the storage and manipulation of various facts. Computer use in accounting and engineering became widespread. Later, typewriters were connected to special computers and word processing was born. **Word processing** is the composition, revision, printing, and storage of documents such as letters and reports.

As time progressed, programs were developed to allow general-purpose computers to do word processing. Then newer word processors such as shown in Figure 7.1 were made to do arithmetic. In fact, word processing machines could be programmed to do all kinds of jobs previously left to computers. After all, a word processor was nothing but a computer specially programmed for handling text. Thus, data processing and word processing began to be integrated and known as **information processing**. It makes a lot of sense, for example, to be able to take figures generated by data processing and place them in documents being created by word processing. As an example of this, the accounting records of an auto manufacturer might contain facts showing which dealers have sold more cars than expected. To send congratulatory letters to these dealers, the word processing operation can take the dealer names, addresses, and sales figures from the accounting records and produce the letters. Figure 7.2 diagrams this process.

Figure 7.1
A word processor doing arithmetic

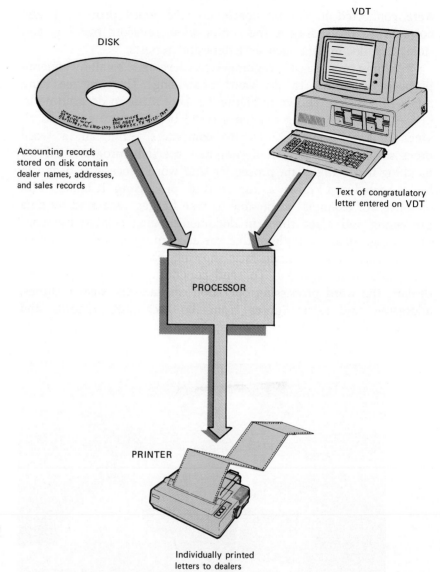

DISK

VDT

Accounting records
stored on disk contain
dealer names, addresses,
and sales records

Text of congratulatory
letter entered on VDT

PROCESSOR

PRINTER

Figure 7.2
Output from data
processing and word
processing can be
combined.

Individually printed
letters to dealers

Another example of the integration of data processing and word processing can be found in the input of data. Frequently, the same input needs to be included in a document and used in further processing. For example, a manager may use a program to estimate how the business should fare in the following year. The numbers from this estimate can then be input into the word processing system to produce a report for top management. They may also be input into the accounting system. Comparisons can then be made between the estimates and the actual figures that will be computed as the year progresses. See Figure 7.3 for an illustration of this process.

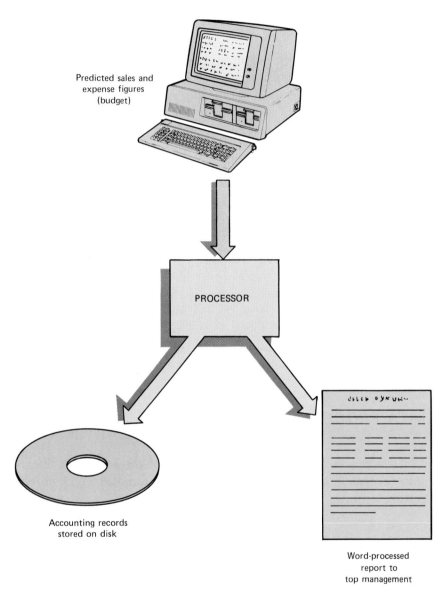

Predicted sales and
expense figures
(budget)

PROCESSOR

Accounting records
stored on disk

Word-processed
report to
top management

Figure 7.3
The same input can
serve both data
processing and word
processing functions.

The benefits of integrating data processing and word processing into information processing include the following:

1. There is less duplication of effort. Data already in the system for one purpose can be used for the other purpose. Data may generally be entered only once instead of twice.

2. Records are more accurate. The more places the same information is recorded, the greater the possibility that some locations will get updated, while others will not. With the integration of data processing and word processing, duplicate recording is reduced.

3. Equipment is better utilized. Trends in office work indicate that computer equipment (such as terminals and microcomputers) is being used more and more by managers, other decision makers, accountants, and secretaries, rather than being operated on a day-long basis by specialized data entry personnel. As a result of this, the in-use time for equipment tends to be less. For example, one study has shown that the average microcomputer in a business office is actually in use about 30 minutes a day. By combining both word processing and data processing functions on one machine, the machine is used more of the time and is, therefore, more economical.

In the remainder of this chapter, we will take a more detailed look at the functions of information processing. We will break the functions into two areas: those typically thought of as data processing functions and those typically thought of as word processing functions. Keep in mind, however, that some of the functions are common to both areas, and that all of the functions are frequently integrated with each other and performed on the same equipment.

DATA PROCESSING FUNCTIONS

Data processing includes one or more of the following operations: recording, coding, sorting, calculating, summarizing, communicating, storing, and retrieving.

Recording

Recording is the process of writing, rewriting, or reproducing data by hand or electronically. Recording includes a very wide range of operations. Some of the operations are handwriting, typewriting, duplicating, microfilming, entering data on a terminal, and recording data on magnetic media such as tape or disks. The employee in Figure 7.4 is recording her work hours with a time clock that communicates the hours directly to the computer.

Figure 7.4   *An employee recording the number of hours worked*

Coding

Coding is the process of assigning a system of symbols, letters, or words to data according to a set of rules. In a school registration system, for example, *1* might stand for freshmen, *2* for sophomores, and so forth. Similar codes may be assigned to major programs of study, names of courses, and job preferences of students.

Stores identify stock items by codes in order to keep accurate sales and inventory records. Items appearing in catalogs have code or stock numbers. ZIP codes on letters are used to sort the letters by cities and various locations in the cities. The names of states have two-letter abbreviations. A single sales slip such as shown in Figure 7.5 may contain several codes. One code may be for the salesperson and another may be for the department. One code may be the customer's account number, and another code may be the stock number identifying the article sold. A telephone number is a code in which some of the numbers stand for a part of the country (area code), some for a city or part of a city, and some for a particular telephone.

Figure 7.5
Typical codes used on a sales slip

Codes speed up processing. They aid in selecting the data needed to solve a given problem. They also save space in a computer. Note the codes used in the partial enrollment summary in Figure 7.6. With the codes shown, the following are facts that could be listed: (1) number of students in each class, (2) number of students in each major, (3) number of female students, (4) number of male students, (5) average age of female students, and (6) average age of male students.

Sorting

Sorting is the process of arranging information according to a logical system. Sorting includes (1) the *sequencing* of names or other data in alphabetic or numeric order; (2) the *grouping* of data by date, product, department, state, or some other classification; and (3) the *selecting* of a certain record from a group of similar records. Sorting may be done on the computer by physically rearranging the data in memory or on an auxiliary storage medium such as a disk. Sorting the data in this manner is one of the most time-consuming operations performed on most computers. For many applications, therefore, programs have been developed that provide the functions of sorting (sequencing, grouping, and selecting) without actually rearranging the data. These programs usually use more memory and auxiliary storage space, but the saving in time is well worth it.

An example of *sequencing* is the arranging of students' names in numeric order according to student number assigned to each student. An example of *grouping* is the bringing together of all the names according to the class of each student. An example of *selecting* is the picking of a specific record from a group of similar records. See Figure 7.7 for examples of sequencing, grouping, and selecting data.

NAME	CLASS	MAJOR	SEX	BIRTHDATE			NUMBER
				MN	DAY	YEAR	
Earle, Timothy	1	1	M	7	5	67	750
Eber, Leslie	2	3	F	12	14	66	313
Edelman, Arthur	1	2	M	3	12	66	485
Edwards, Ann	4	1	F	5	6	64	484
Eiduson, Karen	1	4	F	4	11	65	749
Eng, Michael	3	1	M	9	7	65	751

CODES

Figure 7.6 *Typical codes used on enrollment summaries*

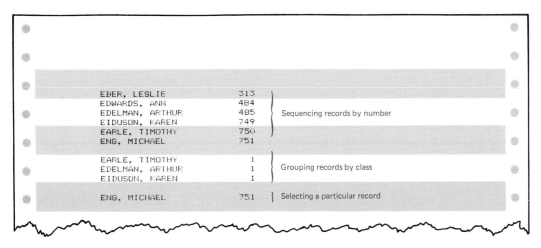

```
EBER, LESLIE        313  ⎫
EDWARDS, ANN        484  ⎪
EDELMAN, ARTHUR     485  ⎬  Sequencing records by number
EIDUSON, KAREN      749  ⎪
EARLE, TIMOTHY      750  ⎪
ENG, MICHAEL        751  ⎭

EARLE, TIMOTHY        1  ⎫
EDELMAN, ARTHUR       1  ⎬  Grouping records by class
EIDUSON, KAREN        1  ⎭

ENG, MICHAEL        751  ⎬  Selecting a particular record
```

Figure 7.7 *Data may be sequenced, grouped, or selected.*

Sometimes the sole objective of a data processing application is the arranging of a list of names in alphabetic order or the grouping of records into separate categories. For other applications, however, sorting speeds up further processing. Before course grades are recorded on student record forms, for example, the grade reports for each student might be grouped together to make the process easier.

Calculating

Calculating is the process of computing in order to arrive at a mathematical result. It includes adding, subtracting, multiplying, dividing, and other mathematical operations. There are many calculations needed to arrive at the wages earned by an employee, for example. Note the results of these calculations in the paycheck shown in Figure 7.8.

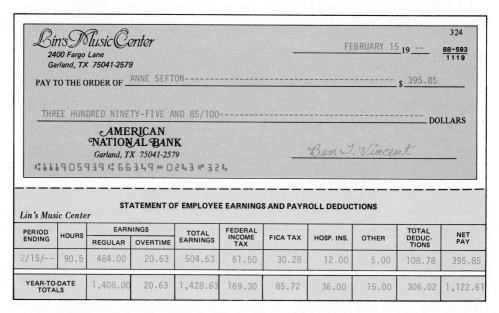

PERIOD ENDING	HOURS	EARNINGS		TOTAL EARNINGS	FEDERAL INCOME TAX	FICA TAX	HOSP. INS.	OTHER	TOTAL DEDUC-TIONS	NET PAY
		REGULAR	OVERTIME							
2/15/--	90.5	484.00	20.63	504.63	61.50	30.28	12.00	5.00	108.78	395.85
YEAR-TO-DATE TOTALS		1,408.00	20.63	1,428.63	169.30	85.72	36.00	15.00	306.02	1,122.61

Figure 7.8 *This paycheck shows typical calculations.*

In Figure 7.8, regular hours worked were added and multiplied by the hourly rate to get the regular earnings. The overtime hours worked were added and multiplied by $1\frac{1}{2}$ times the regular rate to arrive at the overtime pay. The two amounts were added together to get the total earnings. Deductions were then subtracted from the total earnings to arrive at the amount of the paycheck.

Summarizing

Summarizing is the process of converting processed data into brief, meaningful form. Printed reports usually involve summaries. As already explained, many calculations must be made to prepare paychecks for employees of a company. The data from the calculations of all the paychecks can be summarized to make it useful to a business. For example, summaries can list some of the following: (1) total wages paid, (2) total deductions for social security taxes, (3) total number of employees on the payroll, and (4) total earnings for each employee from the beginning of the calendar year to the date of the last check.

Summaries can also consist of such things as percentages, averages, and comparisons of one year's operations with those of other years. For example, the average score on a test is useful in figuring whether a particular score is high, average, or low. Figure 7.9 shows a financial summary.

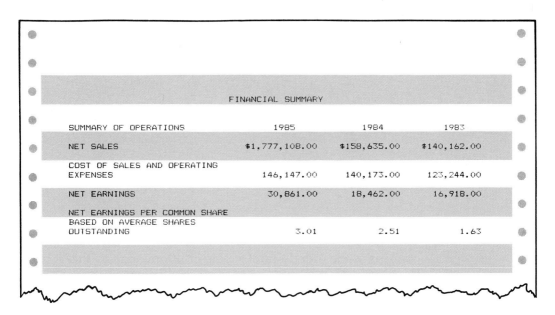

FINANCIAL SUMMARY			
SUMMARY OF OPERATIONS	1985	1984	1983
NET SALES	$1,777,108.00	$158,635.00	$140,162.00
COST OF SALES AND OPERATING EXPENSES	146,147.00	140,173.00	123,244.00
NET EARNINGS	30,861.00	18,462.00	16,918.00
NET EARNINGS PER COMMON SHARE BASED ON AVERAGE SHARES OUTSTANDING	3.01	2.51	1.63

Figure 7.9 *A financial summary*

Communicating

Communicating is the process of transmitting information from one point to another point. Communicating may consist of nothing more than the transfer of reports from one desk to another.

Frequently, however, it includes such activities as the transmission of electronic information by telephone, microwave, satellite (Figure 7.10), and television.

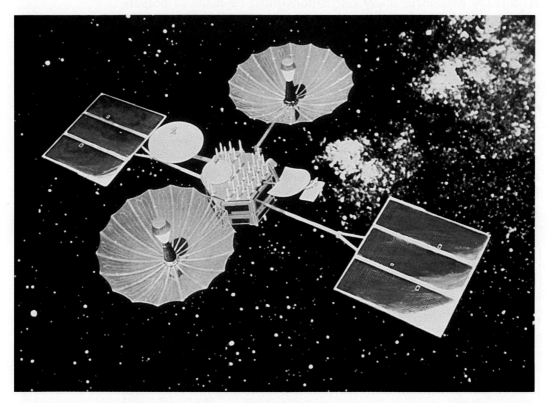

Figure 7.10 *Some data communications are done by satellite.*

Storing

Storing is the orderly safekeeping of information so that it may be used later. The operation should allow for prompt storage of data, for strict following of rules about the use of stored materials, and for destruction of records when they are no longer needed. With a computerized data processing system, storage is done by use of the auxiliary storage devices you learned about in Chapter 6.

Retrieving

Retrieving is the process of making stored information available when needed. Records stored in a computer or on magnetic tape, disks, or COM can be easily retrieved only if the information is properly coded. When it is properly coded, retrieval is accomplished very quickly.

WORD PROCESSING FUNCTIONS

Word processing includes those functions necessary for producing, revising, printing, and storing text in the form of documents. These functions include entering text, revising text, assembling text, merging text and data, communicating the text in the form of a document, and storing and retrieving the document.

Entering Text

Text entry is the process of getting words from the mind of the writer into the computer system. Text is usually entered into the system by using a keyboard and video display, as the operator is doing in Figure 7.11. Any errors made while entering the text are quickly and easily corrected by rekeying. If desired, changes can also be made during the entry process. Eventually the entry of text may be done with speech recognition devices. The entry of text is equivalent to data processing's recording function.

Figure 7.11
Most text is entered on a video display terminal.

Revising Text

Once text is entered, any change made to it is known as a **revision**. Words or characters may be added or deleted, misspellings may be corrected at each point where they occur, or text may be rearranged. Rearrangement may involve moving words, sentences, or paragraphs around to change the order of the text. In making revisions, the correct text does not need to be rekeyed. Refer to Figure 7.12 for an example of revising text.

```
January 22, 19---



Mr. Dale Parker-Smith, Principal
Liberty High School
4409 Century Lane
Boise, ID  83704-2273

Dear Mr. Parker-Smith:

I am writing to tell you how much I enjoyed presenting our
program on animal protection to your student body.

One of your students proposed starting an Animal
Protection Club to help feed and house birds in winter,
volunteer at our society, help educate students in other
schools, and perform other lifesaving tasks.  The other
students were also enthusiastic.

The students were very responsive to the ideas presented,
especially in regard to taking more responsibility for
animal life.  Most students had never thought about the
fact that due to the increasing numbers of people, much of
the natural habitat of animals has disappeared.  This has
not only upset the natural food cycle, but has also
destroyed nesting grounds and winter protection sites.

I commend you again on your wonderful student body.  May
they serve as an example for all our youth to follow.

Sincerely,

Roselyn Kerr

Roselyn Kerr
President
```

Figure 7.12 *One type of text revision is the block move.*

Assembling Text

Frequently in word processing, several different sections of text need to be assembled. **Assembly** is the putting together of different parts of text to form a new document. For example, hundreds of standard prewritten paragraphs may be stored on disk. To compose a reply to a letter, the writer chooses several appropriate paragraphs from the disk and combines them as shown in Figure 7.13. Once the paragraphs are combined, any desired revisions can be made just as if the text had been originally entered from the keyboard.

```
April 5, 19--


Ms. S. R. Finnegan
9873 Ryan Industrial Park        Name and address from keyboard
Eau Claire, WI  54701-2438

Dear Ms. Finnegan:

The information you requested about our log cabins is
enclosed.

The Retreat II model seems to most closely match your
requirements.  It comes as a totally prefabricated unit        Paragraphs
ready for assembly at your site.  It contains 1,200 square      from disk
feet of usable space and is, therefore, ideal for the
larger family or the family desiring a little more space
for its mountain hideaway.  While it is rustic in
appearance, it has space for every modern convenience.

Building the cabin over the creek at your site will
certainly provide a unique setting.  It will also require       Paragraph
a custom-fabricated foundation, probably using steel I          from keyboard
beams.  A local contractor or architect will be your best
source of information on the proper plan.

We are sending your name and address to our local dealer,
Harley Outdoors Company.  A representative will be              Paragraph
contacting you shortly.  In the meantime, please let us         from disk
know if we can provide any additional information.

Sincerely,

M. L. Martin

M. L. Martin
Sales Manager
```

Figure 7.13 *Text from the disk and the keyboard is assembled to form a letter.*

Merging Text and Data

Merging is the process of combining text and data into the same document. Merging is useful in many applications. For example, you may want to send letters to a particular group of people. All the names and addresses you need may already be stored on a disk as data. You can compose the letter with the word processing functions, then have the computer merge together the names, addresses, and letter text. This process works as shown in Figure 7.14.

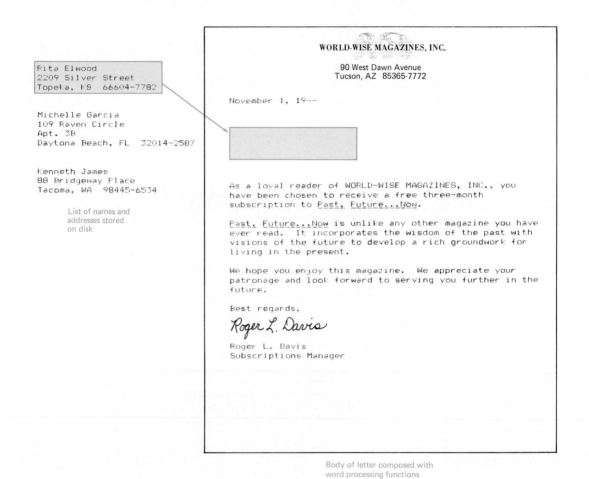

List of names and
addresses stored
on disk

Body of letter composed with
word processing functions

Figure 7.14   Merging data into a letter

Communicating Documents

Once a document has been created, it must be communicated to the intended user. Usually, this means the document is printed, and mailed or delivered. Frequently, however, finished documents are now transmitted to the user in the form of electronic mail. As shown in Figure 7.15, the receiver asks for the mail and the document appears on the screen. The receiver reads the document, then prints a paper copy if one is desired. Communicating a document is quite similar to data processing's function of communicating the results of processing.

Figure 7.15
Requesting the
electronic mail

Storing and Retrieving Documents

The word processing storage and retrieval functions are similar to the data processing storage and retrieval functions. Entire documents or parts of documents may be stored. The storing of documents such as letters and reports has historically been done by keeping the paper on which they were written. However, growing numbers of these documents are being stored on computer media such as disks and COM. As you learned in Chapter 6, these media can store much more information in a smaller space.

SUMMARY

When computers were first used in business, they were used for data processing applications—applications dealing with numbers and facts. Functions carried out by data processing included recording, coding, sorting, calculating, summarizing, communicating, and storing. Later, specialized equipment was developed for processing words. Functions supported by word processors included text entry, revision, assembly of text, merging of data and text, communicating of documents, and storage of documents.

As technology progressed, these two areas of application began to merge. General-purpose computers were equipped with word processing software, while word processors were equipped with programs to allow them to do data processing applications. Provision was made for the data processing and word processing applications to share text and data with each other. The merger of data processing and word processing is known as information processing. Several benefits are derived from information processing, including less duplication of effort, greater accuracy of records, and better utilization of equipment.

REVIEW QUESTIONS

1. What is data processing? (Obj. 1)

2. What is word processing? (Obj. 1)

3. How are data processing and word processing alike? How are they different? (Obj. 1)

4. Describe the benefits to be gained by integrating data processing and word processing into information processing. (Obj. 4)

5. Name and describe the functions of data processing. (Obj. 2)

6. Name and describe the functions of word processing. (Obj. 3)

VOCABULARY WORDS

The following terms were introduced in this chapter:

data processing	recording
word processing	coding

information processing   sorting
calculating   text entry
summarizing   revision
communicating   assembly
storing   merging
retrieving

WORKBOOK EXERCISES

Chapter 7 in the workbook consists of four exercises: True/False, Matching, Completion, and Identification. Complete all four exercises in Chapter 7 of the workbook before proceeding to Chapter 8 in this text.

DISKETTE EXERCISE

Complete the diskette exercise for Chapter 7 before proceeding to Chapter 8 in this text.

8

Systems for Processing Information

Objectives:

1. Describe time-sharing and distributed-processing network systems.

2. Describe real-time systems and batch systems.

3. Describe a typical application for each of the four system categories.

4. Explain the steps in planning and documenting a system.

A **computer information system** is a computer system used for information processing. Some computer information systems are stand-alone units; that is, one processor serves one user. The user may be doing word processing, accounting, or any number of different applications. Other systems, however, must be able to serve more than one user at the same time. An airline reservation system, for example, must be able to keep up with reservation requests from thousands of terminals.

From earlier chapters, you have probably noted differences in the processing of data. Some applications, such as a reservation system, require that data be processed immediately upon its creation. Other kinds of data, such as the number of hours worked by employees, may be saved or accumulated for a while before being processed. In this chapter, we will look at how information systems may be used in the ways just described.

HANDLING MORE THAN ONE USER

In this section, we will classify information systems as either time-sharing networks or distributed-processing networks. A **network** is a collection of processors and terminals that serves more than one user at a time by communicating. Time-sharing and distributed processing refer to how the different hardware is connected together to serve more than one user at a time. At the end of this section, we will find out how communication can take place between parts of a system that are located far apart.

Time-Sharing Systems

In a **time-sharing system**, several input devices (usually terminals) are attached to one processor. The users of the different terminals may be doing the same or different kinds of work with the computer. A time-sharing system can be put together as illustrated in Figure 8.1. This figure shows what is known as a **star network**; that is, the different terminals are connected to the processor as if they were the points of a star. The terminals may be located near the processor and connected directly to the processor with cables. On the other hand, they may be located away from the processor in a different building or even a different country.

The different terminals in a time-sharing system share the processor's time. That is, the processor devotes a very brief amount of time to one terminal, then a very brief amount of time to another terminal, and so on. If the processor is fast and the number of terminals is reasonable, the operator of each terminal will not realize that other terminals are sharing the processor. However, as more terminals are added to a time-sharing system, the **queue** (waiting line) becomes longer and the system seems to run more slowly. The larger the number of terminals, the less processor time available to each of them. Consequently, a time-sharing system can be slowed so much that its speed is unacceptable.

As an example of a time-sharing system, consider the case of a business that sells from catalogs sent to its customers. To place an order, a customer dials a catalog-ordering number. In the company's office is a time-sharing computer with a large number of

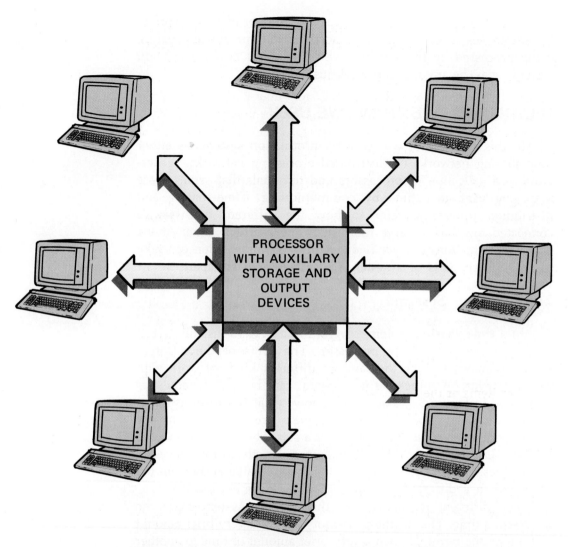

Figure 8.1 *A time-sharing system arranged as a star network*

terminals. Information about all the items the company sells is stored in the computer's auxiliary storage. Information such as the names and addresses of customers is also stored. When an order comes in by phone, an operator uses a terminal to enter the order while talking with the customer. The computer can tell immediately whether the desired item is in stock in the warehouse. If it is in stock, the proper paperwork for shipping the order is done by the computer. If the company is out of the item, the customer can choose a different item, wait until the desired item is received, or cancel the order.

In this particular company, some employees enter orders, while others use terminals to enter price changes that are to go into effect the next day. These price changes have been planned by the company's department managers. For example, the sporting goods manager and the household goods manager may both have decided on price changes for their departments. The changes from each department have been written on paper source documents signed by the department manager. The new prices are entered from these forms.

Much other data must also be input into the computer to fill orders. In addition, there are many other uses for the computer, such as preparation of the payroll and maintenance of the company's financial records. All of these jobs are handled by one computer system. Many different jobs can be going on at the same time; this is known as **multiprogramming**. Also, many different people can be working on the same kind of job at the same time; this is known as **multiprocessing**. All auxiliary storage is controlled by one computer. Multiprogramming and multiprocessing are possible due to the fact that the processor is extremely fast compared with the input and output devices. Therefore, while one program is waiting for input or output to finish, the processor can be working on other items at the same time. Refer back to Figure 8.1 to see an example of this system.

Distributed-Processing Network

Remember that in a time-sharing system, all the terminals are connected to one processor. Since one processor handles all the computing, that processor can have a very large work load. A **distributed-processing network**, on the other hand, uses more than one processor. Instead of having one processor with several terminals, there are two or more processors that are capable of communicating with each other when necessary. They communicate by sending data to each other through cables, phone lines, microwave transmission (similar to radio), or other devices.

In a distributed network, each of the separate processors has its own input devices. It may have its own auxiliary storage and output devices, or it may share these with other computers in the network. There are many different ways to put together a distributed-processing network, and the different computers may be in the same building or spread over a wide area. All distributed-processing networks, however, use more than one processor. This way, the work is shared rather than being carried by one computer.

Two popular ways of setting up a distributed-processing network are the star network and the ring network. A distributed star network uses the same principle as a star network of terminals. There is a processor in the center of the star. Instead of terminals at the points of the star, however, there are small computers. All communication between the different small computers travels through the central computer. In a **ring network**, illustrated in Figure 8.2, there is no central computer. Instead, any one of the computers in the network may communicate with any other computer in the network whenever necessary. If desired, the computers in the network may have multiple terminals of their own, creating a

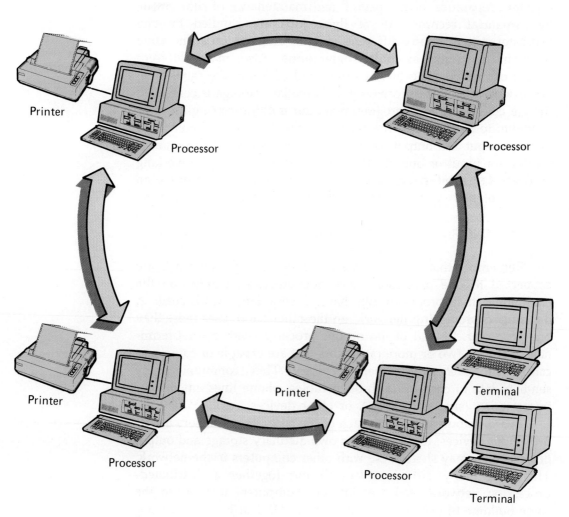

Figure 8.2 *A ring network*

network of time-sharing systems. The computers may have whatever amount and type of auxiliary storage is needed for their particular applications.

For an example of a distributed-processing network, let's look at a school system with several schools. All school records are kept on computer. This includes all student records of courses taken, credits earned, attendance, and so on. It also includes such things as each school's financial records and library inventory. In deciding on the best way to install the computers, the school system first looked at the possibility of placing several terminals in each school. These would be connected to a large computer in the central office by use of phone lines. The idea sounded good until the cost of the phone lines was included. Also, the present computer in the central office would have to be replaced with a larger one in order to handle the additional terminals.

As an alternative, the school system looked at putting a couple of microcomputers in each school. This would eliminate the cost of the phone lines and would eliminate the need to replace the central office computer. Each microcomputer would handle all the processing work that needed to be done. There were several problems with this idea, however. Many students transfer from one school to another during the school year. If a student's records were stored on a microcomputer in one school and the student moved to another school, there would be a problem in getting that student's records transferred to the computer in the new school. There would also be much duplication of records. The same course descriptions, for example, would have to be stored on the computers in all the schools. There are thousands of the same book titles that are stocked by more than one library. If all this data were stored in individual computer systems in each school, a very large amount of money would have to be spent for additional auxiliary storage for all the microcomputers. Furthermore, the problem of getting data from one school to another would still exist. More study showed that much of the data that would have to be duplicated would be used only once or twice a year.

Eventually the school system decided that a distributed-processing network would work best; that is, they put microcomputers in each school. However, each microcomputer is able to communicate over a phone line with the central office computer. The large amounts of data that would have had to be duplicated are stored by the central office computer. On the rare occasions that this information is needed by a local school, the microcomputer can be connected to the central office computer through phone lines to request the information. Another advantage of this solution is that summary information can be transmitted to the central office computer as necessary. For example, information about teacher attendance is maintained at each school during the month, then transmitted to the central office computer in time to prepare paychecks.

The use of the distributed-processing network will not have additional costs for phone lines. Most communication with the central office computer requires only a brief local phone call on existing phone lines. Longer calls for sharing larger quantities of data can be completed at night when no humans are present to need the phone lines.

Data Communications

As you learned earlier, data communications refers to sending data from one unit of a computer system to another. The units may be processors, terminals, or other input or output devices. When the units are located close to each other, they can be connected together by a wire cable. When they are placed in different locations, however, communication by some other method is required.

Most slow- to medium-speed data communication is accomplished by using phone lines. When using a phone line, each character to be sent is coded into a series of bits, as you learned in Chapter 3. The bits are then transmitted over the phone line. Standard phone lines, however, were originally installed to carry voice from one location to another. Therefore, they have trouble with such things as electronic impulses representing 1's and 0's. To resolve the problem, a modem, which was briefly discussed in Chapter 1, is used to connect each computer device to the phone line. Modem is a contraction of "MOdulator-DEModulator," the technical term describing the function of the device. Some modems use what is known as an acoustic (sound) coupler. Other modems are known as direct-connect modems. With an **acoustic coupler**, the modem turns the computer's output into sound. The sound is picked up by the microphone in the telephone handset and converted to the proper electric signal for transmission. To receive data, the process is reversed. The acoustic coupler has a microphone that listens to the sound generated by the telephone handpiece. The sound is then converted into the 1's and 0's expected by the computer. A **direct-connect** modem bypasses the microphone stage. It is plugged straight into a phone line and directly creates the kind of electric signals required. On the receiving end, it directly converts the phone's electric signals back to 1's and 0's. A direct-connect modem may be a separate unit such as shown in Figure 8.3, or it may be mounted inside the computer or other device. It is possible to use an acoustically coupled modem on one end of the phone line and a direct-connect modem on the other end.

Figure 8.3
A modem connects a computer to a standard phone line.

Common speeds for data communication with small computers are 300 bits per second and 1200 bits per second. These speeds are commonly called 300 baud and 1200 baud. **Baud** is another term for bits per second. Therefore, a speed of 1200 baud means that 1200 1's and 0's can be transmitted over the line each second. Speeds up to 9600 baud are usually possible with phone lines. Higher speeds require other means of transmission, such as microwave transmission or satellite transmission. Figure 8.4 shows an earth terminal for a satellite data transmission system.

Figure 8.4
High-speed data communications can be relayed by satellite.

WHEN THE DATA IS PROCESSED

The previous section dealt with how computer systems are connected together to serve more than one user. Now let's look at differences in the timing of processing data. The differences in when processing takes place are dependent on the programs used by the computers, not on how the machines are linked together.

In illustrating the different systems, we will use system flowcharts. A **system flowchart** is a graphic representation of the order of operations in an information processing system. A symbol is used to represent the process taking place at each step.

A system flowchart is like a road map. Through it, in a matter of minutes, you can trace the steps in a plan set up to process data. You can trace information back to its source. You can see the relationship of one step in the plan to another step.

A system flowchart shows what kinds of input go into the system, the steps through which the data passes, and the output produced. Rather than detailed instructions, input, general processing, and output steps are emphasized. Though the amount of detail in a system flowchart can vary depending on the preference of the preparer, detailed instructions are generally handled in the documentation of the computer programs to be used with the system.

The symbols to be used for system flowcharts are illustrated and explained in Figure 8.5. For the most part, system flowcharts are drawn so that they read from left to right and from top to bottom. The symbols are connected by lines. **Arrowheads** and **flowlines** are often used to show the flow of data. If the data flow is in a reverse direction, arrowheads must be used to indicate the direction of the flow. However, you may also use the arrowheads to show normal flow. This takes more time, but often makes the data flow easier to follow when you check over the flowchart.

Input/Output

In system flowcharting in this book, the input/output symbol refers to any type of medium or device bringing data into the system for processing. It may also refer to any type of medium or device on which processing information is recorded or displayed.

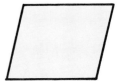

Process

This symbol refers to the processing operations or stations through which data must pass to produce the desired output. The processing operations are not always shown. This basic symbol covers all operations.

Arrowheads and Flowlines

Arrowheads and flowlines are used to show the order of operations and direction of data flow. The arrowheads are required if the path of any flowline does not follow the normal direction, which is left to right or top to bottom. However, arrowheads may also be used to show normal flow.

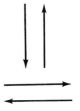

Figure 8.5 *System flowchart symbols*

A short statement identifying what is going on is usually written inside each flowchart symbol. If more detailed explanations are needed, they may be written outside the symbol. Figure 8.6 shows a simple system flowchart for preparing grade reports. It does not show other processing necessary for complete grade record keeping, but it gives an idea of flowcharting principles.

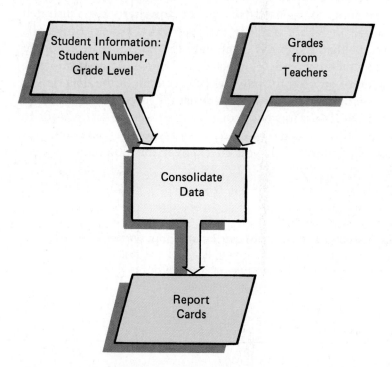

Figure 8.6
System flowchart for preparing grade reports

A system flowchart may start with a symbol that shows the medium or device used for the input of data into the system. However, it can start with an identification of the source data (as is shown in Figure 8.6). The flowchart may end with a symbol showing the output medium or device. It can, however, end with a symbol showing the final output of processed information (again, as in Figure 8.6). The procedure followed is largely a matter of choice on the part of the person describing the system.

If you are asked to flowchart a system, first determine what the output will be and on what medium it will appear. Then ask yourself what data will be input and on what types of media the input data will appear. In your mind, go over the steps the data must pass through in order to become useful information. Then draw the correct flowcharting symbols for the input and output, whenever possible, and for the processing steps. Place these symbols in proper order and indicate the flow of data through the system by using flowlines and arrowheads.

Real-Time Systems

A **real-time system** is one in which data is input and processed immediately upon its creation. Many systems can function only as real-time systems. Imagine what an airline reservation system would be like if it were not a real-time system: You phone the airline and request a seat on a flight. The reservation agent writes down your request. During the day each reservation agent is doing the same for other customers. Then sometime during the night, all the flight requests are fed into the computer. The computer makes as many reservations as possible and prints out long lists of the people who have reservations and the people who don't. The next day, you call the airline again. The agent searches the printout and tells you the desired flight is full. However, there is space on another flight. So, you request the other flight, the agent writes it down, that night your request goes back to the computer, and so on. Compare this to what really happens: When you make your call to the airline, the agent in the airline reservation center (Figure 8.7)

Figure 8.7
Reservation agents using a real-time system

keys in the desired flight. Within a second or two, the availability of the flight is shown on the agent's CRT. Your name and other required information are immediately keyed in and your ticket is reserved.

For a real-time system to work, all the input devices must be on-line to the computer that has the data stored. That is, the input devices must always have communication set up with the computer and auxiliary storage where the data is stored. Beyond that, the computer's program must be written to use real-time processing.

The diagram in Figure 8.8 shows a simplified system flowchart for an airline reservation system. Input to the system consists of flight schedules, aircraft capacity (how many people each aircraft can hold), and reservation requests. Output consists of responses to inquiries; tickets for passengers; lists of passengers; and lists of any special needs, such as no-sugar or low-salt foods for certain passengers.

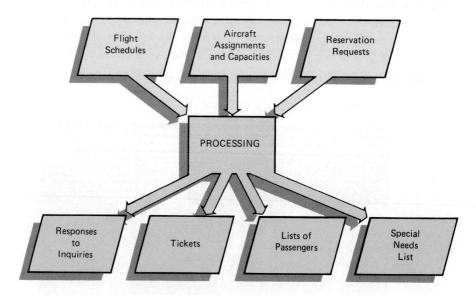

Figure 8.8   An airline reservation system

Batch Systems

Batch systems for information processing are exactly the opposite of real-time systems. Where a real-time system processes data immediately, a **batch system** saves up data and processes it all at once at a later time. Payroll is frequently run as a batch system. A typical batch payroll system is described in the following paragraphs. The system must do the following:

1. Pay employees for the work they do.

2. Provide employees and management with the necessary records of earnings and the deductions from these earnings.

3. Update employees' records at the end of each pay period.

4. Prepare payroll reports required by various government agencies.

Output of the system consists of the following items:

1. A payroll register. A payroll register is a list of all employees, their gross pay, deductions, and net pay. With a computerized system, the payroll register may be printed on paper. As an alternative, it may be stored in auxiliary storage for reference whenever needed.

2. Paychecks. Each paycheck includes a statement of the amounts earned, the amounts of deductions, and the amount of net pay.

3. An updated earnings record for each employee. The earnings record will be stored in auxiliary storage.

4. Totals of hours worked, gross pay, deductions, and so on. These totals are used later in preparing payroll reports required by the government. They may also be used by management in making decisions.

The system functions in the following manner: Each employee of the company uses an automatic time recorder (time clock) to clock in and out of work each day. Such a recorder is shown in Figure 8.9. The recorder stores the number of hours worked on a daily basis. At the end of the week, the paychecks are computed and printed by the computer. Other necessary payroll records are updated at that time. The time recorder provides as input the social security number and number of hours worked for each employee. Data in auxiliary storage provides other necessary information such as each employee's name, the number of withholding exemptions, and hourly rate. Also in auxiliary storage is an earnings record for each employee. The earnings record contains necessary totals for each employee for tax reporting purposes. Such figures as total wages paid for the current quarter, total wages paid for the current year, total tax deductions, and so on are kept in the earnings record. Figure 8.10 shows a flowchart for the payroll system.

Figure 8.9
The number of hours worked is recorded on a time clock.

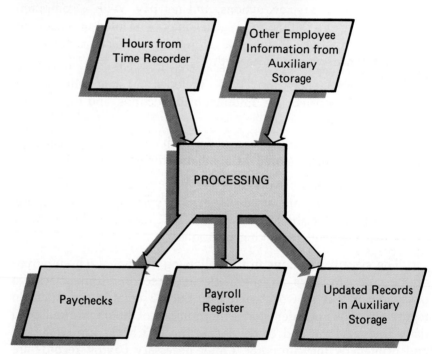

Figure 8.10
A payroll system

The computer goes through the list of employees by reading and writing auxiliary storage as necessary. For each employee, the following steps are taken. (Remember that this process is done once each week and all employees are processed at that time; a paycheck is not calculated each time an employee records hours on the time recorder.)

1. The gross pay is calculated by multiplying the pay rate times the number of hours worked.

2. Deductions for federal withholding tax, state withholding tax, FICA, and other items are computed.

3. Net pay is computed by subtracting deductions from gross pay.

4. Gross pay, deductions, and net pay for the current pay period are added to the figures already in the earnings record so that year-to-date figures are correct through the new pay period.

5. Grand totals for this pay period are updated.

6. A paycheck is printed as shown in Figure 8.11.

Figure 8.11
One of the outputs of the payroll system is paychecks.

When checks have been printed for all employees, the payroll register with grand totals is printed or recorded in auxiliary storage. The checks are then distributed to employees.

PLANNING AND DOCUMENTING A SYSTEM

In this chapter, we have discussed various types of information processing systems. To put any kind of information system into operation, several steps need to be followed. These steps are an analysis of the problem, an analysis of software needs, and an analysis of hardware needs. At each step, findings should be documented by writing them down. The documentation should include all important facts and decisions. System flowcharts are one way of documenting decisions that are made. In Chapter 9 you will learn more ways of documenting the software to be used by the system.

Analysis of the Problem

The first step in forming any system is an analysis of the problem. Analysis of the problem starts with deciding the output of the system. In other words, it's a lot easier to get somewhere if you know where you're going. In this chapter, you have seen several examples of planning the output of systems. The airline reservation system had to respond to inquiries, print tickets, print passenger lists, and print special needs lists. The payroll system had to produce paychecks and other payroll records. Once the required output is known, you should think about the best way to produce that output. Then consider each type of system and the advantages and disadvantages of using each.

Software Needs

Once the analysis of the situation has been made, the next step is to look at the software that will be required. What computer programs will be needed? What must each program do? Can already-written programs be used? Many of these questions will be easier for you after you have studied the software concepts explained in Part Four.

Hardware Needs

Planning for hardware requirements should come only after the situation has been studied and software requirements have been stated. Many times businesses purchase computer hardware first, then analyze the problem and look at software. All too often, the hardware purchased is either not capable of doing the required job or is far more capable than required. In either case, the business has wasted money. In the first case, it will have to buy additional or replacement equipment, in the second it has paid for unneeded computer power. Many times, a new system will run on existing computer hardware. In these cases, the purchase of more equipment is unnecessary. However, the study is still required; otherwise, it will never be known whether more equipment is needed.

In this chapter you have learned about different systems and how to plan and document a new system. Once a system has been planned and documented, it must be implemented. That is, it must actually be created and put into use. After it is in use, a system should constantly be evaluated. For example, is it doing what it is supposed to do? Can it do the job better? Do any features of the system cause problems for users? Any changes that need to be made should be made. Then the evaluation process continues.

SUMMARY

Some computer systems are designed for use by one person at a time. Others are designed to serve many users. Systems serving more than one user may be either a network of terminals or a network of processors. A network of terminals is known as a time-sharing system, while a network of processors is known as a distributed-processing network. Both types of systems have advantages. The choice of one over the other should be based on the situation. In either, data can be communicated either locally or over vast distances. The on-line time-sharing systems can be very expensive, however, if there are many terminals over long distances.

Systems may be either real-time or batch. Real-time systems process data as it is created. In a batch system, data is saved for later processing. In planning either system, system flowcharts may be used. The first step in planning is to analyze the problem. The next step is to decide on the required software. Finally, the needed hardware will be determined. Once a system is in place, it should be evaluated constantly. This ensures that it is performing as desired and aids in the development of improvements.

REVIEW QUESTIONS

1. How are time-sharing networks and distributed-processing networks alike? How are they different? (Obj. 1)

2. What is the difference between a star network and a ring network? (Obj. 1)

3. Why do time-sharing systems seem to slow down under some conditions? (Obj. 1)

4. What is the difference between a real-time system and a batch system? (Obj. 2)

5. What is the function of a modem? What is the difference between an acoustically coupled modem and a direct-connect modem? (Objs. 1, 2)

6. Describe how a system flowchart is constructed. (Obj. 4)

7. What steps should be followed in designing and implementing a computer information system? (Obj. 4)

8. Describe an application for which a time-sharing system is suitable and one for which distributed processing is preferable. (Obj. 3)

9. Describe an application for which a batch system is suitable and one for which a real-time system is required. (Obj. 3)

10. Why should a system constantly be evaluated? (Obj. 4)

VOCABULARY WORDS

The following terms were introduced in this chapter:

computer information system	acoustic coupler
network	direct connect
time-sharing system	baud
star network	system flowchart
queue	arrowhead
multiprogramming	flowline
multiprocessing	real-time system
distributed-processing network	batch system
ring network	

WORKBOOK EXERCISES

Chapter 8 in the workbook consists of three exercises: True/False, Completion, and Crossword Puzzle. Complete all three exercises in Chapter 8 of the workbook before proceeding to Chapter 9 in this text.

DISKETTE EXERCISE

Complete the diskette exercise for Chapter 8 before proceeding to Chapter 9 in this text.

PART FOUR

Software Concepts

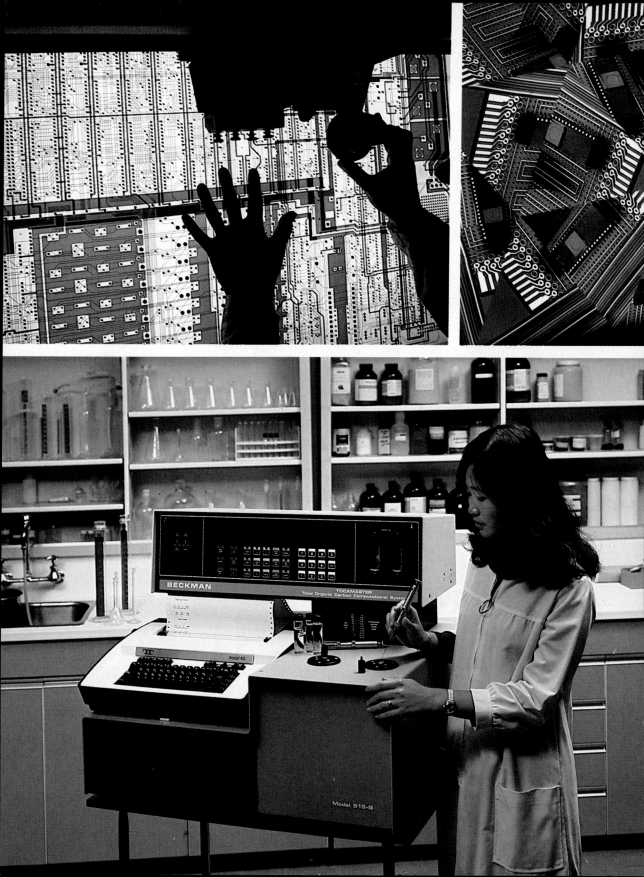

9 Programming Concepts

Objectives:

1. Define systems software.

2. Describe the functions of systems software.

3. Define and give examples of applications software.

4. Explain the differences between machine language, assembly language, high-level languages, and natural language.

5. Describe the process for planning a structured program.

Someone once said that a computer without software might as well be a boat anchor. That statement is very true, for without software a computer is absolutely useless. Software can be purchased prewritten (Figure 9.1), or it can be written by the user or programmer. Prewritten software is commonly known as **canned software**. In this chapter, we will take a detailed look at different classifications of software and find out how to plan a program.

SYSTEMS SOFTWARE

Systems software consists of programs designed to keep the computer functioning and programs to perform many everyday

Figure 9.1   *Canned software is available for many purposes.*

tasks related to the operation of the computer system. That is, systems software is concerned with keeping the computer system working. It also performs general operations rather than operations concerned with solving particular problems of the user. Some of the commonly used systems software is discussed in the following sections.

Operating Systems

The **operating system** is a series of programs that controls the operation of the computer system. Some of the functions of the operating system are as follows:

1. It establishes and controls communication between the processor, auxiliary storage, and input and output devices.

2. It provides a method for copying programs and data into memory from auxiliary storage.

3. It provides a method for saving programs and data from memory to auxiliary storage.

4. It provides a system of commands for telling the processor what to do. These commands may be given one at a time by the operator or may be stored for automatic operation of the computer. For example, commands could be stored so that when the computer is started up, it would automatically execute a program. This program could be designed to call the central computer in a network and request any changed data that might be needed.

Many different operating systems are available, both from computer manufacturers and other vendors. They vary significantly in their capabilities and the ways in which they are used. On some computers, the user never gives commands directly to the operating system. Therefore, the user may not be aware of its existence, but its functions are still being performed. If you are familiar with particular microcomputers, you may be aware of some of the popular operating systems used on these machines. Here are some of the more popular operating systems, along with their developers:

System	Developer
UNIX	Bell Laboratories; UNIX is considered by many to be one of the more advanced operating systems for more powerful microcomputers and minicomputers.
XENIX	Microsoft Corporation; UNIX work-alike operating system.
PC-DOS	International Business Machines Corporation (IBM); a version of MS-DOS, used on IBM's Personal Computer.
MS-DOS	Microsoft Corporation; used on many popular microcomputers.
CP/M	Digital Research, Inc.; used on many popular microcomputers.
Apple-DOS	Apple Computer, Inc.
TRS-DOS	Radio Shack Division of Tandy Corporation.

Utility Programs

Another kind of systems software is utility programs. A **utility program** is a program designed to do a routine job, such as copying data from one disk to another, making duplicate copies of disks, and sorting data into the desired sequence. As an example, suppose you are using a microcomputer with a hard disk drive and a floppy disk drive. Since the hard disk is so much faster and holds so much more data, all your data is stored on that disk. Though the possibility of something going wrong with the hard disk drive is very remote, it can happen. Therefore, at regular intervals you want to copy the data onto floppy disks. By having backup copies, the data can be recovered if disaster strikes. Instead of writing your own program to make the copies, you will most likely use a utility program furnished by the supplier of your operating system. Since it takes many floppy disks to store as much data as is contained on one fixed disk, your backup utility will probably have enough decision-making power built in so that it only copies data that has been changed or added since the previous backup.

Utility programs are available from computer manufacturers, from the vendors of operating systems, and from other companies. Other companies frequently "fill in the gaps" by supplying useful utilities that are not available from the manufacturer or operating system vendor.

User-Interface Shells

Many operating systems and their associated utilities use commands that are somewhat difficult to remember. This did not create a large problem when all computers were operated by specially trained operators who used the commands on a regular basis. As more and more persons began using their own computers, however, an alternative to remembering the commands was needed. As an example, look at the following command line:

FORMAT B:/V/S/1

This is a command line that can be used by one of the most popular operating systems for microcomputers. The command will prepare a new floppy disk so that it can be used. The meanings of the different parts of the command are as follows:

FORMAT   Record the necessary preliminary information on the disk so that it can be used.

B:	Use Disk Drive B (the second drive on the computer).
/V	Verify the disk. (Check the disk to see if there are bad spots on it. If there are, don't use them.)
/S	Place a copy of the operating system software on the disk.
/1	Prepare only one side of the disk.

Since this command may have all, none, or any combination of the characters after the slash marks, the occasional user of the command may have difficulty. Many other commands have a similar number of choices, and that's where user-interface shells come in.

A **user-interface shell** is simply a program that comes between the operating system and the user; it makes the use of operating system commands easier. It is loaded into memory and executed automatically when the computer is **booted up** (started up). The shell uses a series of **menus** (lists of choices) to make operation of the system easier. Look at Figure 9.2 for a very simplified version of such a menu as it might appear on the CRT when the computer is booted up. This example illustrates how easy it is to prepare a new disk using a user-interface shell. You enter an *F* to format a new

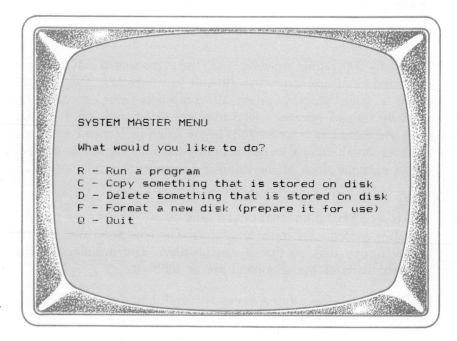

Figure 9.2
Menu of a user-interface shell

disk. When you enter the *F*, the following "conversation" takes place on the screen. Your responses are in blue.

```
Formatting a disk will destroy anything that may already be recorded
on it.

Do you want to continue (Y/N)?  Y

In which disk drive will the disk be placed (A or B)?  B

Do you want the disk to be able to start up the computer (Y/N)?  Y

How many sides of the disk should be formatted (1 or 2)?  1
```

As another example, if a user chooses option *R* to run a program, the user-interface shell prints on the CRT a **catalog** or **directory** (list) of all available programs. The user then selects the desired program from the list.

From these examples, it is obvious that a user-interface shell makes the operating system easier to use. It replaces generally abbreviated and confusing command lines with simple answers to questions. As with all computer software, there is a great deal of variation in the appearance and operation of different user-interface shells.

APPLICATIONS SOFTWARE

In the previous sections, you learned that the operating system establishes communication between the different parts of the computer system and contains the instructions necessary for writing and reading, auxiliary storage, printing, and so on. Utility programs are designed to perform routine functions such as disk copying. User interfaces are programs that make the use of operating system commands easier. In comparison to the software mentioned above, which is essentially directed toward the computer and its operation, applications software is directed toward the problem-solving requirements of the user.

Definition

Instead of controlling the computer or being a general-purpose aid such as a utility, **applications software** consists of programs designed to perform particular work desired by the user. Applications software does work such as accounting, mailing list processing, or serving as a retail store point-of-sale (check-out) system. Applications software may be either canned or custom written. Some canned software can be very easily adapted to different business situations by making choices from among its many capabilities. Other canned software is quite inflexible and can be used only by changing the business' way of operating to suit the software. **Custom-written software** is specially prepared for a particular business and the way it operates. Custom-written software, therefore, is generally much more expensive than canned software. For many applications, however, the use of custom-written programs is the only way to ensure that the job is done exactly as required.

Data Processing Examples

There are literally hundreds of areas in which application programs have been written. Following are a couple of examples.

Accounting   Historically, accounting applications have been among the first to be computerized by a business. You have already seen an example of doing payroll on the computer. Other accounting applications include processing accounts receivable (sending bills to customers and keeping records of the payments) and accounts payable (what the business owes other people), as well as general financial record keeping (known as general ledger accounting).

Spreadsheets   Spreadsheets are one of the fastest growing data processing applications. A **spreadsheet** is a program that uses a table (row and column arrangement) of numbers to perform calculations. Some of the numbers are calculated by performing arithmetic on other numbers in the table. Once the table is set up, all the calculations are done by the program. Since calculation of many of the numbers is automatic, spreadsheets are excellent "what if" tools. The example in Figure 9.3 shows a spreadsheet to forecast the net cash flow (how much cash will be available to spend) from owning a rental house. The items shown in red show the numbers that are entered by the user. Using special instructions, the user also enters the details for calculating the other figures. The calculations of formulas are given in the illustration. Numbers shown in blue are calculated by the program. Note that each of the amounts increases each year by the specified percentage. If desired, the user can change the percentage of increase or change any of the amounts in the first year. All other figures that are dependent on the changed figures will be recalculated automatically.

RENTAL PROPERTY CASH FLOW

	1985	1986	1987	1988
RENTAL INCOME	6,000.00	6,300.00	6,615.00	6,915.75
DEBT PAYMENT	4,000.00	4,000.00	4,000.00	4,000.00
PROPERTY TAX	700.00	735.00	771.75	810.34
INSURANCE	350.00	367.50	385.88	405.17
REPAIRS	500.00	530.00	561.80	595.51
OTHER EXPENSES	300.00	315.00	330.75	347.29
NET CASH FLOW	150.00	352.50	564.82	787.44

The following formulas were used in the calculations. These can be changed by the user as desired.

Net cash flow = rental income - debt payment - property tax - insurance - other expenses.

Rental income will increase by 5% a year.

Debt payment will remain constant.

Property tax will increase by 5% a year.

Insurance will increase by 5% a year.

Repairs will increase by 6% a year.

Other expenses will increase by 5% a year.

Figure 9.3   A spreadsheet is used for forecasting.

Word Processing Examples

In Chapter 7, you learned that word processors aid in the composition and correction of documents. You also learned about merging data files into text to create such items as customized form letters and legal documents. However, there are several other application programs frequently used with word processors. The most common program is the spelling checker. Writing-style checkers are also becoming more popular.

Spelling Checkers   A **spelling checker** program goes through a document one word at a time, looking each word up in a dictionary stored on auxiliary storage. Any word not in the dictionary is called to the attention of the operator. The operator decides whether the word is wrong and needs correction, or whether the word is correct and is just not in the dictionary. Words that are not in the dictionary can be added. Some spelling checkers show the operator words whose spellings are close to that of the word not found; if one of them is the correct word, the program will automatically put it in.

Writing-Style Checkers   Writing-style checkers are a newer development than spelling checkers. They vary more in operation than spelling checkers do. For example, some of them check for overuse of particular words and suggest replacement words whose meaning is similar. Some of them check for overly long sentences. Some even check for such grammatical errors as incomplete sentences.

PROGRAMMING LANGUAGE HIERARCHY

All computer programs, whether they are systems software or applications software, are written in some language. In this section, we will take a look at different language categories, beginning with the hardest to use and ending with the easiest to use.

Machine Language

Originally, computers were programmed in **machine language**, where the instructions were written in the numeric code that is directly understood by the processor. As you already know, all data is represented inside the computer by binary numbers. The only instructions that are understood by the processor are also expressed as binary numbers. Therefore, computer instructions written in machine language are written as a string of binary numbers. Programming in machine language is very difficult and time-consuming. Not only must the instructions be in numbers, the programmer must keep up with the exact memory locations where the data items are to be stored. Programming is done in machine language only when nothing else will work.

Assembly Language

Assembly language is a step up from machine language. Instead of using numbers, the programmer can express instructions in alphabetic terms. For example, *ADD* might mean *add*, or *LAD* might mean *load accumulator direct* (take a number and put it in storage in the processor). Assembly language also allows storage locations in memory to be referred to by names rather than the actual numeric locations. Assembly language is much easier than machine language, but is still rather difficult and time-consuming. It is used when the high-level languages to be discussed in the next section are not suitable.

Before programs written in assembly language can be understood by the computer, they must be translated into machine language. The translation is done by a program called an **assembler**. The assembler is supplied by the computer manufacturer or another vendor.

High-Level Languages

Machine language and assembly language require that the programmer think in terms of the particular processor being used and the instructions the processor requires. **High-level languages**, on the other hand, allow the programmer to think in terms of solving the problem rather than making the processor happy. The programmer is able to write instructions to the computer using English and English-like terms. Because of this ease of use, most application programs are written in high-level languages. Like assembly language programs, however, programs written in a high-level language must be translated into machine language before they can be understood by the processor. The translation is done by either an **interpreter program** or a **compiler program**. The interpreter or compiler is supplied by the computer manufacturer or another vendor.

The operation of an interpreter is somewhat like an English-speaking person talking to a Spanish-speaking person through a human interpreter. The English-speaking person says a sentence, then the interpreter repeats the sentence in Spanish. This process is repeated as long as the English-speaking person talks. In like fashion, an interpreter program for a computer looks at one instruction written in a high-level language, translates the instruction into machine language, and relays it to the processor. The processor then immediately carries out the instruction. Now the interpreter looks at the next instruction and translates it. The process is repeated until all instructions are carried out. Using an interpreter makes it easy for a programmer to debug the program. To **debug** a program means to find and correct the errors in it.

Using an interpreter causes a program to operate more slowly than if a compiler is used.

Compilers also translate high-level languages into machine language. Their operation is similar to a person who translates a book from English to French. After the entire book is translated and written in French, a French-speaking person can read it. A compiler program similarly translates the entire high-level program into machine language and stores the machine-language version. The computer then looks at the machine-language version as it follows the instructions. Programs translated with a compiler operate faster than those translated with an interpreter. Finding problems in the programs, however, is more difficult.

Commonly used high-level languages with which you will become more familiar in later chapters are introduced in the following paragraphs.

BASIC   The **BASIC** language was designed to make interactive programming less difficult. It is usually translated by an interpreter, which makes the identification and correction of programming problems easier. BASIC is considered an easy-to-learn language, partly because of its limited capability. More recent versions of the language, however, are very capable and are suitable for writing application programs in virtually any area. There are many different versions of the BASIC language. BASIC is the acronym for Beginner's All-Purpose Symbolic Instruction Code. You will learn more about this language in Chapter 13.

Pascal   **Pascal** is a relatively new language. It is useful for writing programs for nearly every application. Pascal includes features that make program writing easier. These features are not available in some versions of BASIC. When you learn about structured programming concepts later in this chapter, remember that Pascal is generally considered a well-suited language for doing structured programming. Pascal is generally translated with a compiler, which makes finding and correcting errors more difficult. The Pascal language was named in honor of the mathematician Blaise Pascal, who lived in the seventeenth century. You will learn more about Pascal in Chapter 14.

COBOL   **COBOL** was the first language written for use in business applications. It is still commonly used, especially with minicomputers and mainframes. Its strong point is the handling of large amounts of data stored on auxiliary storage. It is also one of the wordiest languages. While some programmers object to the large number of words required, the English-like sentences make COBOL programs easier to understand than those written in some other languages. COBOL is translated by a compiler. Its name is the acronym for COmmon Business Oriented Language. You will learn more about COBOL in Chapter 15.

Natural Language

The ultimate computer language can be called a **natural language**. At present, natural-language processing is available in a very limited form. Research, however, is progressing. The existence of a comprehensive natural language would mean that you could instruct the computer by using ordinary, everyday English (or Spanish, or whatever language the computer would be programmed to receive).

STRUCTURED PROGRAMMING CONCEPTS

Structured programming is a method of programming in which proven steps are followed in planning and writing a program. Some persons separate the process into **structured design** (the planning of the program) and structured programming (the actual writing of the program). In the remainder of this section, we will turn our attention to the methods used in structured programming. These steps can be used regardless of which high-level language you intend to use. Writing structured programs is easier in some languages, however, than in others.

Top-Down Design / Hierarchy Charts

Top-down design of a program means that you begin to design the program by defining what the program is to do; then you gradually place increasingly more detail in the plan. To do this, you start with a hierarchy chart. A **hierarchy chart** looks like an organization chart for a business which shows the boss at the top and the workers below. To clarify the procedure, let's look at an example.

You decide you want a program that can handle a mailing list for you. So, you draw a box and label it *Mailing List*, as shown in Figure 9.4. Now you start to think about what the program must do to handle a mailing list. You decide that the program must be able to perform four functions: (1) add names and addresses, (2) make corrections in names and addresses, (3) delete names and addresses,

Figure 9.4
The beginning of a hierarchy chart

and (4) print mailing labels. Add a box for each of these functions so that the chart looks like Figure 9.5. You can think of these boxes as being pieces of a computer program. The top box (labeled *Mailing List*) is the boss part of the program. You then have four workers; each of the workers knows how to perform one of the four functions of the program. Each of the workers performs its duty when instructed to do so by the boss.

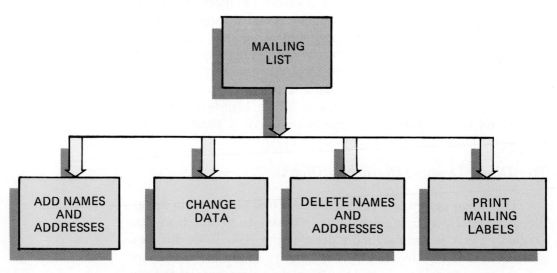

Figure 9.5   *A completed hierarchy chart*

Output Design

Before continuing, you should design the output to be produced by the program. In this case, the output is mailing labels. Use a report spacing chart as shown in Figure 9.6 to draw what the output should look like. Note that the **report spacing chart** is a form arranged in rows and columns with space for each position in which a character can be printed. When completed, it shows the length of each data item that is to appear on the output as well as its location. The spacing for two labels is shown to indicate that the layout is repeated down a page of labels.

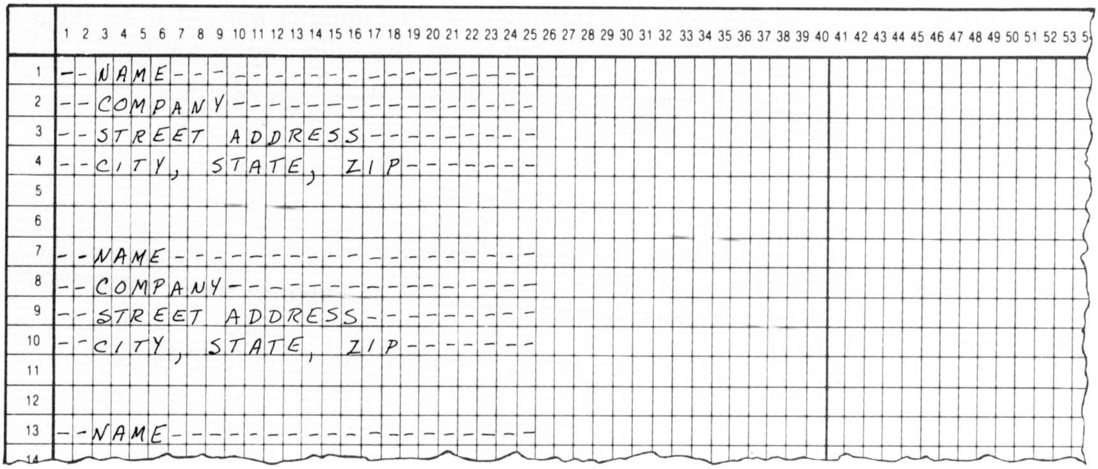

Figure 9.6   Output is designed on a report spacing chart.

Program Design

One of the main ideas of structured programming is that any program can be written using only four kinds of instructions. These four kinds of instructions are described below:

1. **Sequential instructions** are simply steps that are performed one after another. See the following example:

    Clear the screen on the CRT.
    List the possible functions on the CRT.
    Obtain the user's choice of functions.

2. A **case** instruction provides a way for executing one set of instructions out of numerous possibilities included in the program. See the following example:

    Depending on user's choice, perform one of the four functions.

3. **Loop control** instructions are those that are used to make the computer repeat certain instructions. Instructions may be repeated until some condition becomes true, or they may be

repeated as long as some condition remains true. See the following example:

> While user wants to add more people:
> Get name from keyboard.
> Check to see if name is already stored.

4. **If ... then ... else** instructions provide that one thing is to be done if a statement is true; another thing is to be done if the statement is false. See the following example:

> If name is already stored, then inform user
> Else get street address from keyboard
> get city, state, ZIP from keyboard
> store data on disk.

With these kinds of instructions in mind, a program design is made for each of the boxes from the hierarchy chart. Each of the boxes is known as a **module**. A **program design** (also known as **pseudocode**) is a set of the necessary steps that must be performed by each module within a program. The program design is written in ordinary English. By consolidating the steps given in the examples above and adding a couple more instructions, the program design for the **main module** (the top box) is created. The program designs for the Main Module and the Names and Addresses Module are shown in Figure 9.7. Note that what is written in Figure 9.7 is really an outline of the instructions that the computer will execute. In this manner, program designs are written for all the modules.

At this point in designing the program, it is wise to have other persons go over your work in detail, as shown in Figure 9.8. This session, known as a **structured walkthrough**, can find many problems that may be corrected before the pseudocode is converted to computer language.

Coding and Testing

Writing the instructions of a computer program in a computer language is known as **coding** the program. Up to this point in the programming process, we have been unconcerned about the language in which the program is to ultimately be coded. This is because the program design we have written can be converted to virtually any programming language such as BASIC, Pascal, or COBOL. For each of the statements in the program design, we write one or more statements in the programming language. Usually the

MODULE DOCUMENTATION	Program: <u>MAILING LIST</u>	Module: <u>MAIN</u>

Module Function (Program Design):

1. Clear the CRT screen.
2. List the possible functions on the CRT.
3. Obtain the user's choice of functions.
4. Depending on user's choice, perform one of the four functions.
5. If user does not want to quit, go back to Step 1.
6. End.

MODULE DOCUMENTATION	Program: <u>MAILING LIST</u>	Module: <u>NAMES AND ADDRESSES</u>

Module Function (Program Design):

1. While user wants to add more people:

    Get name from keyboard.

    Check to see if name is already stored.

    If name is already stored, then inform user

        Else get street address from keyboard

            get city, state, ZIP from keyboard

            store data on disk.

2. Return to Main Module.

Figure 9.7
Program designs list the program steps in English.

main module is coded and tested first. Then all the other modules are coded and tested. So that you may see the process, Figure 9.9 shows the main module of the Mailing List program converted to the version of BASIC used by the IBM Personal Computer and many other popular microcomputers. Comments are included to help you understand the statements, even if you don't know the BASIC language yet. You will get experience in coding programs when you study programming languages in Chapters 13, 14, and 15.

Figure 9.8
A structured walkthrough can find many problems.

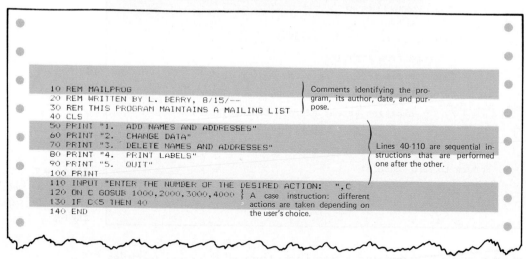

```
10 REM MAILPROG                                    Comments identifying the pro-
20 REM WRITTEN BY L. BERRY, 8/15/--                gram, its author, date, and pur-
30 REM THIS PROGRAM MAINTAINS A MAILING LIST       pose.
40 CLS
50 PRINT "1.   ADD NAMES AND ADDRESSES"
60 PRINT "2.   CHANGE DATA"
70 PRINT "3.   DELETE NAMES AND ADDRESSES"         Lines 40-110 are sequential in-
80 PRINT "4.   PRINT LABELS"                       structions that are performed
90 PRINT "5.   QUIT"                               one after the other.
100 PRINT
110 INPUT "ENTER THE NUMBER OF THE DESIRED ACTION: ",C
120 ON C GOSUB 1000,2000,3000,4000    A case instruction: different
130 IF C<5 THEN 40                    actions are taken depending on
140 END                               the user's choice.
```

Figure 9.9   *A coded BASIC program module*

SUMMARY

Computer software can be divided into several classes. Systems software consists primarily of operating systems, utility programs, and user-interface shells. These are designed to keep the computer functioning and to perform many general operations. Applications software, on the other hand, is designed to solve a particular processing problem of the user. To contrast the two, systems software is designed to keep the computer system going, while applications software is designed to do the processing that will solve the user's problems.

All computer software is written in a computer language, either machine language, assembly language, or a high-level language. Most applications software is written in high-level languages. In putting applications software to use, businesses commonly use accounting programs, word processing programs, and spreadsheet programs. To this list may be added numerous other specialized programs.

All programs should be planned and coded in structured fashion. That is, they should be planned and written according to methods that have been proven to produce programs that work while keeping the computer time required as short as possible. The output should be planned, and the problem should be divided into modules. The necessary program steps should be planned in English before coding them into a computer language. After coding and implementation, the programs should continually be evaluated.

REVIEW QUESTIONS

1. What is systems software? What are its functions? (Objs. 1, 2)

2. Describe three examples of systems software. (Obj. 2)

3. What are the functions of an operating system? (Obj. 2)

4. What is applications software? (Obj. 3)

5. Describe five commonly used types of applications software. (Obj. 3)

6. What are the differences between machine language, assembly language, high-level languages, and natural language? (Obj. 4)

7. What is the difference between an interpreter and a compiler? (Obj. 4)

8. Describe three commonly used high-level languages. (Obj. 4)

9. Describe the process of top-down design. (Obj. 5)

10. Briefly describe the four kinds of instructions with which any program can be written. (Obj. 5)

VOCABULARY WORDS

The following terms were introduced in this chapter:

canned software	debug
systems software	BASIC
operating system	Pascal
utility program	COBOL
user-interface shell	natural language
boot up	structured programming
menu	structured design
catalog	top-down design
directory	hierarchy chart
applications software	report spacing chart
custom-written software	sequential instructions
spreadsheet	case
spelling checker	loop control
writing-style checker	If . . . then . . . else
machine language	module
assembly language	program design
assembler	pseudocode
high-level language	main module
interpreter program	structured walkthrough
compiler program	coding

WORKBOOK EXERCISES

Chapter 9 in the workbook consists of five exercises: True/ False, Matching, Vocabulary Grouping, Hierarchy Charts, and Writing Program Designs. Complete all five exercises in Chapter 9 of the workbook before proceeding to Chapter 10 in this text.

DISKETTE EXERCISE

Complete the diskette exercise for Chapter 9 before proceeding to Chapter 10 in this text.

10 Data Structures

As you learned in earlier chapters, a computer system stores data in its memory for processing. You also learned that the storage locations in main memory are numbered starting at zero. Therefore, data is stored sequentially; that is, in one location after another. For use with high-level languages, however, you can think of the data as being stored in many different arrangements. By thinking in terms of many different data arrangements, the programming of solutions to problems is much easier. The language makes sure that, regardless of the arrangement you think of the data as being in, the data is properly stored in memory in one location after another.

DEFINITION OF DATA STRUCTURE

The arrangement in which a human thinks of data is known as a **data structure**. Each of the data structures visualized by a person can be stored in locations in the computer's memory. The required number of memory locations is set aside by the language and given a name by which the person may refer to the entire group. Each named storage location in the computer's memory is called a **variable**. Suppose a number is to be stored. The location where the number is to be stored may be labeled in a program by a variable name such as *A, B,* or *Number1.*

The following paragraphs describe some of the commonly used data structures. Most of the data structures can be used with either numeric or character data. **Numeric data** consists of numbers with which arithmetic can be done. **Character data** consists of any characters that can be coded using the internal code of the computer—usually either ASCII or EBCDIC.

SINGLE ITEMS OF DATA

The simplest form of data storage is to store just one number or one character string (group of characters). Different languages use different names to refer to such a data item. Some simply refer to it as a variable; others refer to it as a **scalar** (point on a scale) or **elementary item** (an item that cannot be broken down any further). These kinds of storage hold one item of data, such as 40 hours or $15.00. A variable such as this, then, is like a box with one number in it, as in Figure 10.1. Note that the variables have been given names. These are the variable names with which the storage locations could be labeled in the computer's memory.

Figure 10.1
Variables holding
one item

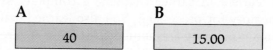

With many computers, storage of a number requires more than one location in memory. Regardless of the exact number of memory locations required, the place for one number is referenced by one variable name. In fact, the programmer usually does not need to be concerned about the exact number of memory locations being used to store a number.

Unless otherwise specified by the programmer, variables are generally elementary items; that is, they are set up by the computer language to hold one value. Keep in mind, however, that any of the data structures discussed in this chapter may be called variables.

CHARACTER STRINGS

One or more characters used together are known as a **character string**. For example, *F, Computer, F987sasd,* and *The Man in the Moon* are all character strings. In small computers, character strings are generally stored with one character per memory location. In some larger computers, more than one character may be stored in a location. With some high-level languages, the variable name used to refer to the character string applies to as many locations as required; the user generally does not need to be concerned about the number of locations. In other languages, the programmer must specify the maximum length of a character string. Figure 10.2 shows how character strings might be visualized. Note that the variables are named *ANIMAL* and *CITY;* the data items stored under those names are *CAT* and *WASHINGTON.*

ANIMAL

CAT

CITY

WASHINGTON

Figure 10.2
Typical character strings

VECTORS

A **vector** is a row or line of data. For example, if four students take a test and make scores of 84, 87, 93, and 87, the scores are a vector. A vector stored in a variable might look as shown in Figure 10.3.

SCORES

1	2	3	4	←Element Numbers
84	87	93	87	

Figure 10.3
A vector of scores stored in a variable

Each of the data items (numbers) in the vector is known as an **element**. If you want the program you are writing to refer to one of the individual numbers, you give its element number. For example, to refer to the 93 in Figure 10.3, you refer to the third element of the vector named *SCORES.* You refer to the element by using a subscript. A **subscript** is a number in parentheses that states which element in a vector or table you are dealing with. To write a reference to the third element (the 93), you may write SCORES(3). Still referring to the same example, SCORES(1) is 84, while SCORES(2) is 87 and SCORES(4) is 87. (Note: Some high-level languages refer to the first element as Element 0 instead of Element 1; in these cases Element 1 is really the second value.)

Some high-level languages also refer to a character string as a vector. In these languages, a character string is visualized as shown in Figure 10.4.

Figure 10.4
Some languages treat a character string as a vector.

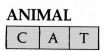

TABLES

A **table** is usually a row and column arrangement of data, such as shown in Figure 10.5. The rows are known as one **dimension** (a measurement in one direction), while the columns are another dimension. This kind of table, therefore, is known as a two-dimensional table. Frequently, only the contents of the table (the numbers in this case) are stored in the table in the computer. In this case, the person writing a program must keep up with what kind of data is stored in each location. The table from Figure 10.5 might be stored in the computer without its headings, as shown in Figure 10.6.

**Number of Items Sold
by Each Salesperson**

	Jan	Feb	Mar
Brock	12	32	12
Carriker	97	14	63
Miller	13	7	98
Reginstein	3	58	49

Figure 10.5
A table is a row and column arrangement of data.

SALES

	1	2	3	←Column Numbers
Row Numbers 1	12	32	12	
2	97	14	63	
3	13	7	98	
4	3	58	49	

Figure 10.6
Tables are frequently stored without headings.

A three-dimensional table can be thought of as shown in Figure 10.7. It is like two or more two-dimensional tables stacked together. A three-dimensional table has planes, rows, and columns. **Planes** refer to the two-dimensional tables that appear to be stacked together. The table in Figure 10.7 has two planes, four rows, and three columns.

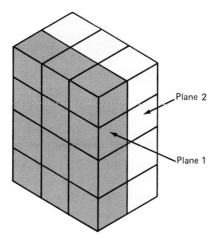

Figure 10.7
A three-dimensional table

It is also possible to have a one-dimensional table, such as shown in Figure 10.8. A one-dimensional table has only one column and serves the same purpose as a vector. Practically speaking, there is no difference between a one-dimensional table and a vector. Internally, some computers may arrange them differently in memory.

PEOPLE

1	Nola
2	Milton
3	Steve
4	Tina
5	Florence
6	Daniel

Figure 10.8
A one-dimensional table has only one column.

As with a vector, the individual data items in a table are known as elements. To refer to an individual element, a subscript must be used for each dimension. That is, one subscript is used for a one-dimensional table, two subscripts are used for a two-dimensional table, three subscripts are used for a three-dimensional table. For example, SALES(4,3) refers to the fourth row and third column of the table called *SALES*. Since the reference to the table used two subscripts, you know the table is a two-dimensional table.

A table may also be referred to as a **matrix** or an **array**. Just about anything that can be written on paper as a table can be represented in the computer as a table. For example, names and addresses, sales figures for each month of the year, and school enrollments can all be stored in table form.

LINKED LISTS

A **linked list** is a table or group of tables in which each data item "points at" the next item that should be processed. The best way to understand a linked list is to look at an example. Suppose you want the computer to keep track of your tape collection. You would like to be able to give the computer the name of a musical performer and receive from the computer a list of all the tapes by that person or group. One way to set up the data would be in the form of a table as shown in Figure 10.9.

TABLE OF PERFORMERS AND TAPES

Performer	Name of Tape 1	Name of Tape 2	Name of Tape 3
The House	The House on Tour	Open House	Foundations
Dandelion	Summer Lights	Mountain/2	
The Harpers	The Harpers on Tour	Tour II—The Harpers	
Jump	Parachute	Sky High	

Figure 10.9
Names of musicians and tapes stored in a table

Storing the data in a table in this manner is easy to understand. However, there are a couple of problems. In the table in the illustration, there is space for three tapes by each performer. If we have only one or two tapes by a performer, there is wasted space. On the other hand, if we have more than three tapes by one performer, there is no place to put the extra tape or tapes.

PERFORMERS TABLE

	Performer	Location of First Tape
1	The House	1
2	Dandelion	3
3	The Harpers	4
4	Jump	5

TAPES TABLE

	Tape Name	Location of Next Tape by Same Performer
1	The House on Tour	2
2	Open House	9
3	Summer Lights	7
4	The Harpers on Tour	6
5	Parachute	8
6	Tour II—The Harpers	0
7	Mountain/2	0
8	Sky High	0
9	Foundations	0

Figure 10.10
In a linked list each numeric pointer points to the next data item.

The problem can be solved by using a linked list. Refer to Figure 10.10 as you study the procedure. Instead of one table containing names of performers and names of tapes, there are two tables. One of them contains the names of all performers, the other contains the names of all the tapes. Whenever a new performer is added, the name is added in the first available space at the end of the table of performers. Whenever a new tape is added, it is simply added to the end of the table of tapes. This seemingly unarranged way of recording things is kept in order by using numbers referred to as "links" or pointers. To see how it works, let's look up all the tapes by Dandelion. First, find Dandelion in the Performer Table. Look to the right of the group's name and you will see the number *3*. This means that the first tape by Dandelion is in Row 3 of the Tape Table. Look at Row 3 of the Tape Table and you will see *Summer Lights*, the name of the album. Look to the right of the name and you will find the number *7*. This means that the next album by Dandelion is in Row 7 of the Tape Table. Look at Row 7 and you find *Mountain/2* . To the right of *Mountain/2* is a *0*. The *0* is an indication that there are no further tapes by Dandelion.

TEXT

All the data structures you have learned so far can be used with either numeric or character data. The data structure known as text can only be used with character data. **Text** consists of one character after another stored in the computer's memory. There is usually no limit on the number of characters except the amount of memory in the computer. Many word processing programs use a text data structure.

SUMMARY

In the memory of the computer, data is stored sequentially; that is, one character after another starting at Address 0 and continuing as far as necessary. For purposes of planning programs, however, the data can be thought of as being arranged in any of several ways.

The simplest form of data storage is known as a variable or elementary item. Some high-level languages call it a scalar. It holds one item of data. The next type of data item is called a vector or one-dimensional table. A vector can be thought of as a list having only a row or a column, but not both. A data structure which usually contains both rows and columns is known as a table. If necessary, tables with three dimensions (planes, rows, and columns) may be used. For complex data-storage requirements, a data structure known as a linked list may be used. A linked list is a table whose rows and/or columns are kept in the desired sequence by numeric pointers that show which item comes next. For applications such as word processing, a data structure known as text may be used. Text is simply a sequential arrangement of any desired characters.

REVIEW QUESTIONS

1. What is a data structure? What is its purpose? (Obj. 1)

2. Name and describe five types of data structures. (Obj. 2)

3. How are vectors and tables alike? How are they different? (Obj. 2)

4. How are tables and linked lists alike? How are they different? (Obj. 2)

5. Explain how a subscript is used. (Obj. 3)

6. List a typical application for each of the data structures. (Obj. 4)

VOCABULARY WORDS

The following terms were introduced in this chapter:

data structure	subscript
variable	table
numeric data	dimension
character data	planes
scalar	matrix
elementary item	array
character string	linked list
vector	text
element	

WORKBOOK EXERCISES

Chapter 10 in the workbook consists of three exercises: True/False, Matching, and Completion. Complete all three exercises in Chapter 10 of the workbook before proceeding to Chapter 11 in this text.

DISKETTE EXERCISE

Complete the diskette exercise for Chapter 10 before proceeding to Chapter 11 in this text.

11 Designing Data Files

Objectives:

1. Define vocabulary words related to data files.

2. Describe sequential files and explain how they are used.

3. Describe random files and explain how they are used.

4. Describe kinds of applications for which each of the file types may be used.

In Chapter 10 you learned about data structures that are used when storing data in the computer's memory. In this chapter you will learn about how data is stored in auxiliary storage.

TERMS USED TO DESCRIBE DATA IN AUXILIARY STORAGE

Several terms with which you may not be familiar are used when referring to data stored in auxiliary storage.

Data Fields or Items

You are aware that individual items of data in the computer's memory may be referred to as scalars or elementary items. Each individual data item in auxiliary storage is also frequently known as a field. Therefore, a person's name is a field. The person's street address is another field.

Records

Suppose that we have the following fields of data about a person: name, street address, city, state, ZIP code, and telephone number. The information about one person may be written on a card as shown in Figure 11.1. When grouped this way, the data becomes a record. We can define a record as a group of related fields. Therefore, we might have a record for Jarrod Stover, one for Pat Ryckley, and one for Robertine Raymond.

```
Stover, Jarrod
1263 Peachtree Drive
Boston, GA  31626-5688
(912)496-7941
```

Figure 11.1
Each card is a record.

Files

A **file** is a collection of related records treated as a unit. Therefore, a group of cards containing customer names and numbers may be grouped into a file as shown in Figure 11.2. When using a computer, this same information could be stored as a file on a magnetic disk, magnetic tape, or other medium suitable to the computer.

Figure 11.3 shows how part of this same customer file might look when recorded on a magnetic disk (if you could see it on the disk). Refer to the figure as we review the terminology used in talking about files. Note that the file is made up of two or more records. Note, also, that all the records contain the same kinds of data. Each record contains a customer's name and number. Each of these items in a record is a field. Thus, a customer's name is one field, and a customer's number is another field.

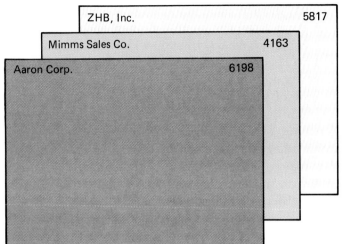

Figure 11.2
A group of records makes a file.

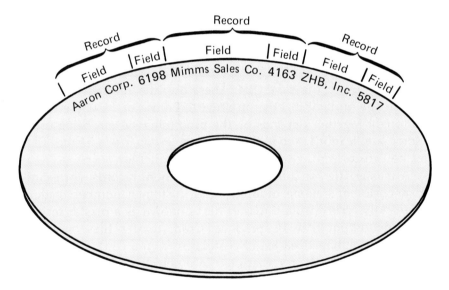

Figure 11.3
Part of a file as stored on magnetic disk

Each record in a file must be distinguished in some way from all other records in the same file. This is a necessary requirement in processing records. In Figure 11.3, you will note that each record can be identified by the customer's name or number. The data in these fields is different on each record. The identifying name or number is used in processing operations, such as sequencing the records in a file or searching the file for a particular record.

The primary goal in information processing is to create and use records. Records take the guesswork out of decision making.

Because incorrect decisions can ruin a business, it is very important that correct records be ready when and where they are needed.

For example, a florist must know how many flowers and plants will be needed during the year. If too many are ordered, the florist loses money. If too few are stocked, business is lost. Last year's records of purchases and sales will help the florist make decisions.

An insurance company needs to know when to send out premium notices (bills) to its policy holders. A teacher needs to know what final grades have been earned by students in each class. A taxpayer needs to keep careful records of earnings and deductible expenses. In these cases and many more, records play a vital role in the decisions that must be made.

The data needed to produce the kinds of information a business or a person needs is logically organized into files, records, and data fields or items.

KINDS OF FILES

The records in files are used to solve information processing problems. Frequently all the data needed in solving a particular problem is not in the same file. Therefore, the records in several files must be brought together in order to be useful. How these files are brought together depends on the processing system being used. In some applications, especially those using batch processing, files may be categorized as master files and detail files.

A **master file** contains relatively permanent records. For example, a customer's name, address, and customer number seldom change. Any record from a master file is known as a **master record**.

Some output may be produced from master files only. For example, an alphabetized list of customers from a certain state may be prepared. Records for that state are selected from the file in alphabetic sequence and printed. Frequently, however, records from several other files will also be needed.

A **detail file** contains records of day-to-day transactions. A sales detail file, for example, contains records of sales to customers. A separate record is needed for each payment received. There may be other detail files, such as a file of stock received or a file of stock shipped out. Any record from a detail file is called a **detail record**.

In some information processing systems, much time is used in sorting file records so that many different reports may be prepared from them. The necessity to physically rearrange data on auxiliary storage, however, has been greatly lessened by the increased use of data base systems. This will be further explained in Chapter 12.

TYPES OF FILE ACCESS

File access is the method by which data is stored and retrieved on auxiliary storage. As you learned in Chapter 6, auxiliary storage devices may be either sequential- or random-access devices. Therefore, it is possible to have either sequential files or random files. Both master and detail files may be accessed by either method.

Sequential Files

The word *sequential* means "one after another." Therefore, the items in a **sequential file** are stored and retrieved one after the other. If two hundred records are to be recorded in a file, the first record must be stored first, then the second record, then the third, and so on. It is impossible to store the tenth record, then the eighth, then the one hundredth, and so forth. When records are to be read from the file, the same principle applies. To get to a particular record, you must read through all of the records in front of it.

By their nature, magnetic tapes are sequential-access storage devices. It is impossible to get to a place in the middle of a file without winding the tape through the first part of the file. Therefore, all files on tape are sequential files. Disks may also be used for sequential-access files if desired.

For many applications, sequential files require less storage space than random files. This is because the records may be of varying lengths. Figure 11.4 shows how data might be arranged in a

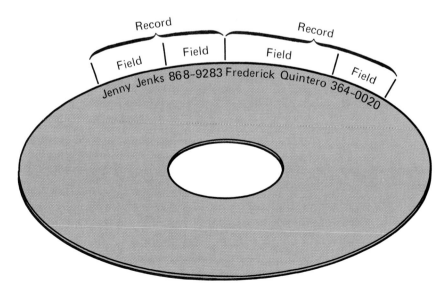

Figure 11.4
A sequential file on disk

sequential file on disk. Since the record for Jenny Jenks is shorter, it takes less space than the one for Frederick Quintero.

For applications in which records are processed in the order they are written, or in which entire data files may be read into the computer's memory at once, the space-saving characteristic of sequential files is an advantage. Applications using sequential files are frequently those using batch processing.

Random Files

Random means "in no particular order." Therefore, the records in a **random file** may be stored and retrieved in any desired order. That is, the tenth record may be processed, then the fortieth, then the second, and so on. For most real-time applications, random files are required.

Figure 11.5 shows how a random file might look on disk. Note that all records require the same amount of space. When the data in a field is shorter than the field length, space is wasted. Requiring all

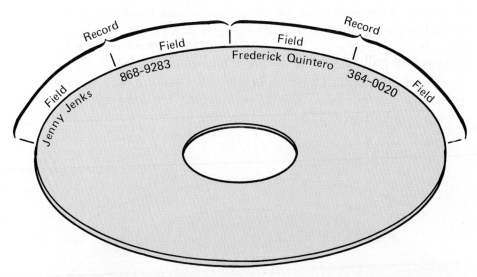

Figure 11.5 A random file on disk

records to use the same amount of space makes it possible to compute exactly where a particular record is located on the disk. For example, suppose that each record contains 64 characters and that each sector on the disk can store 128 characters. This means that two records can be stored in each sector. Assume now that Record 5 is to be stored. The first and second records go in Sector 1. The third and fourth records go in Sector 2. The fifth record goes in the first half of Sector 3. See Figure 11.6 for an illustration of this.

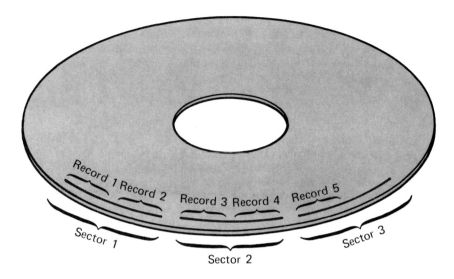

Figure 11.6
Example of two records in each sector

As another example, suppose that each record contains 192 characters and that each sector still contains 128 characters. The first record will require all of Sector 1 and half of Sector 2. The second record will require the second half of Sector 2 and all of Sector 3. This is illustrated in Figure 11.7. The person writing a program in a high-level language does not need to make these calculations. They are done automatically by the high-level language and/or the operating system software.

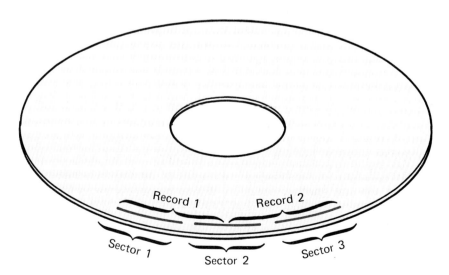

Figure 11.7
Example of one record requiring one and a half sectors

Relative Files   When records in a file are referred to by their numbers as in the examples in the previous paragraphs, the file may be called a **relative file**. That is, each record's location in the file is computed relative to the beginning of the file. If you want to store the one-hundredth record, you refer to it by number and it is placed in the one-hundredth position in the file. If you want to read the fifteenth record in the file, you refer to it by number and the data is retrieved from the fifteenth position in the file.

For some applications, relative files are very appropriate. Suppose that a manufacturer wants a file containing information about the products being manufactured. Each record is to contain the product's stock number, description, and selling price. The storage location of each record is to be determined based on the stock number field. Then, when it is necessary to read information from the file, the stock number will be specified in order to retrieve the information. In this example, the stock number field is the **key field**—the one used for determining the storage location and retrieving the data.

If the products have been given stock numbers starting at 1000 and continuing upward (1000, 1001, 1002, 1003, etc.), it is very easy to write program steps that will convert the key field numbers into record numbers. By subtracting 999 from each stock number, record numbers starting at 1 can be obtained. When such a simple computation is not possible, a more complex math formula may be developed. For example, suppose that the manufacturer's stock numbers are not easy sequential numbers. Instead, they are a combination of alphabet letters and numbers, such as KN3987 or 3N87615. By using the digits and the ASCII or EBCDIC codes of the alphabet letters, record numbers may be computed.

Relative files can access data very rapidly. The disk drive read/write head can move directly to the proper track and quickly transmit the data to the processor.

Indexed Files   For many applications, relative files are not appropriate. An example may be found in a school system that uses a computer to process information about its teachers. On one occasion, it may be necessary to retrieve all the information about one particular teacher by entering the teacher's name. On another occasion, it may be necessary to see a list of all business education teachers. On still another occasion, it may be necessary to locate all teachers who are required to update their education within the next year. For such applications, where the data in the file must be accessed by more than one field, an **indexed file** is a necessity. An indexed file is somewhat like a book with an index. For each record, entries are made in one or more indexes. For example, there might be one index of names and another of social security numbers, both giving the location of the same record in a file. Some high-level languages can automatically set up indexes to files. With other high-level languages, the programmer must write the instructions to set up the indexes.

It is obvious that an advantage of indexed files is the ease with which records can be referred to for storage and retrieval. However, there are some disadvantages. Access is slower than with relative files because of the extra processing required. Also, the indexes take up disk space; this reduces the number of records that may be stored on a disk.

SUMMARY

When a group of related data is stored on auxiliary storage, it is known as a file. Each file is made up of records. Each record contains the data for one person, one inventory item, one sales transaction, or one item of some other type. The individual pieces of data in these records are known as fields. For example, a person's name or phone number is a field.

Files may be either sequential or random in nature. The records in a sequential file must be processed in order, one after the other. The records in a random file may be processed in any order desired. Random files are required for most real-time applications. A random file may be organized on a relative or an indexed basis. A relative file specifies a particular record number to be stored or retrieved. An indexed file makes use of indexes to look up the storage location of the desired records.

REVIEW QUESTIONS

1. What is a field? (Obj. 1)

2. What is a record? (Obj. 1)

3. What is a file? (Obj. 1)

4. What are the distinguishing characteristics of sequential files? (Obj. 2)

5. What are the distinguishing characteristics of random files? (Obj. 3)

6. How are relative and indexed files alike? How are they different? (Obj. 3)

7. For what kinds of applications are sequential files more likely to be used? (Obj. 4)

8. For what kinds of applications are random files more likely to be used? (Obj. 4)

VOCABULARY WORDS

The following terms were introduced in this chapter:

file	sequential file
master file	random file
master record	relative file
detail file	key field
detail record	indexed file
file access	

WORKBOOK EXERCISES

Chapter 11 in the workbook consists of four exercises: True/False, Identification, Analysis, and Designing a Random File Record. Complete all four exercises in Chapter 11 of the workbook before proceeding to Chapter 12 in this text.

DISKETTE EXERCISE

Complete the diskette exercise for Chapter 11 before proceeding to Chapter 12 in this text.

12 Data Base Systems

Objectives:

1. Define a data base system.

2. Explain how a data base system is used.

3. Give the advantages of a data base system.

4. Describe two common types of data base systems.

In Chapter 11 you learned how data is stored on auxiliary storage in the form of files. In this chapter you will learn about data bases. To set the stage for this, let's look at the computer applications of a typical, but fictitious business and see what data files it would use.

APPLICATIONS EXAMPLE USING TRADITIONAL DATA FILES

Let's say that Omega Burger ("the last word in hamburgers") is a rapidly growing hamburger restaurant chain. The developers of Omega realized that the use of computers was a necessity. Omega's first computer application was payroll. To do payroll, the company used a single data file containing the necessary fields.

After payroll was under way, Omega decided to start computer processing of all of its general financial records (general ledger).

Part of the financial records had to do with payroll, so records were set up in a new file to record the total amount of federal and state withholding tax, as well as the total amount of gross pay earned by all employees. To accomplish this, a programmer needed to rewrite part of the payroll program so that data created by that program would be available to the general ledger program.

Next, the company started an employee profit-sharing program. The managers whose stores meet or exceed sales quotas receive stock in the corporation. Each manager is also eligible for free vacation trips if the store's performance is above the goal for two years in a row. This application was set up in stand-alone fashion; that is, all the data for this program is entered by hand on a terminal. The data is then stored in a file containing the appropriate fields.

Because of the growing number of stores, Omega decided next to install a computerized inventory system. This system keeps up with all equipment on hand in the stores. It also updates the quantity of each food item in each store. Store managers report the use of food items to headquarters each week, and the amounts are subtracted from inventory. When headquarters ships food from the central warehouse, it adds quantities back to inventory.

Omega then decided to replace all its cash registers with a computerized point-of-sale system. The system in each store automatically looks up the price of each food item purchased by a customer, thereby reducing errors by cashiers. The system also totals up sales by each cashier and transmits orders to the kitchen so that the proper food can be prepared.

The computer applications used by Omega are shown in Figure 12.1. Let's look at some of the characteristics of the system:

1. Each of the applications is totally separate; each has its own data files. Each of the data files has been designed to meet the requirements of the particular application.

2. The same data may be contained in more than one file. For example, employees' names are found in both the payroll file and the profit-sharing file. Many figures from the payroll, profit-sharing, and inventory files must also be reproduced in the general ledger files. When data exists in more than one place, it is said to be **redundant data**.

3. The data is probably not as accurate as it could be. With the same data in more than one file, it is possible that it may be updated in one file but not in another. When data must be

COMPUTER APPLICATIONS OF OMEGA BURGER

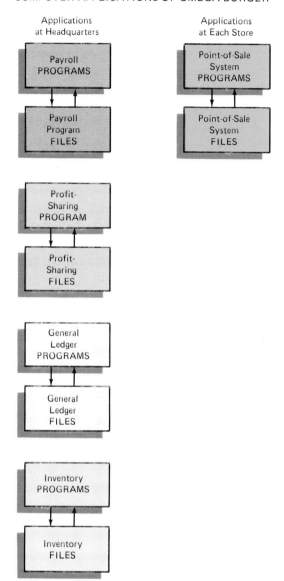

Figure 12.1
Nonintegrated
computer applications

manually transferred from one computer system to another, as with Omega, there is an increased possibility of errors.

4. When a new application is put on the computer, a great deal of effort must go into getting the original data into files. Much of this data may already exist in other files.

5. If the data needed for a particular application changes, it may take a lot of effort to modify data files and programs. For

example, suppose files were created leaving only enough space for a five-digit ZIP code. It would take substantial effort to locate and modify all files that contain ZIP codes to allow space for nine-digit codes. When the data files are changed, all programs that use them must also be changed to reflect the different file contents.

6. The redundant data may cause the company to have to buy more auxiliary storage. While the price of auxiliary storage is less than it once was, it is still a significant expense.

In the way it has implemented the use of its computers, Omega is very much like many other businesses. Even though all the data stored in its computer system is related to operating the business, the data has been divided into separate files. Each computer program has been written to directly access whatever files are needed for that particular application. In other words, programs and data are tied together.

The following section will explain how many of these problems can be reduced by using a data base system.

WHAT IS A DATA BASE?

Considered in a general sense, the term **data base** refers to the group of data necessary to carry on a business. In the computer sense, the term refers to a method of storing data on auxiliary storage so as to minimize the disadvantages that would be present if using data files tied directly to particular programs. In other words, a data base is a method of storing data that separates the data and programs. It makes the data available to many programs, reduces the amount of redundancy, and makes maintenance of accurate data easier.

ADVANTAGES OF DATA BASES

Most of the advantages of data bases are apparent from the definition given above. Some of the programmer advantages of using data bases over separate programs include:

1. Writing programs is easier since there is a separation between the data and programs. Imagine that all the data accumulated by a business is in a series of file cabinets and a human employee is to find the names and addresses of all salespersons who sold more than their quota last month. It

isn't necessary to create a new file cabinet containing only the data necessary to make the report. Instead, the human uses the data as it exists, pulling out the required information. In similar fashion, by using a data base a computer program may access data as it exists without having to create new files. Of course, if the required data is not stored anywhere, it will have to be added to the data base.

2. The amount of auxiliary storage required may be less. Since the data is organized as a group of related information necessary to run the business, there is no need for a series of separate files, many of which would contain the same data.

3. The accuracy of records is increased. This is another advantage that comes from reduced redundancy. Any time an item of data needs to be changed, only one action is necessary to change it wherever it is recorded in the data base.

4. Maintaining the security of data may be easier. When all data is under the control of the data base program, provisions can be more easily made for preventing unauthorized access to the data.

HOW DATA BASE SYSTEMS WORK

A **data base system**, also known as a **data base management system** (DBMS), is a set of computer programs that is available from a computer manufacturer or another vendor. The programs serve the purposes discussed in the previous paragraphs. To get a better idea of what they do, go back to the example of a file cabinet of information with a human handling the filing chores. Now imagine that you own a hamburger business and you have just hired a new employee. You tell the files operator to file the information about the employee. If you want to know how many hamburgers were sold by the store in Boston, you ask the files operator to find the information and give it to you. In similar fashion, application programs request the data base programs to save or retrieve data. Now return to the human example. Suppose your business grows. You buy more file cabinets and hire more files operators. Any files operator can use the data in any file. Likewise, many different application programs can use a data base. The application programs give data to be stored or request data to be retrieved. The data base program serves the function of the files operator searching the files.

KINDS OF DATA BASES

Two frequently used kinds of data bases are network data bases and relational data bases. Each of them has advantages and disadvantages.

Network Data Bases

A **network data base** uses individual files for each of the kinds of data to be stored, and these files are linked together by the use of pointers (similar to the pointers used by the linked lists you learned about in Chapter 10). Figure 12.2 lists some of the files that might be created for Omega Burger's computer system. It also shows how all the applications can access these common files. Compare this figure with Figure 12.1.

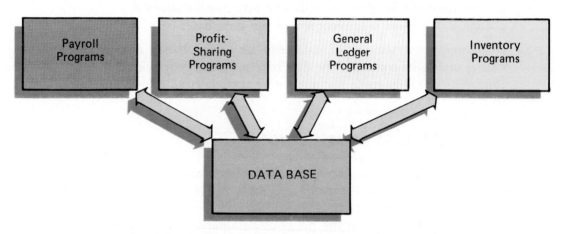

The data base might contain the following files as well as others:

FILE	CONTENTS
Employee File	Master information about employees, including names and addresses, social security numbers, and phone numbers.
Store File	Master information about stores, including addresses and phone numbers.
Sales File	Data from invoices.
Inventory File	Information about each item stocked. This includes its stock number, description, price, quantity on hand, and quantity sold.
Employee Compensation File	Pay rates and earnings records.

Figure 12.2 Omega Burger's data base system

Data in these files is linked together with pointers. See Figure 12.3 for a very simple example. This figure shows a small part of the Employee Master File and a small part of the Store Location Master File. Note that the pointers show the work location of each employee. Likewise, pointers in the Store Location Master File show which employees work there.

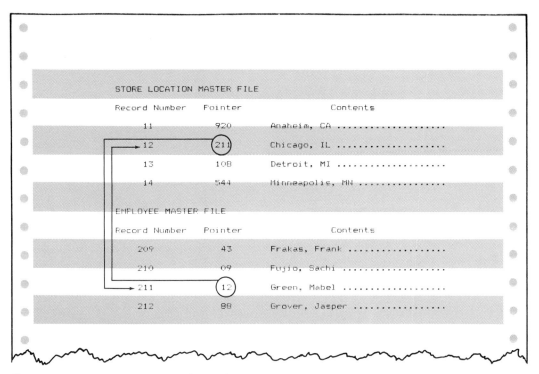

Figure 12.3 *Data is linked together with pointers.*

The data base programs being used include the necessary commands for setting up the relationships between different files and data items. Commands are also included for telling which files need to be accessed by which programs. The work involved in planning the relationships and setting them up is very complex.

Relational Data Bases

The relational data base is the newest form of data base. In a **relational data base**, all data is represented in the form of tables. These tables are known as **relations**. As you would expect, each table contains related data. One table might contain all the data about employees. Another might contain all the data about different stores. There is enough common data in the tables to tie different tables together. For example, in the store table, the number of each store would be recorded. In the employee table, the store number where each person works might be included, thus connecting the data in the two tables. This is illustrated in Figure 12.4.

STORE LOCATION MASTER FILE

Store Number	Location	Other Data
1931	Anaheim, CA	....
3989	Chicago, IL	....
8372	Detroit, MI	....
9312	Minneapolis, MN	....

EMPLOYEE MASTER FILE

Store Number	Name	Other Data
2345	Frakas, Frank	....
3987	Fujio, Sachi	....
3989	Green, Mabel	....
1923	Grover, Jasper	....

Figure 12.4   *Common data ties together the files of a relational data base.*

In the relational data base, there are no pointers from one file to another. The slight amount of redundancy in the data serves the same purpose in a better fashion. The software required to control a relational data base is very complex and tends to be slower than that of other data base systems. However, a relational data base is better suited to complex data manipulation than other systems.

QUERY LANGUAGES AND REPORT WRITERS

Most data base systems provide utilities known as query languages and report writers. A **query language** is a very high-level language that is the closest thing yet to programming in conversational English. The language allows the user to request certain information from the data base without having to go through the formality of writing a program. For example, if Omega Burger's president wants to know which store managers in California have been over quota for the last three years and whose sales have increased at least 15 percent each year, a query language can be used to ask the computer for the answer to the question. The manager in Figure 12.5 is using a query language to update the inventory.

Figure 12.5   *Updating inventory*

A **report writer** is very similar to a query language. Instead of being used for brief answers to questions, however, it is used to define more complex reports to be printed. Using a language provided by the data base system, the user tells which data is to appear in each position on the report.

DATA BASE APPLICATIONS

A data base system can be used with almost any computer that is large enough to do business data processing. Machines all the way from microcomputers with floppy disk drives to mainframe computers can be used. As you would suspect, there are more capable DBMS programs available for larger computers.

Almost any business data processing application can be implemented using a data base system. However, for all but the smallest applications, the task of converting an existing system to a data base system is very complex, time-consuming, and expensive.

SUMMARY

A data base system is a method of storing data on auxiliary storage in which redundancy is reduced and the data is maintained independently from the programs that will be using it. Thus, programming is made easier and data security can be increased. However, creating and maintaining the data base is a large task in itself.

There are several kinds of data base management systems. Two of the most common are the network data base and the relational data base. The network system uses a system of pointers to connect data together. The relational system stores data in tables that have enough common elements to tie them together.

Most data base systems contain query languages and report writers. Query systems provide the user with the capability to ask questions of the computer about the data it has stored. Report writers simplify the generation of reports.

REVIEW QUESTIONS

1. What are the characteristics of a data base system? (Obj. 1)
2. What are the main differences between using regular files and using a data base system? (Obj. 2)
3. What are the advantages of using a data base system? (Obj. 3)
4. How does a network data base organize data? (Obj. 4)
5. How does a relational data base organize data? (Obj. 4)
6. What is the main advantage of using query languages and report writers? (Obj. 3)

VOCABULARY WORDS

The following terms were introduced in this chapter:

redundant data	relational data base
data base	relations
data base system	query language
data base management system	report writer
network data base	

WORKBOOK EXERCISES

Chapter 12 in the workbook consists of three exercises: True/False, Matching, and Planning. Complete all three exercises in Chapter 12 of the workbook before proceeding to Chapter 13 in this text.

DISKETTE EXERCISE

Complete the diskette exercise for Chapter 12 before proceeding to Chapter 13 in this text.

PART FIVE

Applications
Programming
Languages

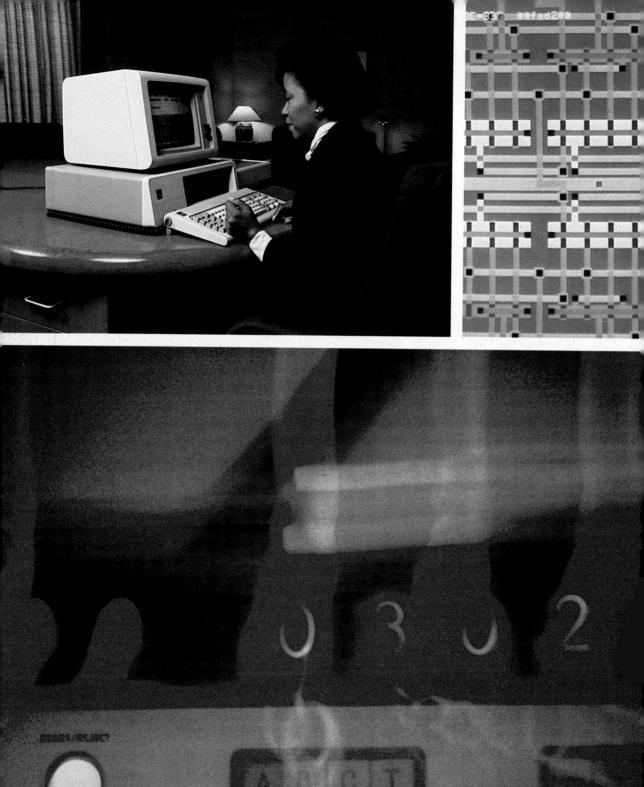

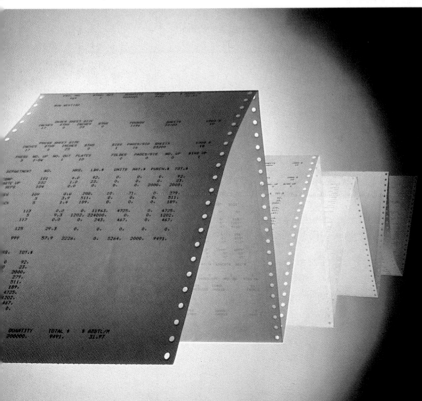

13 Introduction to BASIC Programming

Objectives:

1. List the advantages and disadvantages of BASIC.

2. Distinguish the two different modes available in BASIC.

3. Describe the kinds of data with which BASIC operates.

4. Identify and explain the use of common BASIC keywords.

In Chapter 9, you learned that the BASIC language is useful for writing applications programs in nearly every area. In this chapter, you will learn more about this language, a language which is "standard equipment" on millions of microcomputers.

ADVANTAGES AND DISADVANTAGES OF BASIC

BASIC has many advantages as a programming language. Among them are the following:

1. The BASIC language is especially well suited for doing interactive programming. **Interactive programming** refers to the process of keying a program into the computer and immediately executing (running) the program. This type of

programming is possible only with an interpreted language and with a language that has its own built-in editing program (a program capable of text revision). The built-in editing program allows the programmer to enter the program into the computer's memory. Entering a command then executes the program. Remember from Chapter 9 that a language set up as an interpreter translates the program lines into machine language one at a time as the program executes. Therefore, a separate step for compiling is unnecessary.

2. Because of the interactive nature of BASIC, many programs are much easier to write, and the finding and fixing of **bugs** (errors) is easier than with many other languages.

3. If desired, a program can be compiled with a BASIC compiler to speed up its operation and make it impossible for others to see the program (it is very difficult to read binary machine code). A BASIC interpreter can be used to enter and debug (correct) the program before compiling it.

4. BASIC is available for most small computers. This means that many companies have written programs that run under BASIC. This availability of programs has led to less expensive software, helping to make computer use easier for individuals and small businesses.

5. Many present versions of BASIC are very powerful, making programming of complex problems quite easy.

6. BASIC is a free-form language; that is, there is no particular order for writing a program. The sequence of instructions is determined totally by the required order of instructions for solving the problem and the desires of the programmer.

7. Some versions of BASIC have commands that make the creation of sound and graphics very simplified.

8. BASIC is useful for doing business computations and for solving complex mathematical formulas.

BASIC also has some disadvantages. For many applications, however, the advantages far outweigh the disadvantages. Here are some of the disadvantages:

1. Interpreted languages, including interpreted BASIC, are slower than compiled languages. This disadvantage may be overcome, however, by using a BASIC compiler.

2. Some persons see BASIC's free-form nature as a disadvantage. Since the programmer can write statements in any order desired, this can lead to poor programming habits. The most common bad habit is the use of many "go to" statements from one place in the program to another. When a program is not well planned, such statements are frequently necessary to execute the instructions in the proper order. Needless to say, such programs are difficult to follow when you are trying to find an error.

3. There are many different versions of BASIC from many different manufacturers. Frequently there are differences in the commands used to accomplish the same thing. Therefore, a program written for one version of BASIC probably will not run under another version. A person who knows one version of BASIC, however, finds it quite easy to adapt to other versions.

4. Depending on the version of BASIC being used, the handling of complex data files may be difficult.

5. With older versions of BASIC, the formatting of printed output is somewhat difficult. Newer versions, however, provide extremely easy ways of making the output look the way you want it to look.

OVERVIEW OF BASIC

Understanding more about how BASIC works will make learning the language easier. Since the BASIC language is most frequently set up as an interpreter, this discussion will limit itself to the use of a BASIC interpreter.

Like all high-level languages, BASIC translates English-like instructions into machine language for execution by the processor. Unlike most others, however, BASIC also includes the necessary software for entering a program into the computer's memory and saving it in auxiliary storage. The use of a separate word processor or text editor is not required.

Program Modes

The fact that you can directly enter a program into the computer's memory with BASIC, plus the fact that BASIC is an interpreted language, make two modes (ways of operating) possible.

These modes are the immediate execution mode and the deferred execution mode. The **immediate execution mode** is in effect when an instruction is entered and immediately carried out. The **deferred execution mode** is in effect when the instruction is part of a program and is carried out when the entire program is run.

By using immediate execution mode, you can quickly do many arithmetic problems without writing a program. Let's look at some examples of the things we can do by using BASIC in immediate execution mode. In the examples, **keywords** (words that BASIC understands) are shown in red. Punctuation and symbols that BASIC understands are also shown in red. Words other than keywords which are entered by the programmer are shown in blue. Output produced by BASIC is in black. The keyword **PRINT**, which the computer understands, is used to display words and numbers on the screen as shown in the following examples:

```
PRINT 2+3-1

4


PRINT "THE AVERAGE IS";(90+70+80)/3

THE AVERAGE IS 80
```

If you want to repeat an instruction done in immediate execution mode, you must reenter the instruction.

In deferred execution mode, each instruction is preceded by a line number. This gives BASIC the clue that the instruction is part of a program and is not to be performed until it is commanded to do so by entering the word RUN. **RUN** is the keyword that tells BASIC to follow the instructions that have been entered in the form of a program. Look at an example of using BASIC in deferred execution mode. The input is as follows:

```
40 PRINT "HERE ARE SOME NUMBERS:"

50 PRINT 23,987.32,31.32,29.8

60 PRINT 3783,321.8,9,773.321
```

The output is as follows:

```
RUN

HERE ARE SOME NUMBERS:
    23          987.32      31.32       29.8
    3783        321.8       9           773.321
```

Note that the line numbers of 40, 50 and 60 could have been just about any numbers. The only rule is that the first instruction to be carried out must have the lowest number. The second instruction must have the second lowest number, and so on.

Note that a literal (words enclosed in quotes) is printed by line 40, while constants (numbers) are printed by lines 50 and 60. These are further defined under the section "Constants and Literals." The constants are separated by commas. The commas cause BASIC to move to a new print zone before beginning each number. A **print zone** is an area into which each print line is divided. For example, an 80-column print line might be divided into 5 print zones of 16 characters each. The width of each print zone varies depending on the computer and version of BASIC being used. If items after the keyword PRINT are separated by semicolons rather than commas, the items are printed next to each other rather than in different print zones. Many computers, however, leave one space before each number, even when separation is with semicolons.

Programs which are much more useful than the above example will be introduced later in the chapter.

Variables

In Chapter 10 you learned the definition of a variable. It is a named storage place in the computer's memory. As a program is executed, various data may be stored in this location. In BASIC there are two kinds of variables: numeric variables and character variables.

Numeric Variables A **numeric variable** is a storage place for a numeric value that is not known in advance; that is, a value that will be created or changed while the program is carrying out instructions. Examples of numeric values are student numbers, test scores, total test points for the term, and student averages. Some versions of BASIC make a distinction between variables that hold **integers** (whole numbers) and those that hold **real numbers** (numbers with a decimal point, also known as **floating-point numbers**). In these languages, a numeric variable is set up to hold real numbers unless the programmer specifies otherwise.

Character Variables   A **character variable** is known as an **alphanumeric variable** or a **string variable**. Character variables are used to store any data that contains nonnumeric characters. For example, such data as student names or the names of items stocked by a store is stored in character variables.

A variable whose name ends with a dollar sign ($) is a character variable. To help remember this, imagine the dollar sign as resembling the letter *s* (the first letter in *string*). A variable without a dollar sign at the end of its name is a numeric variable.

Names of Variables   Variable names must begin with a letter of the alphabet. Other characters in the name can be either alphabetic letters or digits. When naming variables, it is desirable to name them for the kind of data they are to store. For example, if you are going to store the name of the city in which a person lives, calling the variable *CITY$* makes sense. Early versions of BASIC (and some current versions), however, restrict the programmer to the use of shorter variable names. Typically, you can use a letter of the alphabet and one digit. This gives names such as *A*, *C1$*, *X3*, or *M*. In this case, about the best you can do in naming a city variable is to call it *C$*, using the first letter of *city*. Many recently developed versions of BASIC allow a total of three characters for a variable name: an alphabet letter followed by any combination of two letters and/or digits. Still newer BASIC versions, such as those used by the IBM Personal Computer and similar computers, allow you to use long names for variables, sometimes using as many as 40 characters. If using one of these versions, the following variable names would be acceptable:

PHONE$, STORE1832, WORKPHONE, ADDRESS$, DISCOUNT3, PRICE, TAXRATE

Constants and Literals

In addition to storing data in variables as discussed above, BASIC also has provisions for storing an item of data that does not change. Such data is known as either a constant or a literal. A **constant** is a number that does not change as the program executes. A **literal** is any combination of characters which is entered between quotation marks. As with a constant, a literal does not change in value during execution of the program.

DEVELOPING EXAMPLE PROGRAMS

The quickest way to become familiar with BASIC programs is to look at some examples. All the statements in the following examples will be explained in detail.

Getting Input from the Keyboard

First, let's see how to get input from the keyboard. Assume that one student in a course has three grades that will be keyed in and averaged. Figure 13.1 shows the steps to the solution of the problem.

1. Get the three grades and store them in variables.
2. Print the average found by summing the grades and dividing the sum by 3.

Figure 13.1   English language program design for grade averaging program

Translating the steps in Figure 13.1 into BASIC gives the program shown in Figure 13.2. Refer to the program as you study the following comments about how it works.

```
10 REM GRADEAVG
20 REM GRADE AVERAGING PROGRAM
30 REM WRITTEN BY CAROLYN BROWN, 11/10/--
40 CLS
50 INPUT "ENTER 3 NUMBER GRADES SEPARATED BY COMMAS:   ";G1,G2,G3
60 PRINT "THE AVERAGE IS ";(G1+G2+G3)/3
70 END
```

Figure 13.2   Grade averaging program coded in BASIC

Lines 10, 20, and 30 contain comments. They have no effect on the program and are not required by the BASIC language. It is good practice to use them, however, as part of good program documentation. The abbreviation **REM** stands for remark. Some BASICs also allow remarks to be indicated by an apostrophe.

Line 40 clears the screen. **CLS**, which stands for "clear screen," is used for this function on the IBM Personal Computer, the TRS-80, and many other computers. The Apple II and Apple IIe require the use of the word **HOME** to clear the screen.

On line 50, the keyword **INPUT** causes the computer to stop and wait for the user to enter data from the keyboard. Since there is a literal following the word INPUT, the computer will print the literal before waiting for the user's response. Such a literal is known as a **prompt** and tells the user what kind of input is required. Once the user enters the required data, the data is stored in the variables whose names appear at the end of the statement. In response to line 50, the user must enter three numeric grades, separating them with commas. The first grade will be stored in Variable *G1*, the second grade will be stored in Variable *G2*, and the third grade will be stored in Variable *G3*.

Line 60 causes the computer to calculate and print the average of the three grades. First, the grades are added up, as indicated by the plus signs between the names of the variables. Note that the parentheses cause the addition to take place before the division. If the parentheses were not used, Grade G3 would be divided by 3, then added to the other two grades. This is because BASIC and most other languages follow the normal math rule stating that multiplication and division should be done before addition and subtraction. As soon as the answer is calculated, it is printed on the screen.

Line 70, the **END** statement, causes the program to stop executing. In most versions of BASIC, the END statement is optional. The program will stop even if there is no END statement.

Note that only one word, INPUT, was required to tell BASIC to get data from the keyboard. Note, too, that only one word, PRINT, was required to display an answer on the CRT. This simplicity of setting up the flow of data from the computer to the operator, as well as from the operator to the computer, is one of the primary advantages of the BASIC language. It was designed specifically for such two-way communication between the computer and the user.

Suppose that a student has grades of 82, 86, and 84. When the program is keyed into the computer, the RUN command may be given as shown below to execute the program. Study the interaction that takes place between the computer and the user. The input from the user is shown in red, while the output printed by the computer is shown in blue.

```
RUN

ENTER 3 NUMBER GRADES SEPARATED BY COMMAS:  82,86,84
THE AVERAGE IS   84
```

Making Decisions

Now let's look at a program that shows BASIC's decision-making power; that is, the power of BASIC to take different actions depending on the circumstances. This program will calculate the amount of commission to pay a salesperson. As you probably know, a commission is figured by multiplying the amount of sales by a rate (expressed as a decimal number). For the example, if a salesperson sells less than $5,000 worth of merchandise for the week, the commission will be figured at a rate of 7 percent (.07 in decimal). If the sales for the week are $5,000 or greater, the commission will be figured at a rate of 9 percent (.09 in decimal). Figure 13.3 shows the steps that must be accomplished by the program if it is to solve this problem.

1. Get the sales amount for the week for one salesperson and store the amount in a variable.

2. If the sales are less than 5000,

    Then calculate commission at 7%

        Else, calculate commission at 9%.

3. Print the amount of commission.

Figure 13.3 Program design for calculating commissions

The program (written from the plan in Figure 13.3) is shown in Figure 13.4. Refer to it as you study the comments in the following paragraphs about how it works.

As in Figure 13.2, the first three statements are remarks. Also, as in Figure 13.2, we have started by clearing the computer's screen in line 40.

Line 50 causes the computer to print the prompt "ENTER THE AMOUNT OF SALES" on the screen. Then the computer waits for

```
10 REM PAY

20 REM THIS PROGRAM CALCULATES COMMISSIONS

30 REM WRITTEN BY HAL SHIELDS, 11/10/--

40 CLS

50 INPUT "ENTER THE AMOUNT OF SALES";SALES

60 IF SALES<5000 THEN LET COMMISSION=SALES*.07
                ELSE LET COMMISSION=SALES*.09

70 PRINT "COMMISSION IS $";COMMISSION

80 END
```

Figure 13.4 *BASIC program for calculating commissions*

user input. Whatever value the user keys in will be stored in the variable called *SALES*. The computation done in line 60 determines how much the salesperson is to be paid. The keyword pair IF . . . THEN makes the decision. If the sales are less than $5,000, the amount is multiplied by .07 (the asterisk indicates multiplication). ELSE (otherwise), the amount is multiplied by .09. Note that only one of the actions will be taken. The choice is dependent on the amount of sales for the week. In either case, the result of the computation is stored in a variable called *COMMISSION*. The keyword **LET** is used to assign the result into the variable. Line 70 then prints the result from the variable.

Note that line 60, even though it is one program statement, takes up two lines on the screen when it is entered. By using two lines and indenting, the statement is easier to read. The ENTER or RETURN key must not be pressed except at the end of the last line when you are entering multiline statements like this. Remember that a BASIC program statement begins with a line number. The program statement ends whenever the ENTER or RETURN key is pressed.

In this program, you have also seen the use of relational operators. **Relational operators** are the symbols used for determining the relationship of one value to another. Figure 13.5 gives the relational operators used in BASIC.

SYMBOL	MEANING
=	equal to
<	less than
<=	less than or equal to
>	greater than
>=	greater than or equal to
<>	not equal to

Figure 13.5
BASIC's relational
operators

Some versions of BASIC do not have the keyword ELSE. For those BASICs, the program in Figure 13.4 can be written as shown in Figure 13.6. In this program, we've also shown the use of brief variable names and the use of the keyword HOME to clear or erase the screen. We have also shown in this example that the keyword LET may be omitted; the statement still works properly.

```
10 REM PAY
20 REM THIS PROGRAM CALCULATES COMMISSIONS
30 REM WRITTEN BY HAL SHIELDS, 11/10/--
40 HOME
50 INPUT "ENTER THE AMOUNT OF SALES";S
60 IF S<5000 THEN C=S*.07
70 IF S>=5000 THEN C=S*.09
80 PRINT "COMMISSION IS $";C
90 END
```

Figure 13.6 *Alternate coding of BASIC commission program*

An Improved Commission Program

It is unlikely that we have only one salesperson. Therefore, it would be beneficial if our payroll program would continue operating, allowing us to figure the commission for several different employees. For this to happen, we must make two changes in the program plan. These changes are shown in Figure 13.7. First, there must be a method of going back and repeating the process. This is indicated in Step 5. Second, there must be some way of telling the program to stop when we are through. We will do this by entering sales of less than zero when we are finished entering the rest of our data. The way the program checks to see if this has happened is shown in Step 2 of the plan.

1. Get the sales amount for the week for one salesperson and store the amount in a variable.

2. If the sales are less than 0, then end.

3. If the sales are less than 5000,

   Then calculate commission at 7%

   Else, calculate commission at 9%.

4. Print the amount of commission.

5. Go back to Step 1 for the next salesperson.

Figure 13.7 *Program design for improved commission program*

Converting our plan into a program gives the result shown in Figure 13.8. Note that we have simply changed line 10 and added lines 55 and 75 to the program from Figure 13.4. Line 75 introduces the **GOTO** statement, which transfers control to a specified statement, in this case, line 50. Once all the data has been input and the program's process has repeated as many times as necessary, the programmer inputs a value less than 0, and, through line 55, the program terminates.

Reading Data

Just as BASIC can get input from the keyboard, it can also get it from lines in the program. As an example of this, let's make a computerized telephone directory. We can put the names and numbers in the program on lines such as shown in Figure 13.9. Each of these lines begins with the keyword **DATA**, which is BASIC's way of identifying them. Data lines don't do anything in a program. They simply hold data so that other lines of the program can read it.

```
10 REM PAY2

20 REM THIS PROGRAM CALCULATES COMMISSIONS

30 REM WRITTEN BY HAL SHIELDS, 11/10/--

40 CLS

50 INPUT "ENTER THE AMOUNT OF SALES";SALES

55 IF SALES<0 THEN END

60 IF SALES<5000 THEN LET COMMISSION=SALES*.07
                ELSE LET COMMISSION=SALES*.09

70 PRINT "COMMISSION IS $";COMMISSION

75 GOTO 50

80 END
```

Figure 13.8   *Improved commission program coded in BASIC*

Each of the data lines consists of a name followed by a phone number, then another name and phone number, and so on. Commas are used to separate the items. On the last data line, we have entered the letters EOD twice where the name and phone number should be placed. EOD is an abbreviation for "end of data." The programmer can use either EOD or fake data that can be used by the program to tell when it has finished reading through all the good data. The fake data items are known as **terminators** since they are located at the end of the data and serve to terminate it.

```
500 DATA SUSAN,783-9873,HENRY,313-9871,RALPH,129-9873,HUBERT,987-3748

510 DATA AARON,348-3382,MARION,338-9938,HELEN,333-3312,IRIS,339-5554

520 DATA.EOD,EOD
```

Figure 13.9   *Data lines used in phone directory program*

In using our computerized phone directory, we want to enter the name of the person whose phone number we need. The computer will then look up the name in the data and print the person's number. Written in English, the plan for the program is shown in Figure 13.10.

1. Get the name to look up in the directory from the keyboard.

2. Read the next name and phone number from the data lines.

3. If the name just read is not the one we're looking for and it's not the data terminator, then go back to Step 2 for more data.

4. If the name read is the name we are looking for, then print the phone number, else print "not found."

Figure 13.10 *Program design for phone directory program*

By translating the English to BASIC, we can get the program listed in Figure 13.11. Refer to the program as you study the description of how it works.

```
10 REM PHONEDIR

20 REM WRITTEN BY W. DANIEL, 11/26/--

30 REM THIS PROGRAM LOOKS UP PHONE NUMBERS

40 INPUT "ENTER THE NAME TO FIND:  ";PERSON$

50 READ NAM$,PHONE$

60 IF NAM$<>"EOD" AND NAM$<>PERSON$ THEN 50

70 IF NAM$=PERSON$ THEN PRINT PHONE$
                    ELSE PRINT "NOT FOUND"

80 END
```

Figure 13.11 *Phone directory program coded in BASIC*

Line 40 uses the keyword INPUT to get a person's name from the keyboard and store it in the variable called *PERSON$*. Line 50 uses the keyword **READ** to read two items from the data (the presence of two variables following READ means to read two items). The first item read is placed in variable *NAM$* (we couldn't use NAME$ because NAME is a keyword with some versions of BASIC). The second item read is placed in variable *PHONE$*. The phone number, if it contains a hyphen as it does here, must be placed in a character variable; the hyphen is a nonnumeric value.

Line 60 uses relational operators to check on the items that were read from the data lines. If the name that was read (variable *NAM$*) is not equal to the fake data item (the terminator) and it is not equal to the name we are looking for, we should go back and execute the READ statement again to get the next two data items. This is done with the IF . . . THEN statement.

If line 60 did not send control back to line 50, it is time to check to see which of two alternative actions should be taken. If the NAM$ read from data is the terminator, it is obvious that the name was not found. Therefore, a "not found" message is printed by line 70. If the NAM$ read from data is the name we are looking for, we obviously will print the matching phone number that goes with the name.

At this point, you have learned some of the elementary ideas about programming in the BASIC language. The language, however, has many other capabilities, including the ability to process large files of data.

SUMMARY

The BASIC language is used on more computers than any other language. It is an interactive language that makes the entry and debugging of programs easy. The newer versions of BASIC provide many advanced features such as the handling of large data files, the use of long variable names, and easy control of the format of output. Since the language is a free-form language, learning it is easy. The lack of required structure in programs can, however, lead to sloppy programming habits. A good version of BASIC is equally at home doing either business- or mathematical-type applications.

REVIEW QUESTIONS

1. What are the advantages of the BASIC language? (Obj. 1)
2. What are the disadvantages of the BASIC language? (Obj. 1)

3. What is the difference between immediate execution mode and deferred execution mode? How does the computer distinguish between them? (Obj. 2)

4. What kinds of variables does the BASIC language use? (Obj. 3)

5. What is the difference between an integer and a real number? (Obj. 3)

6. What is the difference between a constant and a literal? (Obj. 3)

7. How are variables named? What distinguishes a character variable from a numeric variable? (Obj. 3)

8. How do you write a program statement that will get input from the keyboard? (Obj. 4)

9. How do you cause a BASIC program to display output on the screen? (Obj. 4)

10. How does a BASIC program make decisions? (Obj. 4)

11. How do you write program statements to use data that has been stored in the program itself? (Obj. 4)

12. Describe some of the common differences between one version of BASIC and another. (Obj. 4)

VOCABULARY WORDS

The following terms were introduced in this chapter:

interactive programming	RUN
bug	print zone
immediate execution mode	numeric variable
deferred execution mode	integer
keyword	real number
PRINT	floating-point number
character variable	prompt
alphanumeric variable	END
string variable	LET
constant	relational operator
literal	GOTO
REM	DATA
CLS	terminator
HOME	READ
INPUT	

WORKBOOK EXERCISES

Chapter 13 in the workbook consists of two exercises: True/False and Completion. Complete both exercises in Chapter 13 of the workbook before proceeding to Chapter 14 in this text.

DISKETTE EXERCISE

Complete the diskette exercise for Chapter 13 before proceeding to Chapter 14 in this text.

14 Introduction to Pascal Programming

Objectives:

1. List the advantages and disadvantages of Pascal.

2. Describe the kinds of data with which Pascal operates.

3. Describe the general structure of a Pascal program and the procedure for entering and compiling a program.

4. Identify and explain the use of common Pascal procedures and identifiers.

In Chapter 9, you learned that the Pascal language is well suited for applications in many areas. In this chapter, you will learn more about this increasingly popular language.

ADVANTAGES AND DISADVANTAGES OF PASCAL

Pascal has many advantages as a programming language. Among them are the following:

1. The primary advantage of the Pascal language is that it encourages the use of good programming techniques. For example, each program must be named, all variables must be

specified before using them, and most program parts may be written without using GOTO commands. The reduced use of GOTO commands makes programs much easier to follow.

2. The programmer may invent data types. This advantage will be discussed further in the section on commonly used data types.

3. The primary structure of the Pascal language is standard, meaning that programs that do not go beyond the standard features are quite easily executed on computers made by different manufacturers.

Like any language, Pascal also has some disadvantages. Here are some of them:

1. Since Pascal is not a free-form language, it is harder to learn than BASIC. Remember, however, that the required structure leads to programs that are easier to understand.

2. Standard Pascal is rather weak in some areas, such as the handling of strings of nonnumeric characters. Therefore, nearly all suppliers of Pascal have added extensions to their versions of the language. These extensions are frequently different from one another, making it impossible to run programs written for one version of the language under another version.

3. Pascal is not an interpreted language. Therefore, it is necessary to use a word processor or text editor to enter programs. Finding and correcting problems is not as easy as with BASIC.

OVERVIEW OF PASCAL

This section will give you a better understanding of some of the general ideas about the Pascal language. The reading of this section should make the specific programming examples easier to understand.

Program Translation

Like all high-level languages, Pascal must be translated into machine language for execution by the computer. A Pascal program must first be entered into the computer and stored on auxiliary storage. Unlike BASIC, Pascal does not include a built-in editor, although some implementations of the language include a separate editor as part of an overall package. Therefore, a program must be entered with a word processor or text editor for storage on disk. The program you enter into the computer is known as a **source program** since it is the source from which the translation is to be made.

After the source program is stored, the Pascal compiler is used to translate the program into an **object program**, the result or object of the translation. Depending on the implementation of Pascal, the translation may be directly into machine code or into an intermediate type of code. If the translation is into machine code, the translated program can be executed directly and will run at a high speed.

If the translation is into intermediate code, the situation is different. The source program you write is translated into "pseudo commands" (made-up processor commands that do not necessarily match the machine code commands of any processor). A special interpreter program then translates these commands to machine code at the time the program is executed. The advantage of this procedure is that the same translated Pascal code can be used regardless of the processor on which the program is to run. It is only necessary to provide a different run-time interpreter for each different model of processor. The disadvantages are slower program execution and the requirement that the interpreter program always be available on the disk.

Data Types and Variables

As you learned in Chapter 10, a variable is a named storage location in the computer's memory. As a program is executed, various data may be stored in this location. One of Pascal's strong points is the many different types of data that may be stored in variables. In addition to the data types provided as standard equipment with the language, the programmer may define other types. When writing a program, the names of all variables must be specified, along with the type of data each variable is to hold. The exact types of data that may be stored depend upon the particular version of the language being used. The following section describes some commonly used types of data.

Commonly Used Data Types with Pascal

Four of the most commonly used data types are the integer, real, character, and boolean data types. As with BASIC, the two most common numeric data types are integer numbers and real numbers. Remember from Chapter 13 that an integer is a whole number, while a real number is a number with a decimal point.

Character data consists of any character that can be represented by the coding system being used, such as ASCII. Character variables are thus used to hold alphabet letters and punctuation marks, as well as any special characters that may be available. A character variable in standard Pascal holds only one character at a time unless it has been defined as a table. Various extensions to this limitation have been implemented by the different suppliers of the language, however.

Boolean data, stored in variables, consists of one of only two possible values: true or false. Thus, these variables are used in many decision-making circumstances within a program.

In addition to the data types described above, there are many others available, including ones defined by the programmer. Allowing the programmer to define new data types opens up many interesting possibilities for improving the clarity of programs. For example, if you were writing a program for use by a bakery, you could define a data type known as PIES. You could then specify that this data type could have only the values *CHOCOLATE, COCONUT, LEMON,* and *PECAN*. In the program you could then have a statement that says, in effect, "Print sales figures for all the pies." The program would then give you figures for chocolate, coconut, lemon, and pecan pie sales. Obviously, there is a lot of detail that has been overlooked in this example, but the idea is what we are interested in at this point.

Names of Variables

The variables used in Pascal are given names known as **identifiers**. Each name must begin with an alphabet letter and may be followed by any combination of alphabet letters and digits. You may remember that these are the same naming rules used by better versions of BASIC. Also like BASIC, the maximum length of a variable name depends on the particular version of Pascal being used. Two popular versions allow 8 and 31 characters, respectively. Underscores (_) can also be used in variable names. Whether Pascal pays attention to the underscores or simply ignores them depends on the version of the language.

Simple Program Construction

Pascal programs require identification of all their parts and all the variables they use. This is part of the required structure that keeps Pascal programs more understandable than some of the free-form programs that can be written in BASIC. The required structure for a simple program is shown in Figure 14.1. Note that no line numbers are used. On the first line is the word **PROGRAM** followed by the name you wish to call the program. Program names, like variables, are named with words called identifiers. The rules for the construction and length of program names, therefore, are the same as for variables. Following the name of the program, and in parentheses, is an indication of whether the program uses input, output, or both. These **parameters** are indicated by placing either INPUT, OUTPUT, or both words in the parentheses. This step is unnecessary with some versions of Pascal. Note that the program line ends with a semicolon. This is Pascal's way of saying it is the end of the statement. Statements can be written in whatever physical layout is desired (more than one line per statement, for example) since a semicolon designates the end of each statement.

```
PROGRAM NAME OF THE PROGRAM (PARAMETERS);
BEGIN
     FIRST STATEMENT;
     SECOND STATEMENT;
     ETC. . . . .;
END.
```

Figure 14.1
Required structure for a simple Pascal Program

On the line following the name of the program in Figure 14.1, you see the word **BEGIN**. At the end of the program you see the word **END**. These two words delimit (show the beginning and end of) the action to be taken by the program. Between these two words, all statements that the program must perform are included. Note that END is followed by a period, indicating that this is the end of the entire program rather than just the end of a statement.

Producing Simple Output

Now that you're familiar with the elementary structure of a program, let's add the necessary processing steps to produce an entire program that prints some words on the screen (see Figure 14.2). The figure includes both the program and the output that will be produced when the program is executed. In all program examples in this chapter, line numbers have been placed in front of the statements in order to make reference to the programs easier. Remember, however, that line numbers are not used when entering Pascal programs. Once a program is entered, several steps must be taken to compile the program before executing it. These steps are not shown in the figures, however.

```
Line:              Program code:

1                  PROGRAM SIMPLE (OUTPUT);
2                  BEGIN
3                     WRITELN('This output is being produced');
4                     WRITELN('by a Pascal program.');
5                  END.


                   Output when program is executed:


                   This output is being produced
                   by a Pascal program.
```

Figure 14.2   A simple Pascal program

First, look at line 1 of Figure 14.2. Note that the name of the program is SIMPLE. As indicated by the parameter in parentheses on the title line, the program will do output, but no input. Once the program is named, the BEGIN statement (line 2) indicates where the processing begins. This is followed by the actual printing instructions. The **WRITELN** (write line) procedures are used on lines 3 and 4 to print output on the screen. Note that we referred to WRITELN as a procedure. A **procedure** is something that Pascal is able to perform. In this case, Pascal is able to write a line on the screen when we use the procedure named WRITELN. Following the name of the procedure, and enclosed in parentheses, is the data to be printed. In this program, the data for the WRITELN procedures consist of literals. Note that each literal is enclosed in single quotes (apostrophes) rather than regular quotation marks. Some versions of Pascal allow you to use either single or double quotes.

Finally, after all the other program statements, the END statement (line 5) indicates the end of the program. Note that, unlike some versions of BASIC, Pascal requires the END statement.

Getting Input from the Keyboard

Now that we know how to print output on the screen, let's find out how to get input from the keyboard, store it in variables, and do simple computations with it. Let's use the grade averaging problem that you learned in the chapter on BASIC. A student in a course has three grades that will be keyed in and averaged. For a review, look at the program design for the problem in Figure 14.3.

1. Get the three grades and store them in variables.
2. Print the average found by summing the grades and dividing the sum by 3.

Figure 14.3   English language program design for grade averaging program

Refer to Figure 14.4 as you study the following explanation. This figure shows both the grade averaging program and the result of its execution. In the execution part, items printed by the program are shown in blue. Items entered by the user are shown in red. The program begins just as the previous one began, by naming the program (line 1). Following the name, both INPUT and OUTPUT appear inside the parentheses, since both functions will be occurring in this program. When previously coding this program in BASIC, we were able to simply begin with the steps to be performed. With Pascal, this is not possible. Remember, we said that Pascal forces a degree of structure on you to require at least the appearance of good programming habits. That structure requires you to declare all variables before using them.

Declaring a variable means that you list its name and tell what kind of data it is to hold. As you can see from the program, the declaration of variables is done before writing BEGIN, which starts carrying out the processing steps. The declaration of variables is done on line 2. We have used variable names of *G1*, *G2*, and *G3*. The term **VAR** at the beginning of the line stands for *variables*. This is followed by the names of the variables, separated by commas. Following the last variable name is a colon. Following the colon, the word REAL specifies that the variables named before the colon are to hold real numbers. We declared them as real variables in case a teacher gives a test grade of 87.5. Otherwise, they could have been declared as integer variables. If there were other types of variables to declare (integer variables, for example), they would be declared following the semicolon, on the same or the next line.

Now that the variables have been declared, we can begin with the processing steps. Line 3 indicates the beginning. Remember

```
Line:        Program code:

  1    PROGRAM GRADEAVG (INPUT, OUTPUT);

  2    VAR G1,G2,G3: REAL;

  3    BEGIN
  4         WRITE('Enter 3 numeric grades separated by spaces:    ');
  5         READLN(G1,G2,G3);
  6         WRITELN('The average is ',(G1+G2+G3)/3:5:1);
  7    END.
```

Output when program is executed:

```
Enter 3 numeric grades separated by spaces:    95 92.5 87.5
The average is 91.7
```

Figure 14.4 *Pascal grade averaging program*

from the program design that the first step is to get the three grades and store them in variables. To accomplish this, we first print a prompt, as shown on line 4. Notice that we use a WRITE procedure instead of WRITELN. The only difference is that WRITELN causes the cursor to drop to the beginning of the next line after the printing has been done. **WRITE** keeps the cursor on the same line following completion of the printing.

After the prompt is printed, the **READLN** procedure (line 5) is used to get input from the keyboard and assign the data into the variables previously declared. When the program is executed, the first number entered on the keyboard is placed in Variable *G1*, the second number is placed in Variable *G2*, and the third number is placed in Variable *G3*.

With the scores in variables, the WRITELN procedure (line 6) is used to do the computation and print the average. The parentheses around the variable names are necessary to make Pascal add the grades together before dividing by 3. The colons and numbers following the divisor specify how the answer is to be printed. The first colon and number (:5) specify that a total width of 5 columns is to be used for printing the number. The second colon and number (:1) specify that there is to be one place to the right of the decimal point. Note that a number may be rounded, if necessary, to make it fit the number of decimal places specified. The rounding applies only to the printout; it has no effect on the number stored in the computer.

Making Decisions

Now let's take a look at a program that shows Pascal's decision-making power. As in Chapter 13, this next program calculates the amount of commission to pay a salesperson. If a salesperson sells less than $5,000 worth of merchandise for the week, the commission will be figured at a rate of 7 percent. If the sales for the week are $5,000 or greater, the commission will be figured at a rate of 9 percent. Review the program design as shown in Figure 14.5. Refer to the program design and the program (Figure 14.6) as you study the comments in the following paragraphs about how the program works.

1. Get the amount of sales for the week for one salesperson and store the amount in a variable.

2. If the sales are less than 5000,

   Then rate is 7%

   Else, rate is 9%.

3. Calculate commission by multiplying sales times rate.

4. Print the sales and the commission.

Figure 14.5   *Program design for calculating commissions*

As is usual with a Pascal program, the first line contains the name of the program. On the second and third lines, the method of writing comments is introduced. The comments are indicated by braces, {}, in the program and are ignored by Pascal when the program is compiled. The comments, which are for the benefit of people reading the program, may be enclosed by a combination of parentheses and asterisks, (* *), if the keyboard being used cannot make braces.

Next, in line 4 the variables are declared. This program is using only real variables. The program instructions begin with line 5. Line 6 prints a prompt, followed on line 7 by the READLN procedure to get a sales amount from the keyboard and place it in the variable *SALES*.

Once the input is received from the keyboard, it is time for the program to make a decision on whether the commission rate is 7 percent or 9 percent. This is done in line 9 by using the **IF** ...

Line: Program code:

```
1        PROGRAM PAY (INPUT,OUTPUT);

2            {Written by Harmon Perez, 11/10/--}
3            {This program calculates commissions}

4        VAR SALES, COMMISSION, RATE: REAL;

5        BEGIN

6            WRITE('Enter the amount of sales:   ');
7            READLN(SALES);
8            WRITELN;              {This prints a blank line.}

9            IF SALES<5000 THEN RATE:=0.07
                        ELSE RATE:=0.09;

10           COMMISSION:=SALES*RATE;

11           WRITELN('RATE:   ',RATE:3:2,'    COMMISSION:   ',COMMISSION:7:2);

12       END.
```

Execution of the program with sales less than $5,000:

```
Enter the amount of sales:   4750.18

RATE:   0.07   COMMISSION:   332.51
```

Execution of the program with sales greater than or equal to $5,000:

```
Enter the amount of sales:   7432.98

RATE:   0.09   COMMISSION:   668.97
```

Figure 14.6   *Pascal program for calculating commissions*

THEN . . . ELSE statement. Here, one of two alternative actions may be taken. As stated in the program design, the rate is 7 percent (.07) if the sales are less than 5,000; otherwise, the rate is 9 percent (.09). Notice that the relational operator *less than* ($<$) is used to state the condition of the decision. Other relational operators may also be used in programs. Line 9 also introduces the **assignment operator**. This operator, written as a colon and equal sign ($:=$), places a value in a variable. In this case, it places the selected rate into the variable that stores the rate. Line 10 multiplies this rate times the sales amount and places the product into the variable that holds the amount of commission. On line 11, the WRITELN procedure is then used to print the result.

More Advanced Program Construction

Remember that a procedure is something that Pascal knows how to do. The procedures you have used thus far (WRITELN, WRITE, READLN) are built-in parts of the language. However, for anything Pascal does not already know how to do, you may define your own procedures. In other words, you can teach new things to Pascal.

The ability to teach Pascal new procedures makes the language especially valuable for writing programs in the modular form you learned about in Chapter 9. Remember from that chapter that more complex programs may be broken into different modules that work together. In Pascal, each of these modules may be a set of instructions defined by the programmer as a procedure. There are also sets of instructions known as functions. Functions are quite similar to procedures but are not discussed in this text.

Now let's look at an example of a program designed in modular form and coded in Pascal. This will be a cash register program. Item prices will be entered on the keyboard one after another until the user enters a price of zero. As each price is entered, it is added to a subtotal. When a zero is entered, the sales tax and total amount due are computed. The subtotal, tax, and total are then printed. Remembering the procedure from Chapter 9, we will first create a hierarchy chart as shown in Figure 14.7. We will call the program CASHREG, short for cash register. The two functions are (1) get an item, and (2) total up the sale.

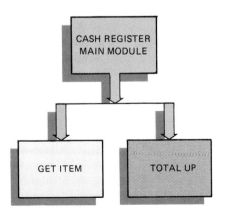

Figure 14.7
Hierarchy chart for cash register program

Once the hierarchy chart is complete, the work to be done by the three modules is defined. Now we will complete the program design for the main or control module. Then we will do the other modules (submodules). The designs of the modules for the cash register program are shown in Figure 14.8.

Main Module:
1. Initialize (put zeros in) variables that will contain totals.
2. Repeat Get-Item Module until price of zero is entered.
3. Perform the Total-Up Module.

Get-Item Module:
1. Get a price from the keyboard.
2. Add the price to the subtotal variable.

Total-Up Module:
1. Figure sales tax by multiplying subtotal by 5 percent.
2. Figure total by adding the subtotal and the sales tax.
3. Print the subtotal amount.
4. Print the sales tax amount.
5. Print the total amount.

Figure 14.8   Program design for the modules of the program CASHREG

From the program designs of the modules, the program can be coded. In coding the program, the required structure of Pascal that we have learned thus far must be considered. To that structure, we will add one more item. Generally, programmer-defined procedures (the two submodules of this program) appear before the main module when the coded program is entered. That is, you tell Pascal the meaning of a procedure before you try to use it. It is good programming practice, however, to code the main module first, then code the submodules.

Keeping this structure in mind, study the program as coded in Figure 14.9. Comments in the program indicate where the definition of the procedures begins and where the main body of the program begins. Note that Pascal allows a very straightforward translation from the English of the program design. Indeed, it is quite possible in many circumstances to write the original program designs in Pascal.

Line:	Program code:

```
1        PROGRAM CASHREG (INPUT,OUTPUT);

2        VAR PRICE, SUBTOTAL, TAX, TOTAL: REAL;

3        {The following code defines the procedures (modules)}

4        PROCEDURE GET_ITEM;
5            BEGIN
6                WRITE('Price (0 if done):  ');
7                READLN(PRICE);
8                SUBTOTAL:=SUBTOTAL+PRICE;
9            END;


10       PROCEDURE TOTAL_UP;
11           BEGIN
12               TAX:=SUBTOTAL*0.05;
13               TOTAL:=SUBTOTAL+TAX;
14               WRITELN('SUBTOTAL: ',SUBTOTAL:10:2);
15               WRITELN('TAX:      ',TAX:10:2);
16               WRITELN('TOTAL:    ',TOTAL:10:2);
17           END;


18       {Following is the main body of the program (the main module)}

19       BEGIN
20           SUBTOTAL:=0;
21           TOTAL:=0;
22           REPEAT GET_ITEM UNTIL PRICE=0;
23           WRITELN;
24           TOTAL_UP;
25       END.
```

Execution of the program:

```
Price (0 if done):   12.41
Price (0 if done):   29.63
Price (0 if done):   18.48
Price (0 if done):   0

SUBTOTAL:      60.52
TAX:            3.03
TOTAL:         63.55
```

Figure 14.9 *Pascal cash register program*

In studying the program, begin with the main module (line 19). Lines 20 and 21 place zeros in the totaling variables. Unlike BASIC, Pascal does not automatically place a value in a variable when it is created. Therefore, if you don't place a beginning value in a variable being used for accumulating a total, there is no telling what number you will wind up with in the variable. Line 22 keeps telling the Get-Item Module to do its work until the user enters a price of zero. Once a price of zero has been entered, line 23 prints a blank line. Then simply by using the name of the procedure (line 24), the Main Module tells the Total-Up Module to do its work.

SUMMARY

The Pascal language is growing in popularity. The primary reason for this is its structured format, which encourages good programming techniques. The structure requires that programs and program parts be named and that all variables be declared before using them. There are also many different data types, including those defined by the programmer.

The things that Pascal is able to perform, such as WRITE a line on the video display or READ input from the keyboard, are known as procedures. If there is not a suitable built-in procedure for what needs to be done, the programmer may write one. This expandability of the language is another primary advantage of the language. Also, Pascal allows a much more direct translation than other languages from the English program design to the high-level computer language.

REVIEW QUESTIONS

1. What are the advantages of the Pascal language? (Obj. 1)

2. What are the disadvantages of the Pascal language? (Obj. 1)

3. What are the characteristics of integer data? (Obj. 2)

4. What are the characteristics of real data? (Obj. 2)

5. What are the characteristics of character data? (Obj. 2)

6. What are the characteristics of boolean data? (Obj. 2)

7. Describe the procedure for entering and compiling a Pascal program. (Obj. 3)

8. What is the primary difference in the way different Pascal compilers operate during the compilation and execution of programs? (Obj. 3)

9. Describe the general structure of a Pascal program. (Obj. 3)

10. Name and describe Pascal's procedures for displaying data and for accepting input from the keyboard. (Obj. 4)

11. Name and describe one of Pascal's methods of handling decision making in a program. (Obj. 4)

12. What is a procedure? (Obj. 4)

13. In what order are program modules written when using Pascal? (Obj. 4)

VOCABULARY WORDS

The following terms were introduced in this chapter:

source program	WRITELN
object program	procedure
boolean data	declare
identifier	VAR
PROGRAM	WRITE
parameters	READLN
BEGIN	IF ... THEN ... ELSE
END	assignment operator

WORKBOOK EXERCISES

Chapter 14 in the workbook consists of three exercises: True/False, Sequencing, and Completion. Complete all three exercises in Chapter 14 of the workbook before proceeding to Chapter 15 in this text.

DISKETTE EXERCISE

Complete the diskette exercise for Chapter 14 before proceeding to Chapter 15 in this text.

15 Introduction to COBOL Programming

Objectives:

1. List the advantages and disadvantages of COBOL.

2. Describe the steps in coding, entering, and compiling a COBOL program.

3. Describe how COBOL uses the computer's memory.

4. Identify and explain the purpose of each of the divisions of a COBOL program.

You learned in Chapter 9 that COBOL is a high-level programming language that is widely used for business applications. When you finish studying the language in this chapter, you will not be able to actually program in COBOL. You will, however, have a better understanding of COBOL.

ADVANTAGES AND DISADVANTAGES OF COBOL

COBOL has distinct advantages as a programming language. Some of them are described as follows:

1. COBOL was designed to process and maintain large files. In fact, the word FILE is used many times in the programs. COBOL files can be recorded on any of the auxiliary storage media described earlier, such as disks or tapes. In COBOL, data going to the printer is also known as a file. With some versions of COBOL, data coming to and going from the terminal may also be known as a file.

2. The steps of a COBOL program are stated in a near-English language. The word ADD orders the computer to add numbers. MOVE tells it to move data from one variable to another. *NUMBER* can be used as a variable name for a student number. The use of a near-English language makes COBOL easier for the programmer to understand than other programming languages that use short names and symbols. Therefore, the logic of programs is easier to follow.

3. COBOL is generally considered a standard language. A COBOL compiler must contain certain standard capabilities. With some exceptions (the reference manual for the version of COBOL being used will point out variations from the standard), the COBOL program that runs on one computer can be easily changed to run on another computer. For this reason, COBOL is said to be a machine-independent language.

4. COBOL programs are easier to maintain and modify because of the near-English language in which they are written.

COBOL also has some disadvantages. However, for business data processing, the advantages outweigh the disadvantages. Some of the disadvantages are as follows:

1. COBOL compilers require more memory (main storage) than some other languages. For this reason, COBOL cannot be used with computer systems having a very small amount of memory.

2. COBOL programs are usually longer than programs in other languages. The near-English language that makes COBOL easy to read also creates long sentences. In addition to long sentences, divisions and detailed data descriptions are required. These also add to the length of the programs.

3. COBOL is harder to learn than some other languages, like BASIC. However, once the rules are understood, COBOL's readability makes it easier to understand and maintain.

OVERVIEW OF COBOL

Understanding how to write COBOL programs will be easier if you have an idea of how the computer's memory is organized under COBOL. Assume that you have a computer system set up as shown in Figure 15.1. Note that the system consists of a processor with main storage, a monitor, a disk drive, a keyboard, and a printer.

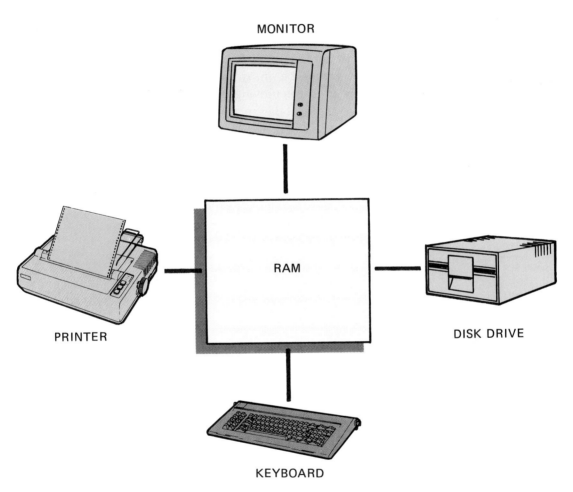

MONITOR

RAM

PRINTER

DISK DRIVE

KEYBOARD

Figure 15.1   A computer system

With COBOL, sections of memory called buffers are set aside for use with the different devices, such as the disk drives and printer. This can be visualized as shown in Figure 15.2, illustrating how the memory can be divided. Each file on auxiliary storage has its own area of memory reserved. Therefore, if two data files on disk are to be in use, there are two areas of memory reserved for them. All data to be recorded in a file must be moved into the reserved part of memory before it can be written to the storage device. Likewise, all data to be printed must be moved into the area of memory reserved for the printer before it can be printed. With some versions of COBOL, the same holds true for the terminal. All data to appear on the screen or to be input from the keyboard passes through the screen section of memory. Part of the memory not reserved for the storage of file data may be used for **working storage**; that is, it may be used for any variables that are not associated with a file. For example, intermediate variables used in computations would be in working storage. Many of COBOL's commands are used for moving data from one memory location to another as processing takes place.

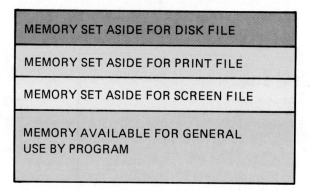

Figure 15.2
Memory usage by COBOL

MEMORY SET ASIDE FOR DISK FILE

MEMORY SET ASIDE FOR PRINT FILE

MEMORY SET ASIDE FOR SCREEN FILE

MEMORY AVAILABLE FOR GENERAL USE BY PROGRAM

WRITING A COBOL PROGRAM

As is true with any programming language, you should plan a COBOL program before coding it. Once the program is planned according to the program design steps you learned about in Chapter 9, it is coded and entered through the keyboard to the CPU.

Coding a COBOL Program

Once a COBOL program has been planned, it is coded. Unlike BASIC, where program statements can be written in just about any order desired, all COBOL programs are written in four parts, known as divisions. These divisions and their titles must appear in every program in the following order:

1. **IDENTIFICATION DIVISION**. This division gives the title of the program, known as the **PROGRAM-ID**, which is required. The title is then followed by the name of the programmer and the date the program is written, both of which may be omitted if desired.

2. **ENVIRONMENT DIVISION**. This division specifies the type of computer on which the program is to run. It also names the input and output files and may specify the input and output devices to be used.

3. **DATA DIVISION**. This division describes the data files and data structures to be used by the program.

4. **PROCEDURE DIVISION**. This division specifies the actual steps the computer is to follow in processing the data to solve a problem. This part of a COBOL program is the part most like a BASIC program.

The words used in writing a COBOL program are of two types: those on a reserved word list and those supplied by the programmer.

A **reserved word** is a word that has a specific meaning to a COBOL compiler. The compiler reserves such words for given purposes. Reserved words may be divided into several groups. For example, verbs are action words such as ADD, MOVE, and WRITE. Modifiers and connectors are such words as TO, FROM, AFTER, and BEFORE. Other reserved words are used to name various divisions and sections of a program or to describe files. There are reserved words in every COBOL program. The choice of words depends on the problem to be solved and the type of computer being used. When you study an example program later in this chapter, you will become familiar with some of the reserved words.

Programmer-supplied words are any nonreserved words used in a program. These words are used as variable names in files and working storage descriptions, and as labels for some sections of the program. Unlike variables in BASIC, which are defined simply by using them, programmer-supplied words in a COBOL program must be defined in the Data Division of the program.

COBOL programs may be written on plain sheets of paper. In practice, however, a program is written on a **COBOL Program Sheet**. Such a sheet is illustrated in Figure 15.3. Note that the sheet contains space for 80 columns of information. These columns correspond to the 80 columns of a typical video display. One program line will be entered from each completed line of the COBOL Program Sheet. Information from each of the numbered columns on the program sheet will be entered into the corresponding column of the display.

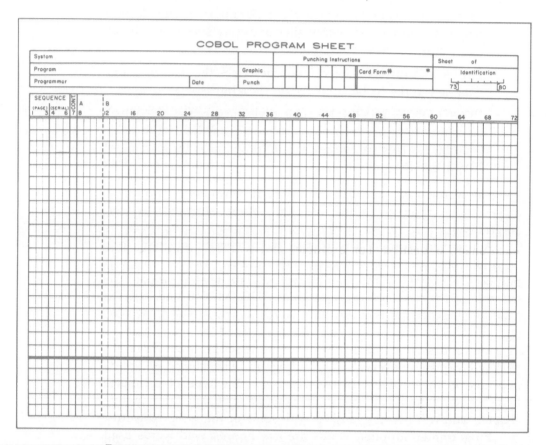

Figure 15.3 *A COBOL Program Sheet*

Figure 15.4 shows enlargements of parts of the COBOL Program Sheet. Note the boxes in the upper left-hand corner of the figure. These boxes are not numbered on the program sheet. The information written in these boxes will not be entered into the computer. This information is for quick reference only. The name of the program and the programmer can be written in whatever fashion desired.

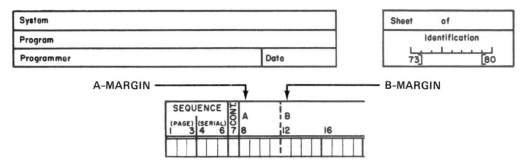

Figure 15.4 *Enlarged sections of a COBOL Program Sheet*

The box labeled *Identification* in the upper right-hand corner of the program sheet (Figures 15.3 and 15.4) will contain information that may be entered in Columns 73-80. These spaces are for identifying (naming) the program; their use is not required with some versions of COBOL. Above the identification area is space for writing in the page number. The first sheet of a program should be numbered as 1, the second sheet as 2, and so on. Once the entire program is finished, the total number of pages may be entered on each sheet, if desired. For example, *sheet 3 of 12* means the third page of a total of 12 pages. The page number may also be written in Columns 1-3 of the program sheet under *SEQUENCE*. Columns 4-6 may be used for the numbers of the instructions. Column 7 may be used for either of two purposes: (1) a hyphen is placed in the column if it is necessary to divide a program line between two lines on the program sheet; or (2) an asterisk is placed in the column to indicate that the line is a remark and should be ignored by the compiler.

The actual statements making up a COBOL program are written in Columns 8-72. Note in Figure 15.4 that Column 8 is labeled *A* for the **A-Margin**, while Column 12 is labeled *B* for the **B-Margin**. Some COBOL statements must begin at the A-Margin, while others must begin at the B-Margin.

Entering and Translating a COBOL Program

As is true with all high-level programming languages, COBOL must be translated into machine language before processing can take place. The translation is handled by a compiler program. As you learned in Chapter 14, a program written by the programmer is known as the source program. The machine language code produced by the compiler is known as the object program. The object program contains the instructions that will be carried out by the computer. The steps in producing the object program are as follows:

1. Enter each line of the COBOL source program into a text file.

2. Run the COBOL compiler program. From the source code that is input, this program produces the object code. Figure 15.5 shows this process.

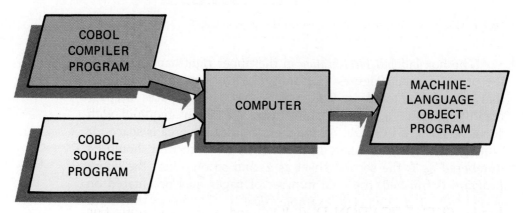

Figure 15.5 *Translation process of a COBOL program*

DEVELOPING EXAMPLE PROGRAMS

Now that you have a general idea about how a COBOL program is written, let's look at some examples.

Example 1

Suppose that we want to record student data in a file on disk. For each student, the file is to contain the name, class code, and three test scores. Figure 15.6 shows the format of the desired file contents.

Now let's look at the four required divisions of a COBOL program that will accomplish the desired task (Figures 15.7 through 15.10). In each program part shown as an example, the reserved COBOL words are printed in red. Programmer-supplied words are printed in blue. The program is written in Microsoft COBOL, which is available for many microcomputers[1].

---

[1]Microsoft is a registered trademark of Microsoft Corporation.

STUDENT RECORD	MAXIMUM LENGTH
Name	Maximum of 20 characters
Class Code	1 digit (enter 1, 2, 3, or 4)
Score 1	Maximum of 3 digits (range 0-100)
Score 2	Maximum of 3 digits (range 0-100)
Score 3	Maximum of 3 digits (range 0-100)

Figure 15.6 *Desired contents of data file on disk*

Identification Division   Figure 15.7 shows the Identification Division as printed out by the COBOL compiler during compilation. The line numbers were supplied by the compiler; therefore, the programmer did not need to enter sequence numbers on the program sheet. Each line shown in this division begins at the A-Margin (Column 8). Some compilers require only the division header (IDENTIFICATION DIVISION) and program identification (PROGRAM-ID) lines in this division. If using one of these compilers, you could omit the lines giving the author's name and the date written.

```
Line:        Program code:

1            IDENTIFICATION DIVISION.
2            PROGRAM-ID.    ENTSCO.
3            AUTHOR.        HENDERSON.
4            DATE-WRITTEN.  NOVEMBER 6, 19--.
```

Figure 15.7 *Identification Division*

Environment Division   The amount of required information in the Environment Division varies depending on the compiler being used. In the example in Figure 15.8, note that the division has been broken into two sections: the CONFIGURATION SECTION and the INPUT-OUTPUT SECTION.

Line:	Program code:
5	ENVIRONMENT DIVISION.
6	CONFIGURATION SECTION.
7	SOURCE-COMPUTER. IBM-PC.
8	OBJECT-COMPUTER. IBM-PC.
9	INPUT-OUTPUT SECTION.
10	FILE-CONTROL.
11	SELECT SCORES-FILE, ASSIGN TO DISK.

Figure 15.8 Environment Division

The Configuration Section gives the name of the **source computer** (the computer that will be used for translating the program) and the name of the **object computer** (the computer that will be used for running the machine-language code). Some compilers allow you to omit this information.

The Input-Output Section contains the names that will be used by the program to identify files. The reserved word FILE-CONTROL is COBOL's way of saying it is about to identify the files. Following this word is the SELECT statement that actually names the file and tells which input or output device it will use. In the example program, there is one file. This file, called SCORES-FILE (the hyphen is there because you cannot use two words as the name of a file), will be on a disk drive, named simply as DISK. The device names vary from one computer to another.

Data Division   The Data Division describes the arrangement of data to be used by the program. Study Figure 15.9. The division is broken into sections. The FILE SECTION describes the files. That is, this section names memory locations to be set aside for use by data on its way to and from files on various auxiliary storage and input/output devices. The WORKING-STORAGE SECTION describes data structures. Working storage is COBOL's way of saying "variables in memory." In a more complex program, there may be additional sections in the data division. In versions of COBOL that set up the screen and keyboard as a file, a SCREEN SECTION is defined in this division.

Now let's take a more detailed look at the file section of the Data Division:

1. On line 14, FD SCORES-FILE means we are about to write a file description (FD) of the file known as SCORES-FILE.

```
Line:              Program code:

 12                DATA DIVISION.
 13                FILE SECTION.
 14                FD   SCORES-FILE
 15                     LABEL RECORDS STANDARD
 16                     VALUE OF FILE-ID IS "A:SCORES".
 17                01   STUDENT.
 18                     05   STUDENT-NAME    PIC A(20).
 19                     05   CLASS-CODE      PIC 9.
 20                     05   SCORE-1         PIC 999.
 21                     05   SCORE-2         PIC 999.
 22                     05   SCORE-3         PIC 999.
 23                WORKING-STORAGE SECTION.
 24                77   CONTINUE-OPTION      PIC X.
 25                     88 FINISHED VALUE IS 'N'.
```

Figure **15.9** *Data Division*

2. On line 15, LABEL RECORDS STANDARD means that COBOL should follow its standard rules in identifying each record on the disk.

3. On line 16, VALUE OF FILE-ID IS "A:SCORES" connects the file name used in the program with the file name used on the disk. Note that the file name used in the program, SCORES-FILE, is 11 characters long. The operating system of the computer on which this example is being run, however, limits the length of file names to 8 characters. Therefore, this line says that the name SCORES-FILE will be abbreviated on the disk to the name SCORES. The *A:* specifies that the file will be on the disk located in the first disk drive.

4. Line 17 begins with 01, which means that we are naming a record in the file. Therefore, each record in this file will be known by the name STUDENT.

5. Now we will look at lines 18-22. The record called STUDENT is described in detail. In other words, it is broken down into fields. The line numbers with 05 at the beginning of them show that these data names are part of the record identified with 01. PIC is short for PICTURE and tells what the data looks like. The meaning of each line is as follows: A field called *STUDENT-NAME* is to exist; it is to be alphabetic with a maximum length of 20 characters. This description is specified by PIC A(20); the *A* stands for alphabetic. A field

called *CLASS-CODE* is numeric and is one digit in length, as specified by PIC 9. The 9 means numeric, and a single 9 means only one digit. *SCORE-1*, *SCORE-2*, and *SCORE-3* are fields of three digits each, as specified by PIC 999. If desired, this could have been written as PIC 9(3). Note that only **elementary items** (those that are not broken into smaller units) have picture clauses. If desired, we could have defined the record differently. For example, we could have set the scores up as a **group item** (group of elementary items) and called it *GRADES*, as shown below:

```
01   STUDENT.
     05   STUDENT-NAME     PIC A(20).
     05   CLASS-CODE       PIC 9.              GRADES is a group item made up
     05   GRADES.          ◄─────────── of the elementary items below it.
          10   SCORE-1     PIC 999.            Note that only elementary items
          10   SCORE-2     PIC 999.            have PICTURE clauses.
          10   SCORE-3     PIC 999.
```

Note that programmer-supplied names consisting of more than one word have hyphens between the words. This is because no name may contain a space.

6. Lines 23-25 describe the working storage to be used by the program. The 77 on line 24 is a special number used in COBOL to identify an elementary working storage item (in this case, CONTINUE-OPTION) that is not broken into smaller parts. On line 25, the 88 is a special number used in COBOL to name a condition. A **condition** involves a comparison of two values. In this example, when the variable *CONTINUE-OPTION* has an "N" placed in it, the FINISHED condition will be true. This variable will be referred to later in the Procedure Division to indicate when the user has entered all the names and scores desired.

Procedure Division Planned in English, the processing steps required in the Procedure Division might be as shown in the next section. To see how these English steps are translated into COBOL, refer to Figure 15.10 as you study the steps. After each English step, the numbers of the COBOL lines pertaining to the step are listed. On the program listing, note that headings or labels start at the A-

Margin to designate the beginning of each section. The program is designed in two modules: the main module, and a submodule to do the detail processing.

Main Module   The program design for the Main Module is as follows:

1. Start the job by opening the output file (line 28 of the COBOL listing in Figure 15.10).

2. Perform the Detail Processing Module until the user has finished entering all desired data (line 29 of Figure 15.10).

3. At the end of the job, close the data file and stop (lines 30-31).

```
Line:          Program code:


 26            PROCEDURE DIVISION.
 27            MAIN-MODULE.
 28                OPEN OUTPUT SCORES-FILE.
 29                PERFORM DETAIL-PROCESSING-MODULE UNTIL FINISHED.
 30                CLOSE SCORES-FILE.
 31                STOP RUN.
 32            DETAIL-PROCESSING-MODULE.
 33                DISPLAY 'ENTER STUDENT NAME:'.
 34                ACCEPT STUDENT-NAME.
 35                DISPLAY 'ENTER CLASS CODE (1,2,3 OR 4):'.
 36                ACCEPT CLASS-CODE.
 37                DISPLAY 'ENTER THE FIRST SCORE:'.
 38                ACCEPT SCORE-1.
 39                DISPLAY 'ENTER THE SECOND SCORE:'.
 40                ACCEPT SCORE-2.
 41                DISPLAY 'ENTER THE THIRD SCORE:'.
 42                ACCEPT SCORE-3.
 43                WRITE STUDENT.
 44                DISPLAY 'ANY MORE SCORES (Y/N)?'.
 45                ACCEPT CONTINUE-OPTION.
```

Figure 15.10   *Procedure Division*

Detail Processing Module   The program design for the Detail Processing Module is as follows:

1. Get a student's name from the keyboard and put it in the part of memory set aside for data going to the disk (lines 33 and 34). Note that **DISPLAY**, like BASIC's PRINT, puts information on the screen, while **ACCEPT** is similar to BASIC's INPUT. ACCEPT is followed by *STUDENT-NAME*,

the name we gave to a 20-character elementary item in line 18 of the program. Remember that this data name is in the section set aside for the output file.

2. Get the class code from the keyboard and put it in memory set aside for data going to the disk (lines 35-36).

3. Get the three scores for one student and put them in memory set aside for data going to the disk (lines 37-42).

4. Take the data that has been stored in memory and write it on the disk (line 43). Note that all the fields that make up the record called STUDENT are written to the disk at once.

5. Find out if the user wants to enter more scores. Put the response of Y or N in the working storage variable called *CONTINUE-OPTION* (lines 44-45). The Main Module step on line 29 will look at this variable to determine whether to repeat the Detail Processing Module. Remember that a value of N placed in the variable means the user is finished.

Example 2

For the second example, let's write a program that uses the detail file created in Figure 15.6 of Example 1. The program will read the data from the disk and print a report giving each student's name, class code, and average score. Figure 15.11 shows how the output of the program should look.

Identification Division   As shown in Figure 15.12, the Identification Division is identical to Figure 15.7 in Example 1 except for a different program name.

Environment Division   The Environment Division, as shown in Figure 15.13, is very similar to that of Example 1. Note that after the SELECT clause for the SCORES-FILE (line 11), a STATUS clause has been added. Each time COBOL writes or reads a file, it places two characters in a variable of the programmer's choice to indicate whether the file operation was successful. The variable to be used for this purpose is to be called *FILE-STATUS*. The variable will be used to determine when all data has been read from the file. Note that in addition to the SCORES-FILE, a file known as PRINTED-REPORT-FILE is selected and assigned to the printer (line 12).

Data Division   Refer to Figure 15.14 as you study this section. The description of the SCORES-FILE is identical to that used in Example 1. After all, it is exactly the same file. A new file

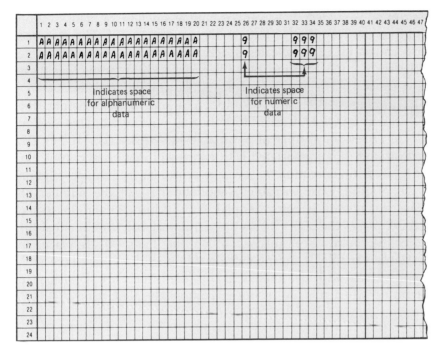

Figure 15.11
Output written on a report spacing chart

Line:	Program code:
1	IDENTIFICATION DIVISION.
2	PROGRAM-ID. PRTAVG.
3	AUTHOR. HENDERSON.
4	DATE-WRITTEN. NOVEMBER 6, 19--.

Figure 15.12 *Identification Division*

Line:	Program code:
5	ENVIRONMENT DIVISION.
6	CONFIGURATION SECTION.
7	SOURCE-COMPUTER. IBM-PC.
8	OBJECT-COMPUTER. IBM-PC.
9	INPUT-OUTPUT SECTION.
10	FILE-CONTROL.
11	SELECT SCORES-FILE, ASSIGN TO DISK, STATUS IS FILE-STATUS.
12	SELECT PRINTED-REPORT-FILE, ASSIGN TO PRINTER.

Figure 15.13 *Environment Division*

description is added, however, beginning on line 24. This section describes the format of a line on the printed report. The reserved word called **FILLER** indicates space between columns of variable data. For example, on line 28 a filler of PIC X(5) means that there are 5 spaces between the NAME-PRINT column and the CODE-PRINT column. After the description of the printed output, the WORKING-STORAGE SECTION begins on line 32. This section first describes the format of a variable known as *TOTAL-SCORE*. This variable is not associated with either an input or an output file, but is used in computing the average score. Next is the description of the *FILE-STATUS* variable. Remembering that the number 88 means a condition is being defined, look at lines 35 and 36. When COBOL places the digits '10' in the status variable, it means that the end of the file has been reached. When the digits '00' are placed in the status variable, it means that the file operation was successful. These values will be looked at by the Procedure Division to determine when the file has been completely read.

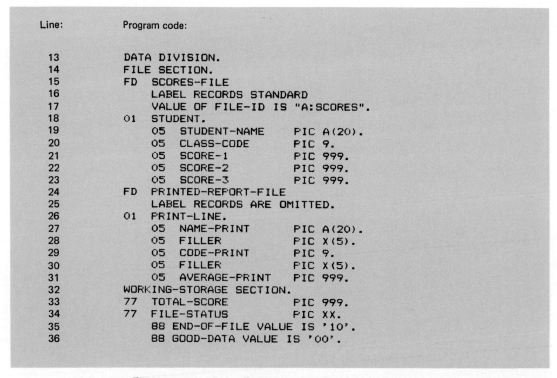

```
Line:           Program code:

  13            DATA DIVISION.
  14            FILE SECTION.
  15            FD   SCORES-FILE
  16                 LABEL RECORDS STANDARD
  17                 VALUE OF FILE-ID IS "A:SCORES".
  18            01   STUDENT.
  19                 05   STUDENT-NAME      PIC A(20).
  20                 05   CLASS-CODE        PIC 9.
  21                 05   SCORE-1           PIC 999.
  22                 05   SCORE-2           PIC 999.
  23                 05   SCORE-3           PIC 999.
  24            FD   PRINTED-REPORT-FILE
  25                 LABEL RECORDS ARE OMITTED.
  26            01   PRINT-LINE.
  27                 05   NAME-PRINT        PIC A(20).
  28                 05   FILLER            PIC X(5).
  29                 05   CODE-PRINT        PIC 9.
  30                 05   FILLER            PIC X(5).
  31                 05   AVERAGE-PRINT     PIC 999.
  32            WORKING-STORAGE SECTION.
  33            77   TOTAL-SCORE            PIC 999.
  34            77   FILE-STATUS            PIC XX.
  35                 88 END-OF-FILE VALUE IS '10'.
  36                 88 GOOD-DATA VALUE IS '00'.
```

Figure 15.14 *Data Division*

Procedure Division   As in Example 1, the Procedure Division is divided into a Main Module and a Detail Processing Module. The program designs for each module are shown below. To see how these English steps are translated into COBOL, refer to Figure 15.15 as you study the steps.

Main Module   The program design for the Main Module is as follows:

1. First, open the SCORES-FILE for input (line 39).

2. Open the PRINTED-REPORT-FILE for output (line 40).

3. Once the output file is opened, spaces are moved to the record known as PRINT-LINE (line 41). **SPACES** is a reserved word meaning blank space. Spaces are moved to the print line in case any "garbage" (data from a previous program) is in the area of memory to be used for printing. If garbage remains in the filler areas, it will appear on the paper when the printout is produced.

4. Perform the Detail Processing Module until all the data is read from the scores file (line 42).

5. Close the files and stop the run (lines 43-44).

Detail Processing Module   The program design for the Detail Processing Module is as follows:

1. Read a record from the disk (line 46). When a record is read from the file, all the data automatically goes into the fields identified as part of the record. That is, the student's name goes into the variable known as *STUDENT-NAME*, the class code goes into *CLASS-CODE*, Score 1 goes into *SCORE-1*, and so on. It is not necessary to separately specify where the data goes; that was handled in the data division. If there is no more data in the file, COBOL automatically places the digits '10' into the file status variable.

2. Line 47 sets up the processing to be done, but only if the effort to read data from the file was successful in line 46. This condition is indicated by the condition name of GOOD-DATA. Following the condition (on lines 48-52) are the steps to be performed:
   a. Complete the arithmetic. Two ways of stating arithmetic are illustrated. One way uses the reserved word COMPUTE followed by a formula (line 48). The other way (line 49) specifies the arithmetic, then specifies the

258   *Part Five ■ Applications Programming Languages*

reserved word GIVING followed by a variable name into which the answer should be placed.
b. Move the student name from the disk input area to the printer output area of memory (line 50).
c. Move the class code to the printout area (line 51). Without these moves, the name and code would not be printed.
d. Print a line on the printer (line 52).

```
Line:          Program code:

37             PROCEDURE DIVISION.
38             MAIN-MODULE.
39                 OPEN INPUT SCORES-FILE.
40                 OPEN OUTPUT PRINTED-REPORT-FILE.
41                 MOVE SPACES TO PRINT-LINE.
42                 PERFORM DETAIL-PROCESSING-MODULE UNTIL END-OF-FILE.
43                 CLOSE SCORES-FILE, PRINTED-REPORT-FILE.
44                 STOP RUN.
45             DETAIL-PROCESSING-MODULE.
46                 READ SCORES-FILE.
47                 IF GOOD-DATA
48                     COMPUTE TOTAL-SCORE = SCORE-1 + SCORE-2 + SCORE-3,
49                     DIVIDE TOTAL-SCORE BY 3 GIVING AVERAGE-PRINT,
50                     MOVE STUDENT-NAME TO NAME-PRINT,
51                     MOVE CLASS-CODE TO CODE-PRINT,
52                     WRITE PRINT-LINE.
```

Figure 15.15 *Procedure Division*

SUMMARY

The COBOL language is especially well suited for processing large files of business data. Since programs are written in English-like sentences, they are easy to understand. However, they also tend to be quite long. COBOL is a compiled language. Therefore, programs are entered into a text file for translation into machine language by the compiler program.

Each COBOL program must be written in four divisions. The Identification Division gives the name of the program, as well as the name of the programmer and the date the program is written. The

Environment Division describes the computer equipment on which the program is to run. The Data Division describes all the data files and data structures to be used by the program. The actual processing instructions the computer is to follow are then given in the Procedure Division.

REVIEW QUESTIONS

1. What are the advantages of the COBOL language? (Obj. 1)

2. What are the disadvantages of the COBOL language? (Obj. 1)

3. For what kinds of applications do the advantages of COBOL outweigh the disadvantages? (Obj. 1)

4. What are the steps in coding, entering, and compiling a COBOL program? (Obj. 2)

5. Describe the different parts of the COBOL Program Sheet. (Obj. 2)

6. Explain the relationship between the computer's memory and its input/output and auxiliary storage devices when using the COBOL language. (Obj. 3)

7. Describe and give the purpose of the Identification Division. (Obj. 4)

8. Describe and give the purpose of the Environment Division. (Obj. 4)

9. Describe and give the purpose of the Data Division. (Obj. 4)

10. Describe and give the purpose of the Procedure Division. (Obj. 4)

VOCABULARY WORDS

The following terms were introduced in this chapter:

working storage	B-Margin
Identification Division	source computer
PROGRAM-ID	object computer

Environment Division	elementary item
Data Division	group item
Procedure Division	condition
reserved word	DISPLAY
programmer-supplied word	ACCEPT
COBOL Program Sheet	FILLER
A-Margin	SPACES

WORKBOOK EXERCISES

Chapter 15 in the workbook consists of four exercises: True/ False, Matching, Completion, and Sequencing. Complete all four exercises in Chapter 15 of the workbook before proceeding to Chapter 16 in this text.

DISKETTE EXERCISE

Complete the diskette exercise for Chapter 15 before proceeding to Chapter 16 in this text.

PART SIX
Careers

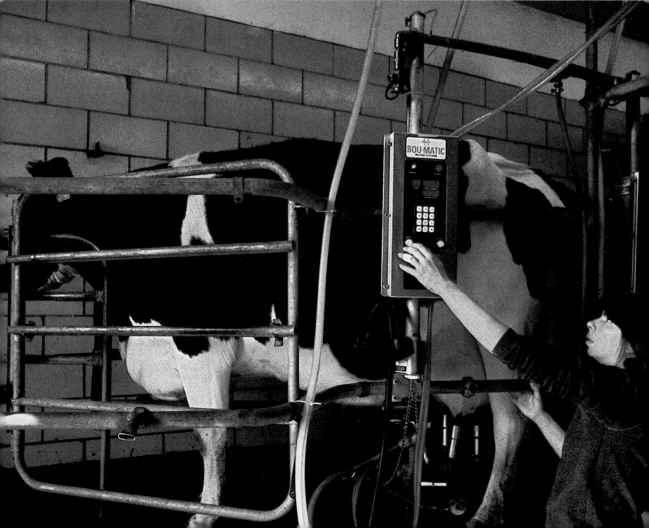

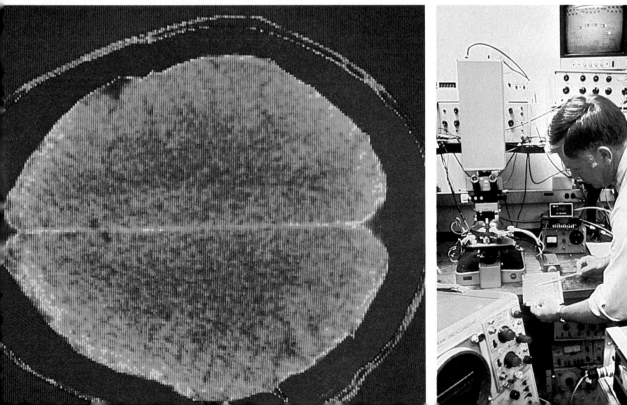

16 Careers in Information Processing

Objectives:

1. Name the different information processing jobs available at each educational level.

2. Describe five common job categories in information processing.

3. Describe the skills and education usually required for each of the common job categories in information processing.

4. Describe the career ladders for the common information processing careers.

The use of computers is not limited to persons who work in the information systems department of a business. The secretary using a word processor is using a computer. The retail salesperson may be using a cash register that is a computer. The inventory clerk may enter stock quantities into a computer or into a terminal connected to a larger computer. A personal computer may be on the president's desk to aid in financial analysis.

Are all of these jobs information processing jobs? As increasingly more workers use computers to perform some of their job duties, how can information processing jobs be identified? The use of the computer is not sufficient to cause a job to be called a business data processing job.

TYPES OF INFORMATION PROCESSING JOBS

Two features may be helpful in identifying certain jobs as information processing jobs. The first feature is the amount of work time actually spent using computers. The second feature is the job qualifications required of persons who hold the positions. A major portion of the work in information processing jobs involves computer usage. Furthermore, special computer training is generally necessary for information processing occupations.

Four generally distinct types of jobs exist in information processing:

1. Jobs involving planning or managing computer use in a company.

2. Jobs requiring computer programming skills.

3. Jobs requiring computer operating skills.

4. Jobs requiring inputting data into computers.

The need for qualified persons in information processing has been so great that qualified and experienced job seekers call it a "seller's market." Job openings in this field are now greater than the supply of qualified persons. This has had the effect of pushing some beginning salaries higher than the beginning salaries of jobs in other fields. In addition to jobs related to the use of large computers, the rapidly increasing use of microcomputers within businesses, schools, and homes has created an increased need for qualified people to create prewritten software for these machines. Many job opportunities exist for persons who can program business applications, educational courseware, and games which can run on several different brands of microcomputers. Many young programmers have started their careers by learning to program on the microcomputers available in their schools or homes.

There are generally more job openings in cities than in rural areas. However, as more small businesses acquire computers, the situation is likely to improve rurally. Persons interested in working with modern technology who are willing to train in school and on the job will find employment opportunities.

JOB ENTRY AS RELATED TO EDUCATIONAL LEVEL

The job level at which a person may enter the field of information processing primarily depends on the amount of education completed. In this section, we will look at the kinds of jobs which may be available with various amounts of education.

Secondary Education

Courses taken in high school can help you decide if you are interested in an information processing career, as well as prepare you for some entry-level jobs. Some appropriate courses are those involving an introduction to information processing, programming, keyboarding, and word processing. Other courses, such as accounting and an introduction to business, are also helpful.

Generally the jobs available to high school graduates who have the necessary skills are in word processing, data entry, and computer support. Computer support jobs are those jobs that are related to the computer in some way, but require no special computer skills. They include such responsibilities as filing computer media, accepting and logging in source documents, and distributing printouts. Some jobs as computer operators and programmers are available to high school graduates who completed appropriate course work while in high school. Part-time jobs in these areas are frequently available to persons who are continuing their education at technical schools or colleges.

Community College or Technical School Education

If you obtain more education at a community college or technical school, you will be able to enter the information processing field at a higher level or at a higher starting salary than would be possible with a high school education alone. Two years or less of specialized training should enable you to know whether or not information processing really interests you. With information processing training beyond high school, many more opportunities are available in the areas of computer operation and programming. Also, many businesses prefer that their word processing operators have education beyond the high school level.

College or University Education

Job opportunities in information processing will be more extensive if you complete a four-year bachelor's degree in a major related to computers and business information management. Data processing, information systems, management information systems, computer science, and office systems management are such majors.

Many businesses require bachelor's degrees for positions in programming and systems analysis, as well as for promotions to supervisory and management positions. Many top-level positions require extensive on-the-job experience in addition to a bachelor's degree.

A LOOK AT FIVE INFORMATION PROCESSING JOBS

In this section, five information processing jobs will be described in detail. The major tasks and personal qualifications to perform these tasks will be explained. A different amount of formal education is required for each position. Descriptions of the positions will also clarify the basic functions needed to plan, develop, and operate an information processing system.

The starting point for using a computer in information processing is planning the procedures to be used for solving a problem. Therefore, the systems analyst's job will be described first. Once the information system has been planned, the detailed programming of the parts of that system must be completed by the programmer. Perhaps the programs and data will be entered into the computer by a data entry operator. The word processing operator may then perform several different roles within the information processing system, depending upon the business application. This person may use a prewritten software package recommended by the systems analyst. In addition, programlike commands to the word processing equipment may be written. Data entry may also be the responsibility of the word processing operator.

Systems Analyst

The systems analyst usually works under the supervision of the manager of the information processing center. The primary role of the systems analyst is the design and creation of an information processing system. Systems analysts are frequently promoted to other positions in information processing departments. One possible promotion is to the position of data base administrator (Figure 16.1). The data base administrator is the person in charge of setting up the company's data base and controlling the relationships among the data. Another promotion possibility is into the overall management of the information system.

Figure 16.1   *The data base administrator is in charge of setting up a company's data base.*

Duties   In designing a system, the systems analyst must perform many duties. Managers who will be using the new system should tell the systems analyst what their needs are. The systems analyst can then work with the managers as the following steps are carried out to design and implement a system to meet their needs.

Determining Output Required and Input Needed   As you are aware, the first step in planning any system is to determine what output is desired. After this, the input necessary to produce the required output must be determined. To get answers to questions about the output desired and the input needed, the systems analyst must frequently talk with employees, as the analyst in

Figure 16.2 is doing. These persons must be questioned and their cooperation obtained if complete and accurate information is to be gathered.

Figure 16.2 *A systems analyst obtaining information from an employee*

Determining Required Resources Once the systems analyst fully understands the output needed from a system, the steps required to produce the output are developed. Some of these steps may involve the use of a computer, others may not use the computer. With the steps in mind, the resources to carry them out are planned. These resources are human resources, computer software, and computer hardware. The exact roles to be performed by employees and by the computer are identified. The requirements that must be met by computer software are determined. Usually a search is made to determine if prewritten software is available that will do the job; prewritten software is frequently more economical, if it is available. Finally, a decision is made about the hardware necessary in order to run the required programs. Hardware already on hand may be adequate, or other equipment may need to be purchased.

At all points in the planning process, evaluation is taking place. If at any point it is decided that the expense of developing the system is greater than the benefits to be gained, the system may be eliminated.

Planning and Producing the Programs   If it is necessary to write new programs to implement the system, the systems analyst plans the required programs in detail. The input and output of each program is carefully specified through the use of documentation forms. Programmers are then assigned to write the programs. Next, the programs are tested and debugged. The systems analyst monitors the entire process.

Implementation   Once a system has been designed and the programs have been written, the programs must be put into use. Users of the programs must, therefore, be trained in how to use them. In addition, an evaluation must be made to determine whether or not the system is indeed performing as desired. These steps in the implementation phase are frequently supervised by the systems analyst.

As more company employees outside the information processing department use personal computers or terminals, special training and assistance may be provided by the systems analyst. The systems analyst may be responsible for planning the use of different types of computing equipment within a company. This planning is necessary to prevent duplication of information systems. Extra coordination of equipment and software purchases is necessary to make sure equipment and data files are compatible. Equipment and files compatibility is necessary when information is to be shared by different company employees or other users of the system.

Education and Skills Required   In order to perform successfully as a systems analyst, a person needs a strong background in business as well as in the technical aspects of computer systems and programming. A bachelor's degree is usually required. This degree may be in information systems or in a related academic program that emphasizes a broad business management background. The systems analyst should know at least one programming language. Knowledge of more than one language is preferred.

A keen interest in solving problems and an ability to think logically are mandatory for the systems analyst. Furthermore, a creative mind is a must in order to see new ways of doing things. The ability to compare the costs of several different ways of solving problems with and without the computer is necessary. The systems analyst must also be able to communicate well with users in order to plan a successful system. Once the system is planned, more communication is needed as the users become familiar with the system. The systems analyst's verbal and written communication skills should be well developed, and he or she should be able to communicate with others without using computer jargon. For persons wanting to advance into management positions within the company, a solid foundation in business administration is necessary, as is a broad general knowledge of the operation of the company.

Programmer

Programmers generally work under the supervision of a systems analyst. There may also be supervisors with other titles, such as lead programmer or project leader. Depending on the complexity of a programming assignment, a programmer may work alone or as part of a team. Experienced programmers may be promoted to systems analyst positions.

Duties   The exact duties of a programmer depend on the business for which the programmer is working. In a larger business, the programmer may receive complete details about a program from the systems analyst. In this case, the programmer simply writes the steps required by the program in computer language, along with completing necessary documentation. The programmer in Figure 16.3 is performing such a task. In other instances, the programmer may be required to complete detailed plans for a program before beginning the coding process. In some cases, a programmer performs all the duties of a systems analyst before beginning to code a program. Regardless of the starting point at which the programmer begins, the result of the programmer's work should be a correctly functioning, well-documented program. In smaller businesses, the programmer may also serve as the computer operator. For security reasons, however, the jobs of programmer and computer operator should be separated whenever possible.

Figure 16.3
Programmer at work

Education and Skills Required   Most programming jobs require education beyond the high school level, although there are some beginning jobs available to high school graduates. Depending on the company, either a technical school diploma or a bachelor's degree is usually required.

A programmer must know at least one programming language. Because it is not always possible to predict the language a programmer will need when employed, the training of programmers often includes several high-level languages. Many courses of instruction also include assembly language programming, which can be a valuable asset in many programming positions.

There is a growing trend for programmers to enter or modify their programs directly on keyboards, rather than first writing them on paper. Programmers also frequently need to write documentation. Because of this, it is important for programmers to have keyboarding skills.

Successful programmers think logically and like working with precise details. They can concentrate on a programming problem until it is solved. In the past, it was thought that programmers should be good mathematicians. However, logical thinking seems to be the essential trait.

Computer Operator

The computer operator usually works under the supervision of a lead operator or the manager of the information processing center. In some installations, the operator may have other duties, such as filing media or entering data.

Duties   Once programs have been written, the next step is running the programs on the computer. The computer operator (Figure 16.4) is responsible for sequencing the jobs and running them in the order of their importance. On a large computer system, some programs may be running continually, while others are executed only occasionally.

Figure 16.4
Computer operator at work

The computer operator must follow instructions closely. Messages will be received from the computer during the running of programs. The operator must make correct responses to these messages and must enter commands to carry out the desired actions. If errors or problems occur during the running of a program, the operator must know how to handle them.

In addition to actually running the computer, the operator is responsible for making sure that the correct disks or tapes are mounted on auxiliary storage. It is also the operator's responsibility to make sure that the printer has the correct paper and that the output of a job is complete.

Education and Skills Required   Technical training in equipment operation and introduction to computer programming can often be learned at a two-year technical school or community college. Some employers will hire operators with only a high school education and provide them with on-the-job training for the particular computer being used. Many computer operators continue their education to obtain the skills necessary to work as programmers.

Word Processing Operator

In some companies, certain persons are employed only as word processing operators. In other companies, word processing is part of a job that also includes other duties.

Duties   The work of a word processing operator includes entering text, modifying text, and formatting text for printout in the form of letters, reports, legal papers, or other documents. The word processing operator may use a microcomputer, a word processor (Figure 16.5), or a terminal attached to a larger computer. When the word processing equipment is connected to another computer, the operator can input data into the larger computer system. This may permit an employee who is originating or is familiar with the source documents to prepare the computer input. The advantages in doing this are accuracy and speed. If some items of the input data are contained in other written documents, it may save time to combine the preparation of letters or reports with data entry. The sharing of data can also work in reverse. The word processing operator may get data directly from the files of a larger computer to enter into written documents. Time is saved and accuracy is greater when the data from the larger computer system does not have to be printed out separately and then reentered by the word processing operator.

Figure 16.5
A word processing
operator entering text

The word processing operator cannot be considered a computer operator merely because the word processor itself is a computer. The job becomes more like a computer operator's job, however, when applications other than word processing are carried out on the word processing equipment. Some of these applications include sending electronic mail, updating files of records, preparing accounting reports, and performing financial analyses. The word processing operator should then be able to follow established procedures for performing these functions.

Some word processing jobs require that the operator actually program the word processing equipment to perform special tasks. Many word processors or word processing software packages use "glossaries," "macros," or "word processing languages." These are sets of instructions that can be carried out by the word processor automatically. The instructions are like small computer programs in that they are entered only once and reused many times.

Since word processors are computers, it is also possible to write programs for many of them in high-level languages such as BASIC, COBOL, and Pascal. A word processing operator who has the skills to use these languages may progress to other programming jobs. Frequently, however, word processing operators choose to apply for promotions into the area of office administration, rather than the field of information processing.

Education and Skills Required   Technical training in using word processing equipment may be obtained in technical institutes or community colleges. Many high schools also teach introductory courses in word processing equipment operation. However, acquiring excellent language skills and keyboarding skills are equally as important as learning equipment operation. Businesses are frequently willing to teach the use of specific word processing equipment to potential employees who can demonstrate good English transcription skills. Since many secretaries in business offices use some type of word processing equipment, persons with good secretarial skills and knowledge of using word processing equipment will have many job opportunities.

Data Entry Operator

Once a computer program is written, it must be entered into the computer for recording on an auxiliary storage device. Usually the original entry of a program is done on a keyboard. Data to be processed by the program must then be entered on a regular basis. At one time, almost all programs and data were keyed in by data entry operators. Now, however, more and more entry is being done by other persons. For example, programs may be entered by programmers, and accounting data may be entered by accountants.

Duties   The data entry operator enters programs or data into the computer system. In doing so, the operator works with different source documents, such as handwritten forms, typed forms, or specially marked sheets of paper. The data on these source documents is entered by using a keyboard. The operator must understand the layout of the records and know how to enter the data from the source documents. Understanding the equipment and following directions carefully are important.

In companies using data entry operators, the high volume of data often makes data entry a 24-hour activity. For this reason, data entry operators may have a choice of day or night working hours.

Education and Skills Required   The main requirement for the data entry operator is the ability to type or key data rapidly and accurately. Persons in this position should enjoy working with modern data entry equipment and doing the same kind of work for long periods of time. They should be able to gain satisfaction from producing a large volume of high-quality work. Data entry operators must be able to follow detailed instructions carefully and work under time pressure when needed. Also, as technology advances and changes in equipment take place, operators must be able to adjust to these changes.

Persons wishing to begin work as data entry operators can learn to use data entry equipment in high school or technical school. Some businesses provide on-the-job training. If a person has good keyboarding skills, data entry training on the job may take only three to six weeks.

CAREER ADVANCEMENT

Figure 16.6 reviews some of the different job titles in the information processing field and shows the approximate amount of education needed. Once people enter this field, they may advance to different higher-level positions. Advancement may depend upon their interests, education, experience, and willingness to learn on the job. The amount of preparation may vary, depending on the size of the information processing installation. The figure gives only a general idea of the education needed.

Many entry-level jobs are available in information processing that need little or no training beyond high school. However, almost all positions beyond the entry level do require specialized training and/or experience. In looking at Figure 16.6, note that most entry-level positions are in the area of operations. In many cases, there is an opportunity for a worker to continue an academic program while working. Many employees in information processing departments are also part-time students.

The jobs shown at the bottom of Figure 16.6 are entry-level jobs that may be available with a high school education. The next division shows the positions available with a postsecondary technical or community college education. The third section shows the jobs that can be obtained with on-the-job training or additional education toward a bachelor's degree. The top section shows the jobs that require at least a bachelor's degree.

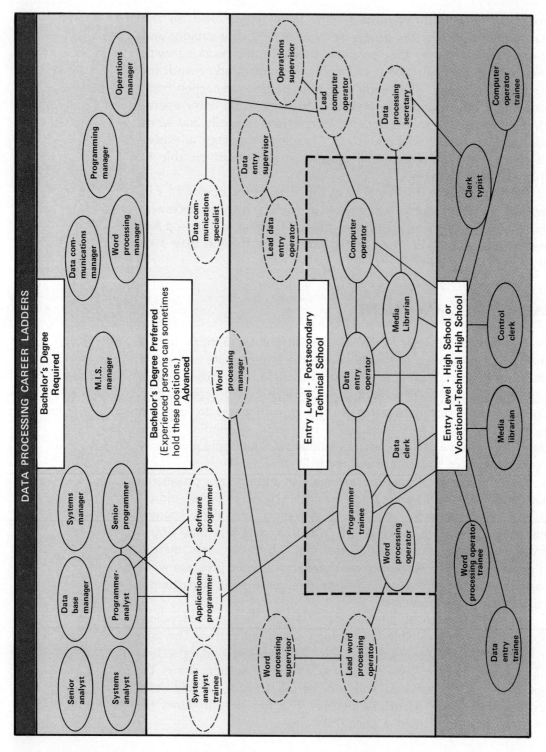

Figure 16.6 *Data processing career ladders*

For the positions in the top two sections of Figure 16.6, persons who have had on-the-job training while working toward a degree are more likely to be hired than are those who have had academic training only. Persons with on-the-job experience may advance to other positions in the companies that employed them while they were going to school. Other companies are also interested in persons who have experience using the same types of computers that they have in their companies. On-the-job programming experience in a particular language is also important to an employer.

In Figure 16.6, the jobs inside the symbols with broken lines are possible promotions from another level. Symbols with solid lines are used for entry-level jobs. For example, a programmer trainee might eventually become an applications programmer. Some of the jobs in the top level of the diagram are shown inside solid lines because they are entry-level jobs for which a bachelor's degree is needed. However, these jobs are sometimes available as promotions to persons with on-the-job training.

INFORMATION PROCESSING SALARIES

The salaries available to persons in information processing jobs vary considerably. Some of the factors affecting salaries are as follows: (1) amount of job experience; (2) size of the company; (3) industry of which the company is a part, such as manufacturing, banking, retail sales, or government; and (4) geographic location of the company.

Figure 16.7 shows the ranges of typical salaries received by information processing employees in 1983. In each job column, the bottom figure is the national average for the job in small companies (companies where the annual sales are less than $1 million). The top figure is the national average in large companies (companies where the annual sales are over $1 million). The middle figure is the national average salary for all persons having that particular job.

Notice the wide range of salaries in the job categories shown. Remember that these figures, reported by *Datamation* magazine, are averages. The salaries for individual positions may be higher or lower than the averages, depending on the circumstances. Although it is impossible to predict how much these salaries will increase, recent experience suggests adjusting the amounts upward about ten percent a year when updating the figures.

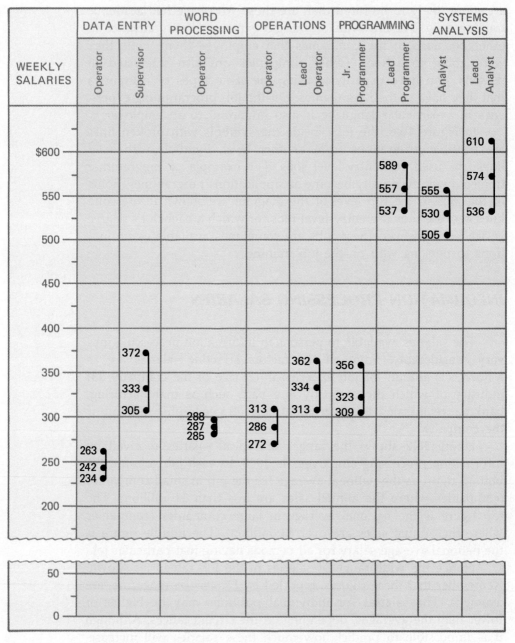

NATIONAL AVERAGE SALARY RANGES
FOR SELECTED DATA PROCESSING JOBS

SOURCE: *Larry Marion, "1983 DP Salaries—The Key Word Is Perks,"* Datamation *(September, 1983), pp. 82-97.*

Figure 16.7 *The average weekly salaries vary according to the size of the installation and geographic location.*

SUMMARY

A very high demand for information processing employees will continue to make jobs plentiful for persons interested in careers in this growing field. Entry-level jobs are open to persons with high school, technical school, or community college education. The jobs include data entry trainee, word processing operator trainee, data entry operator, media librarian, data clerk, computer operator trainee, computer operator, and programmer trainee.

It is possible for persons to obtain more specialized training on the job or at a four-year college or university. This training can qualify them for more advanced jobs in programming or systems analysis. On-the-job training and more education can also help a person become a supervisor or manager in data entry, word processing, operations, programming, or systems analysis.

The general shortage of information processing employees has caused salaries to rise in relation to the salaries of other business and office jobs. This means that many people are likely to be attracted to careers in information processing. The best jobs will go to those who are well prepared and who are willing to continue to learn as changes come. The persons who enjoy the challenges of working with computer technology will be able to find satisfying careers in business information processing.

REVIEW QUESTIONS

1. What kinds of information processing jobs are available to persons with a high school education? (Obj. 1)

2. What kinds of information processing jobs are available to persons with a technical school or community college education? (Obj. 1)

3. What kinds of information processing jobs are available to persons with a bachelor's degree? (Obj. 1)

4. Describe the duties of a systems analyst. (Obj. 2)

5. What kinds of skills and education are usually necessary for employment as a systems analyst? (Obj. 3)

6. Describe the duties of a programmer. (Obj. 2)

7. What kinds of skills and education are usually necessary for employment as a programmer? (Obj. 3)

8. Describe the duties of a computer operator. (Obj. 2)

9. What kinds of skills and education are usually required for employment as a computer operator? (Obj. 3)

10. Describe the duties of a word processing operator. (Obj. 2)

11. What kinds of skills and education are usually necessary for employment as a word processing operator? (Obj. 3)

12. Describe the duties of a data entry operator. (Obj. 2)

13. What kinds of skills and education are usually necessary for employment as a data entry operator? (Obj. 3)

14. For each of the jobs of programmer trainee, computer operator, and word processing operator, list a job to which a promotion would likely be possible. (Obj. 4)

15. Describe the typical promotion path that might be taken to get to a position in data base administration or information systems management. (Obj. 4)

16. Referring to Figure 16.7, compare the salary levels for different jobs in information processing. (Obj. 4)

WORKBOOK EXERCISES

Chapter 16 of the workbook consists of two exercises: True/False and Completion. Complete both exercises in Chapter 16 of the workbook before proceeding to Chapter 17 in this text.

DISKETTE EXERCISE

Complete the diskette exercise for Chapter 16 before proceeding to Chapter 17 in this text.

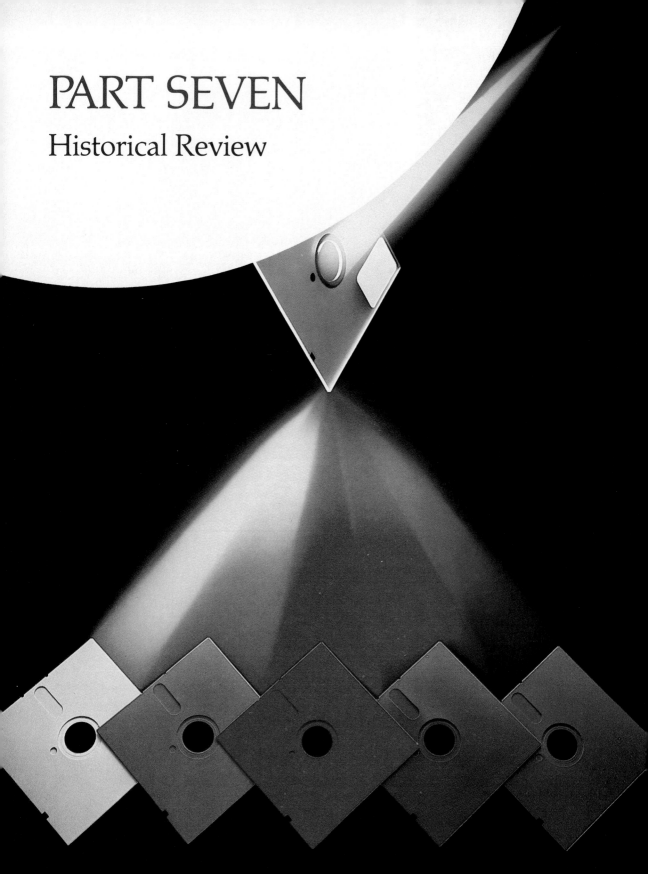

PART SEVEN

Historical Review

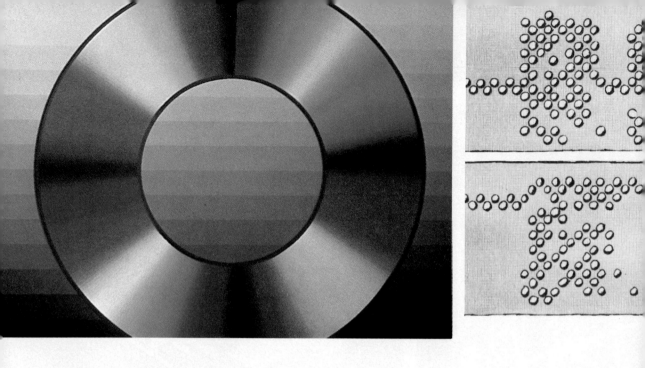

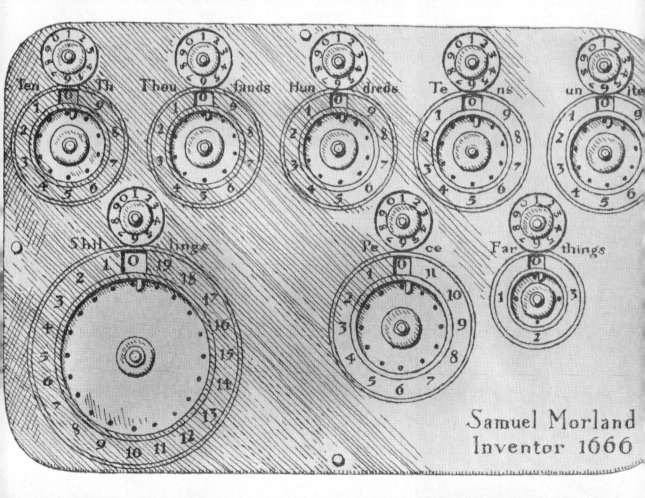

Ten Th Thou fands Hun dreds Te ns un ite

Shil lings Pe ce Far things

Samuel Morland
Inventor 1666

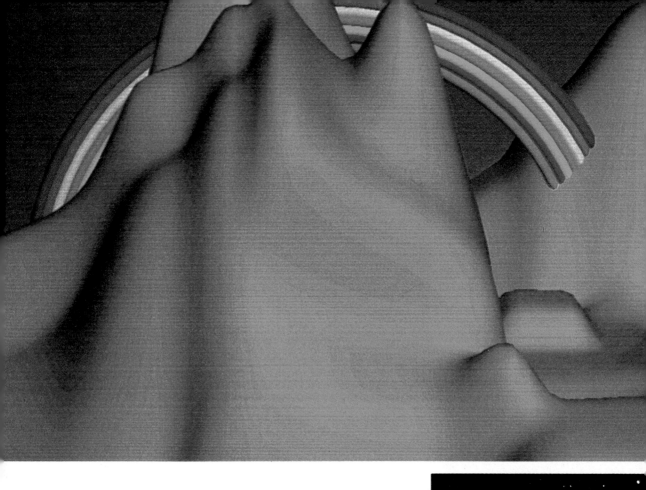

17 A Brief History of Computing

Objectives:

1. Trace the historical development of computing.

2. Describe the different generations of computers.

FROM FINGER COUNTING TO ELECTRONIC COMPUTERS

The first digital computer used in business was installed in 1954. Although slow compared to today's computers, it made computations automatically and rapidly. What did people do before that date to speed up calculations and make them less tiresome?

Finger Counting

Before the nineteenth century, most calculations were made in a person's brain. The first computations were simple counting, and no doubt the person used all ten fingers to help. The early Roman schools actually taught finger counting and devised a method of multiplying and dividing using the fingers.

Abacus

From the use of fingers, persons moved to aids such as pebbles, sticks, and beads for computations. More than three thousand years ago the **abacus**, the first counting machine, was invented. It consists of a frame in which rods strung with beads are set. The beads represent digits and the rods represent places: units, tens, hundreds, and higher multiples of ten. In the abacus illustrated in Figure 17.1, each bead in the top compartment has an assigned value of five; each bead in the bottom compartment, a value of one. The beads in both compartments have a counting value when they are pushed toward the board that separates the two compartments. In the illustration, the beads represent a total of 249.

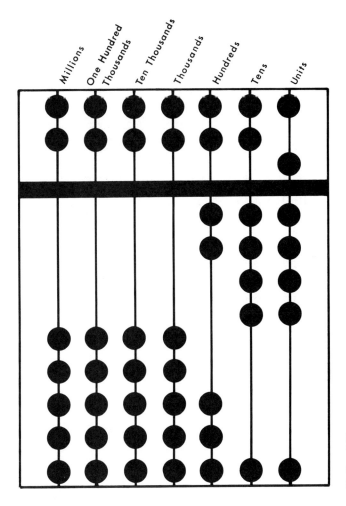

Figure 17.1
The abacus was first used more than three thousand years ago.

The origin of the abacus is uncertain. Some say it is a product of the ancient Hindu civilization. Others say it came from Babylon or Egypt. Some believe that the Chinese invented it. The Chinese modified and adopted it early in their history; it has, therefore, generally become known as a Chinese invention.

The Japanese also modified and adopted the abacus. The Japanese model (Figure 17.2) is known as a **soraban**. It differs from the abacus in that it has only one bead on each rod in the upper compartment and five beads on each rod in the lower compartment. Note in Figure 17.1 that the abacus has two beads on each rod in the upper compartment and five beads on each rod in the lower compartment. The abacus and the soraban are still used in some countries. In skilled hands, they are amazingly rapid and efficient in making computations.

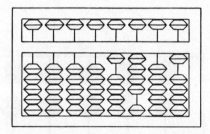

Figure 17.2
A Japanese soraban

Napier's Bones

In the 1600s, John Napier invented a device consisting of rods or strips of bone on which numbers were printed. The device became known as "**Napier's bones.**" By means of these rods or bones, computations could be performed, including the extraction of square and cube roots. See Figure 17.3.

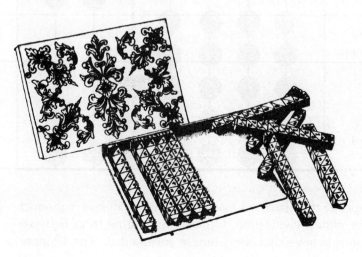

Figure 17.3
Napier's bones could be used for computations.

Slide Rule

The **slide rule**, conceived by William Oughtred in 1622, consists of an outer rule and a central sliding rule. Both rules are divided into scales. The rules are moved either backward or forward until a selected number on one scale lines up with a selected number on the other scale. The desired result is then read from a third scale. The slide rule, shown in Figure 17.4, was widely used by engineers and scientists until recently. The electronic calculator put the slide rule out of business.

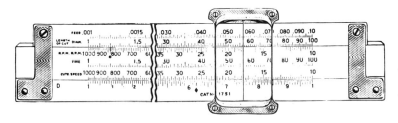

Figure 17.4
The slide rule was made obsolete by the hand-held calculator.

Inventors of Early Calculators

The development of mechanically operated adding machines and calculators began in the 1600s. Some of the early developers are discussed in the following sections.

Blaise Pascal   In 1642, Blaise Pascal invented the first mechanical adding machine, shown in Figure 17.5. It was capable of carrying tens automatically. His machine consisted of wheels with cogs or teeth, on which the numbers 0-9 were engraved. The first wheel on the right represented units; the second, tens; the third, hundreds; and so on. As the wheels were turned, the numbers appeared in a window at the top of the machine. When the units wheel was turned beyond Digit 9, the tens wheel at the left would reflect the carry. For example, to add 7 and 4, the 7 was stored on the first wheel by turning the wheel until the 7 appeared in the window. Then the wheel was turned again through four places. This procedure resulted in a carry, which was accomplished by a series of gears arranged in such a way that they turned the next wheel. As a result, 1's appeared in the windows above the tens and units wheels.

Figure 17.5
The first mechanical adding machine, invented by Pascal

Gottfried von Leibnitz   In 1671, Gottfried von Leibnitz drew the plans for a calculator that could multiply and divide as well as count, add, and subtract. A drawing of the machine is shown in Figure 17.6. In 1694, a machine was actually built using his plans, but it did not work very well. The plans were correct, but the technology capable of making precision parts had not yet been developed.

Figure 17.6
Von Leibnitz's calculator

Charles Xavier Thomas   For the next two hundred years, many attempts were made to improve on the Pascal and von Leibnitz inventions. Progress was made, although it was slow and sometimes painful. Gradually, calculators became faster, smaller, more reliable, and at least partially automatic. In the 1820s, Charles Xavier Thomas invented a calculator that was the first to add, subtract, divide, and multiply accurately. It was widely copied by other inventors and was thus considered to be the ancestor of the mechanical calculators that preceded today's electronic calculators. Figure 17.7 shows a typical 1880 machine; it was capable of performing the four principal arithmetic operations.

Figure 17.7
A typical 1880 calculator

Early American Inventors All early calculator inventors were Europeans. In 1872, however, Frank S. Baldwin developed the first calculator to be invented in the United States. The invention of this machine, shown in Figure 17.8, marked the beginning of a rapidly growing calculator industry in this country. The first practical adding machines which listed amounts and sums on paper were invented in the late 1800s by Dorr Eugene Felt and William S. Burroughs.

Figure 17.8
First U.S. calculator, invented by Baldwin

Oscar and David Sundstrand invented the ten-key adding-listing machine in 1914. This machine introduced the keyboard arrangement that became the standard for calculators used in business offices. The same basic keyboard arrangement is used on most of today's electronic calculators.

Punched-Card Machines

While development was proceeding on calculating machines, a new idea in processing data was being introduced in the late 1800s. It was the punched card.

Herman Hollerith   Using **punched cards** to record factual information, Herman Hollerith developed an entirely new system of processing data. Punched paper tape and punched cards had been used as early as 1728 to control weaving machines. The punched-card principle for weaving patterns in rugs on the first automatic loom was perfected in 1801 by Joseph Jacquard. The principles of these early applications were adapted by Hollerith for use by the U.S. Census Bureau. Hollerith was an independent inventor who was contracted by the Bureau in 1880 to help speed up the sorting and tabulating of census data. (It had become apparent that it would take over ten years to tabulate the next census figures without some type of automation.) By 1887, he had worked out a code of representing census information through a system of punched holes in paper strips. He later changed to a standard-sized card because the paper strips did not work very well. Thus, Hollerith developed the first machine capable of processing statistical information from punched cards. The system included the cards, a card punch, a sorting box, and a tabulator equipped with electromagnetic counters. With this equipment, cards could be sorted at the rate of about 80 cards per minute. Data appearing in the cards could be tabulated and counted at the rate of 50 to 75 cards per minute. Figure 17.9 shows Hollerith's punched-card machine.

The Hollerith system was used to process the 1890 census. As a result, the 1890 census was completed in one fourth the time needed to compile the 1880 census. Hollerith then organized a company to manufacture and market his system. This company later became known as the International Business Machines Corporation (IBM).

The Punched-Card Era   Over the years many improvements were made on the original punched-card machines. The machines

Figure 17.9
Hollerith's punched-card machine

for punching holes in the cards were improved and equipped with a number of automatic devices. A calculator that could read the punched cards and multiply or divide the data was developed. Various models of machines were developed for sorting the cards and printing reports from data contained in them.

From the 1920s through the mid-1970s, punched–card equipment was widely used for business data processing. Cards were punched on a card-punch machine (also known as a keypunch) with a keyboard similar to that found on a present-day computer or terminal. A later model **card-punch machine** is shown in Figure 17.10. Cards to be punched were placed in the card hopper and

Figure 17.10
Machines such as this one punched holes in cards.

passed through the machine one card at a time as the operator entered the data on the keyboard. Each character was punched according to a predetermined code. The most commonly used code was known as the Hollerith code and is shown on the card in Figure 17.11. The standard card was divided into 80 columns, and one character was punched in each column. Note that a digit was recorded by punching one hole in a column, while an alphabet letter was recorded by punching two holes.

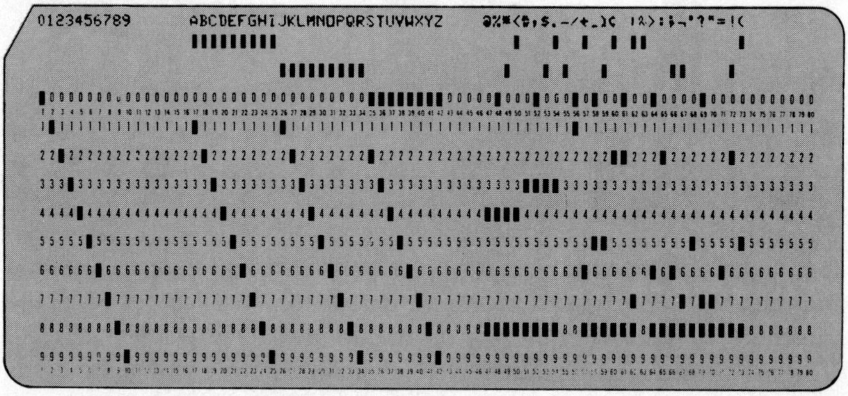

Figure 17.11
Hollerith's punched-card code

The different items of information in a punched card were divided into fields in the same manner that a record from a disk file is divided into fields. A card field was a vertical column or group of consecutive columns set aside to record a single fact. A field could contain a name, an amount, or a code, for example.

Once the cards were punched, they were arranged or sorted with a **sorter** such as shown in Figure 17.12. A **tabulator** (Figure 17.13) was then used to print reports from the data. The important thing to remember about all these machines is that, although they could do arithmetic and print reports, they were not computers. They contained many mechanical parts and did not make use of stored programs to control their operation.

EARLY COMPUTERS

Now let's take a look at some of the developments leading up to the stored-program computer as we know it today.

The Analytical Engine

Turn your clock back briefly about one hundred and fifty years to the middle 1800s and meet another inventor, Charles Babbage.

Figure 17.12
A sorter

Figure 17.13
*A tabulator was
used to print reports.*

Babbage had some entirely new and advanced ideas on designing a computer. "I am going to construct a machine," wrote Babbage, "which will incorporate a memory unit system, an external memory unit, and conditional transfer. I am going to call this device an 'Analytical Engine.' " What Babbage described with startling accuracy is the computer.

Babbage was a mathematician of good reputation, who spent his life and his fortune, as well as large sums of money from the British government, on the design of an automatic computer. The machine designed by Babbage was to have four basic parts. One part, consisting of the memory, was to be used to store the numeric data used in calculations. A second part, consisting of gears and cog wheels on which digits were engraved, was to be used for computing. A third part, consisting of gears and levers, was to be able to move numbers back and forth between the memory and computing units. Finally, Babbage planned to use punched cards for getting information into and out of his machine.

Babbage believed he could use cards to program his machine to handle computations automatically. He also seemed able to envision the possibility of programming his machine to change from one series of steps to another when certain conditions were encountered. This, of course, is one of the most valuable abilities of a computer.

Babbage did not complete his machine, a drawing of which is shown in Figure 17.14, but he did leave for a new generation of

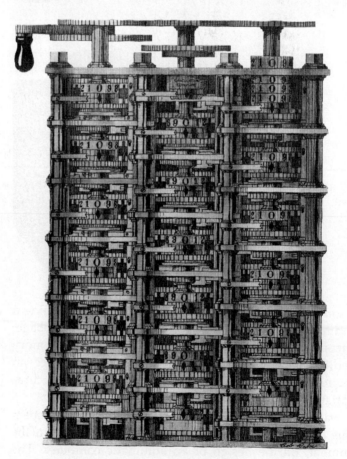

Figure 17.14
Babbage's analytical engine

inventors a great many details of his plan. Due to the technological conditions existing then, the various parts of his machine simply could not be made to the exact specifications required. He was ahead of his time. Had he been successful, his machine would have been the first true computer. As it was, his work was largely forgotten until the 1940s, when new attempts were made to design and build a rapid automatic computer.

Mark I

In 1944, Howard Aiken developed a calculator called the **Mark I**. The Mark I obtained data from punched cards, made calculations with the aid of mechanical devices, and punched the results into a new set of cards. The most unusual aspect of the new machine, however, is that it was controlled automatically by instructions punched into paper tape attached to the computer. Thus, it was the first machine to use a stored program to control its actions. The Mark I, although it can be regarded as the first successful computer, was not an electronic computer. It was mechanically operated.

ENIAC

Another early pioneer working on computers was Dr. John V. Atanasoff, who can be given credit for developing the ideas on which the first electronic computers were based. Many of these ideas were used in ENIAC, developed by Dr. John W. Mauchly and J. Presper Eckert, under a contract from the U.S. Army. The first electronic computer to go into operation, **ENIAC** (the Electronic Numerical Integrator and Calculator) contained thousands and thousands of vacuum tubes. To program ENIAC required changes in thousands of wires and switches. In other words, its program was hard-wired to memory, instead of being read into memory as with today's computers. ENIAC, shown in Figure 17.15, was completed in 1946 and was used for several years.

EDSAC and EDVAC

The first electronic computers to utilize the stored-program concept were the **EDSAC** (Electronic Delay Storage Automatic Calculator) and **EDVAC** (Electronic Discrete Variable Automatic Computer). Though the EDVAC (Figure 17.16), developed by Dr. John von Neumann, was conceived first, the EDSAC was completed first, in 1949.

Figure 17.15   ENIAC, *the first operable electronic computer*

Figure 17.16
*EDVAC, the first
computer designed to
use a stored program*

COMPUTER GENERATIONS

ENIAC, EDSAC, and EDVAC were largely experimental or military machines. The first computer available for data processing use was the **UNIVAC I**, a machine developed by Eckert and Mauchly after ENIAC was finished. Remington Rand bought Eckert and Mauchly's company and the UNIVAC I. Remington Rand thus became the first company in the business of selling computers. The first commercially used UNIVAC I was installed at the U.S. Census Bureau in 1951. In 1954, General Electric became the first business to use a computer when they purchased a UNIVAC I. The UNIVAC I is illustrated in Figure 17.17.

Figure 17.17 UNIVAC I was the first commercially available computer.

IBM, which for years had dominated the market for electromechanical data processing machines for business use, announced their first commercially available computer in 1953. They shortly overtook Remington Rand in sales. Since then, IBM has continued to be the leading company in the computer business.

First Generation

All the early computers are known as first-generation computers. They used vacuum tubes in their circuitry. For this reason, the machines were very large in size, were very slow by today's standards, and required almost constant maintenance.

The large number of vacuum tubes in these early computers created many problems because of the amount of heat generated by the tubes. This heat problem made it necessary to install heavy-duty air conditioning units. The first-generation computers were mostly computational machines. Their input/output capabilities were usually limited to keyboard and/or punched-card input and printer and/or punched-card output, although some used magnetic tape.

First-generation computers could make over 100 thousand calculations per second. Although this may seem extremely fast, the speed of a Control Data Corporation computer introduced in 1983 is almost 800 million calculations per second, or 8,000 times faster.

Second Generation

Second-generation computers, first available in the late 1950s, used transistors in place of vacuum tubes. This change brought many improvements. The cost of computers decreased, and more businesses could afford them. The amount of heat put out by the machines was much less, reducing air conditioning requirements. The use of transistors also made it possible to reduce the size of the equipment. This change further increased the computer's computational speed. Also, the transistors proved to be much more reliable than vacuum tubes. Figure 17.18 shows the transistors of a second-generation computer in addition to typical components of a vacuum tube computer system.

A typical second-generation computer was the IBM 1401 (Figure 17.19). Introduced in 1959, it was designed for business use. This machine used transistor circuitry.

Removable disk storage units and magnetic tape input/output units were developed for use on second-generation computers. The

Figure 17.18
First-generation
vacuum tubes and
second-generation
transistors

Figure 17.19 *A representative second-generation computer, the IBM 1401*

speed of the line printers was increased from three hundred lines per minute, which was fairly common on first-generation computers, to one thousand lines per minute. The speed of card readers and card punches was also increased, although not as dramatically as that of the printers. These changes in the computer made it more useful as a tool in business because of the large volume of data to be processed and the lengthy printed reports required.

Third Generation

Third-generation computers introduced the use of very small electronic circuits called integrated circuits, rather than transistors. This change further decreased the size of the computer, while increasing its speed. The speed of the first-generation computers was described in milliseconds (1/1,000 of a second). The speed of the second-generation computers was described in microseconds (1/1,000,000 of a second). The speed of the third-generation computers was described in nanoseconds (1/1,000,000,000 of a second). The speed of line printers on many third-generation computers was increased to two thousand lines per minute, while one printer could print over twenty thousand lines per minute.

Fourth Generation

Fourth-generation computers use what is known as **VLSI** circuitry. The abbreviation VLSI refers to *very large scale integration*. This means that extremely large numbers of electronic components are crammed into each integrated circuit chip. It is possible to place all the components required for an entire computer on one circuit chip. Figure 17.20 shows a chip containing all the circuitry required for a computer.

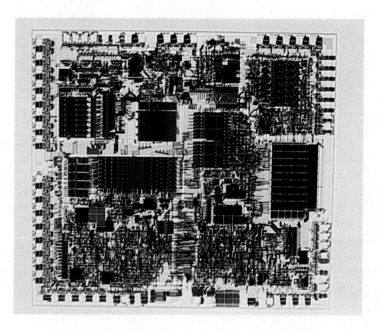

Figure 17.20
A processor with all circuits on one chip

IMPROVEMENTS IN DATA ENTRY

At the same time computers themselves were undergoing tremendously fast development, the methods of getting data into the computers were also changing. As indicated earlier, most of the first-generation computers used keypunch machines and punched cards to input data.

For years, the keypunch was the mainstay of data entry. A **keypunch machine** punched data into cards as punched holes and printed the meanings of the punched holes at the tops of the cards. Usually data was keyed twice: once for the original input, and again to verify its accuracy.

The first data entry improvement over punched cards was the **key-to-tape machine**, shown in Figure 17.21. This machine records data on magnetic tape instead of punched cards. The machine has a typewriterlike keyboard. Data is keyed as digits, letters of the alphabet, and special characters. Data is recorded on the tape as magnetized spots in a form of binary code. Some key-to-tape machines have cathode-ray tube displays. The transaction appears on the screen as it is being entered and is transferred to tape once it is complete.

Figure 17.21
A key-to-tape machine

Following the key-to-tape machine was the key-to-disk machine. The general principles remained the same. Instead of recording on tape, however, the **key-to-disk machine** records its data on magnetic disks. The present trend in data entry is toward using input devices connected directly to the computer.

SUMMARY

Development of computational machines has been going on for over three thousand years, beginning with the abacus. The first machine capable of adding, subtracting, multiplying, and dividing was developed in the 1820s. Another giant step forward occurred in the 1880s when Herman Hollerith invented a punched-card method of processing data. Punched cards were the mainstay of business data processing through the middle part of the twentieth century.

The first electronic computer was developed in the late 1940s. From that point, development has been incredibly rapid. Each major improvement in technology has led to the development of a new "generation" of computers. Since the first commercial use of the computer in the early 1950s, four different generations of computers have been developed. The fifth generation is currently under development and may become available at any time. With each generation, computers have become much faster and much more capable. At the same time, they have become unbelievably small. Substantial price reductions have accompanied each advance in technology. The computer has truly become a universal machine.

REVIEW QUESTIONS

1. Name and describe each of the major steps in the development of computing equipment, beginning with the abacus and continuing through the early computers. (Obj. 1)

2. In what contribution to data processing did each of the following men participate? (Objs. 1, 2)

   a. Blaise Pascal

   b. Charles Babbage

    c. Herman Hollerith

    d. Howard Aiken

    e. John Atanasoff

    f. J. Presper Eckert and John Mauchly

    g. John von Neumann

3. What are the main features of each generation of computers? (Obj. 2)

VOCABULARY WORDS

The following terms were introduced in this chapter:

abacus	ENIAC
soraban	EDSAC
Napier's bones	EDVAC
slide rule	UNIVAC I
punched card	VLSI
card-punch machine	keypunch machine
sorter	key-to-tape machine
tabulator	key-to-disk machine
Mark I	

WORKBOOK EXERCISES

Chapter 17 in the workbook consists of three exercises: True/False, Time Line, and Identification. Complete all three exercises in the workbook.

DISKETTE EXERCISE

Complete the diskette exercise for Chapter 17.

Glossary

abacus: an ancient calculating device consisting of a frame in which rods strung with beads are set; by sliding the beads, computations can be done

ACCEPT: A COBOL command used to get input from the keyboard

acoustic coupler: a device used by some modems that uses a microphone and speaker to connect the computer to the phone line by means of sound

alphanumeric variable: same as a character variable

A-Margin: Column 8 of a coding sheet or video display; COBOL headings are written beginning at this column

applications software: programs designed to perform particular work desired by the user

array: another name for a table

arrowhead: a symbol that shows the direction of data flow in a flowchart

ASCII: the American Standard Code for Information Interchange, a popular code used for representing information in a computer system

assembler: the program that converts assembly language programs into machine code

assembly: the process of putting together different parts of text to form a new document

assembly language: a language a step above machine language in which the instructions to the processor may be represented by alphabetic abbreviations

assignment operator: the operator used to place a value into a variable

auxiliary storage: supplementary storage areas that hold data outside the memory of the computer

backup: a copy of important data from an auxiliary storage device

band printer: a printer that contains characters on a rotating band

bar-code scanner: an input device that reads bars of varying widths that are printed on a product; the various widths of bars are interpreted to a unique identification number for the product

base: the number by which a digit is multiplied when it is moved a column to the left

BASIC: Beginner's All-Purpose Symbolic Instruction Code; an easy-to-learn, general-purpose, high-level language

batch system: a system in which data is saved up or accumulated for later processing

baud: bits per second; the rate of communication

BEGIN: the word used to indicate the beginning of a procedural part of a Pascal program

binary: a number system having a base of 2 and using the digits 0 and 1

bit: a binary digit, either a 1 or a 0

B-Margin: Column 12 of a coding sheet or video display; many COBOL statements begin at this margin

boolean data: data that can take on only one of two values, true or false

boot up: start up, as in turning on the computer

bubble memory: an auxiliary storage device consisting of a chip containing a surface across which magnetic "bubbles" move in the patterns required for representing characters

bug: an error in a program

byte: eight bits, the number of bits usually used to store one character

CAD/CAM: computer-aided design/computer-aided manufacturing

calculating: the process of computing in order to arrive at a mathematical result

canned software: prewritten software

card-punch machine: a machine used to punch holes in a punched card

case: a type of instruction that provides a way for executing one set of instructions out of numerous possibilities

catalog: a list of the items stored on a disk

cathode-ray tube: a televisionlike display device used for computer output

chain printer: a printer that contains characters on a rotating chain

channel: a recording path along magnetic tape

character data: any character that can be coded using the internal code of the computer (usually ASCII or EBCDIC)

character string: one or more characters used together

character variable: a variable that stores alphanumeric (character) data

check digit: a digit that is calculated from the other digits in a number; it can be used to check the accuracy of the entry of the other digits

CLS: the keyword used to clear the screen on many computers

COBOL: COmmon Business Oriented Language; a high-level language designed for use in business applications such as accounting

COBOL Program Sheet: a sheet of rows and columns upon which a COBOL program is coded

coding: (a) assigning numbers, symbols, or words to data according to a set of rules; (b) writing the steps of a problem solution in computer language

communicating: transmitting information from one point to another point

compiler program: a program that translates an entire high-level language program into machine code at once

computer: a device in which data and the instructions for processing it are represented as electronic codes or impulses

computer information system: a computer system used for information processing

computer output microfilm: an output method in which data is placed on microfilm rather than on paper

condition: a situation involving the comparison of two values

constant: an unchanging number

control character: a character that generally is not visible on an output device; instead, a control character is designed to control the communication between a computer and another device, such as a terminal or printer

CRT: cathode-ray tube

cursor: a marker on a video display

custom-written software: software that is specially prepared for a particular business and the way it operates

cylinder: an imaginary cylinder shape on a disk pack consisting of all the tracks of a given number; for example, Track 3 on all disk surfaces

daisy wheel printer: a printer that uses a print wheel containing characters on the ends of "petals"

data: facts in the form of numbers, characters, or words

DATA: the keyword used to store data on a program line

data base: the group of data necessary to carry on a business, or a group of information that may be accessed by a computer

data base management system: same as a data base system

data base system: a group of computer programs used to create and access a data base

data communications: the process of sending data from one computer system or device to another

Data Division: the division of a COBOL program that describes all the files and data structures to be used by the program

data processing: converting facts into usable form

data structure: the arrangement in which a human thinks of data

debit card: a card used in place of cash to pay for purchases; the amount of the purchases is immediately deducted from one's checking account

debug: to find and correct errors in a program

declare: to specify a variable name and tell what kind of data it is to hold

deferred execution mode: the mode in which instructions are preceded by line numbers and are carried out when the RUN command is given

detail file: a file that contains records of day-to-day transactions

detail record: any record from a detail file

digitizer: an input device used to trace shapes and transmit their numeric representation to the computer

dimension: a measurement in one direction; rows of a table are one dimension, columns are another dimension

direct access: another name for random access

direct connect: a type of modem in which conversion of electric signals between the phone line and computer is done by electronic circuitry rather than the use of sound

directory: a list of the items stored on a disk

disk drive: the most common form of auxiliary storage

disk pack: a group of disks on a spindle

DISPLAY: a COBOL command that puts information on the screen

distributed-processing network: a network having more than one processor

dot matrix: a row and column arrangement of dots used to form characters

EBCDIC: the Extended Binary Coded Decimal Interchange Code, a popular code used for representing information in a computer system

EDSAC: the first stored-program computer to be finished

EDVAC: the first stored-program computer to be designed

EEPROM: electronically erasable programmable read-only memory

element: each of the numbers stored in a vector or table

elementary item: (a) a data item that is not divided into smaller portions; (b) a variable that holds one value at a time

END: (a) the keyword that causes a program to stop executing; (b) the word used to indicate the end of a procedural part of a Pascal program

ENIAC: the first electronic computer; however, it did not use a stored program

Environment Division: the division of a COBOL program that describes the computer equipment being used

EPROM: erasable programmable read-only memory

ergonomic: a term used to describe devices that are comfortable and nontiring to use, resulting in increased productivity

field: (a) a space or group of spaces needed to record a single fact; (b) an individual item of data

file: a group of related records

file access: the method by which data is stored and retrieved on auxiliary storage

FILLER: a reserved word in COBOL that indicates space between columns of variable data

flexible disk: a magnetic disk made from pliable plastic material

floating-point number: a decimal number

floppy disk: another name for a flexible disk

flowline: a line used in a flowchart to show the flow of data

GOTO: the keyword used to send program control to a different line

graphic: a chart, drawing, or picture

group item: a group of elementary items

hard disk: a disk made from rigid material which does not bend

hardware: the physical equipment or components in a computer system

hexadecimal: a number system having a base of 16 and the digits 0-9 and A-F

hierarchy chart: a chart similar to an organization chart, showing the functions to be performed by a computer program

high-level language: a language in which instructions are expressed in English-like expressions

high-resolution graphics: a term used to describe displays that can show extremely detailed graphics

HOME: the keyword used to clear the screen on many computers

Identification Division: the division of a COBOL program that names the program, gives the name of the programmer, and gives the date the program is written

identifier: the name of a variable or procedure

if . . . then . . . else: a type of program step that takes one action if a statement is true and a different action if the statement is false

IF . . . THEN . . . ELSE: a statement used for making a decision within a Pascal program

immediate execution mode: the mode in which an instruction is carried out immediately as it is keyed in

impact printer: a printer that strikes the paper to form images

indexed file: a file in which each record is entered into one or more indexes for purposes of storage and retrieval

information processing: the job of putting data into usable form

information system: a system that processes data

information utility: a business that has huge groups of information stored in its computers and makes this information available to subscribers who pay a fee for the service

ink-jet printer: a printer that forms characters by squirting ink onto the paper

input: data that enters a system

INPUT: the keyword used to get input from the keyboard

input device: a device that receives data and feeds it to the processor

integer: a whole number

integrated circuit: any electronic "chip" that contains a large number of electronic components; microprocessors and memory, for example, use integrated circuits

interactive: a term used to describe a computer system that is set up for two-way communication between the user and the computer

interactive programming: keying a program into a computer and immediately executing the program

interface: the connection between a computer and a device

interpreter program: a program that translates a high-level language into machine code one statement at a time, then relays it to the processor, which immediately executes each statement as it is received

keyboard: a commonly used input device that sends data to the processor each time a key is struck

key field: the field used for determining the storage location of a record in a random file

keypunch machine: another name for a card-punch machine

key-to-disk machine: a data entry machine with which data is recorded on magnetic disks for later input to a computer

key-to-tape machine: a data entry machine with which data is recorded onto magnetic tape for later input to a computer

keyword: a word that the BASIC interpreter or compiler understands

laser disk: an auxiliary storage device in which characters are represented by coded holes burned in the surface of the disk by a laser beam

laser printer: a printer that uses a laser beam to "write" characters on a light-sensitive drum that then transfers the characters to paper in a manner like that used by a copying machine

LET: the keyword used to assign values to variables

light pen: an input device used to specify positions on a CRT; the pen is pressed against the screen and the computer calculates the position against which it is pressed

linked list: a table or group of tables in which each data item "points at" the next item to be processed

literal: unchanging character data

loop control: a type of program statement that makes the computer repeat certain instructions

machine language: a language in which instructions are written in the numeric code that is directly understood by the processor

magnetic disk: an auxiliary storage medium on which data is magnetically recorded on a disk covered with microscopic bars of magnetizable material

magnetic ink character recognition: an input system used by banks to read magnetic numbers printed across the bottom of checks and deposit slips

magnetic scanner: an input device that reads magnetically encoded data from a short strip of magnetic tape such as used on the back of credit cards

magnetic tape: a long strip of flexible plastic that is coated with microscopic bars of a magnetizable material

mainframe: a large-sized computer

main module: the top box of a modular program

main storage: another name for memory

Mark I: the first programmable calculator

master file: a file that contains relatively permanent records

master record: any record from a master file

matrix: row and column arrangement; another name for a table

media: the materials upon which data is recorded prior to being sent to the computer

medium: the singular form of media

megabyte: one million bytes

megahertz: a million cycles per second

memory: storage locations that are directly addressable by the processor

memory mapped: a method in which a video display serves as a "window" into the computer's memory

menu: a list of operations from which the user may choose

merging: combining data and text into a document

microcomputer: a computer that uses a processor whose circuits are all on one integrated circuit chip

microfiche: small rectangular sheets of microfilm

microprocessor: a processor whose processing circuits are all contained on one piece known as an integrated circuit

minicomputer: a computer that is smaller and less powerful than a mainframe

modem: a device (MOdulator/DEModulator) used to connect computer equipment to telephone lines

module: a small part of a computer program

monochrome: only one color

mouse: a pointing device that is moved across a surface; as it is moved, a pointer on the video display moves in the same direction

multiprocessing: handling more than one person working on the same job at the same time

multiprogramming: handling more than one job at the same time

Napier's bones: a calculating device invented by John Napier in the 1600s; it consisted of rods or strips of bones

natural language: a programming method in which ordinary English may be used to instruct the computer; available only to a very limited extent

network: a collection of processors and terminals that serves more than one user at a time by communicating

network data base: a data base in which pointers are used to make connections between data stored in different files

nibble: four bits, or half of a byte

nonimpact printer: a printer that forms characters without actually striking the paper

nonvolatile memory: memory that does not lose its data when the power is turned off

numeric address: the numeric label or name applied to a location in memory

numeric data: numbers that can be used for arithmetic computations

numeric variable: a variable that stores numbers

object computer: the computer that will be used for running the machine-language code

object program: the machine-language program or intermediate-language program produced by the compiler

on-line: connected directly to the computer

operating system: a series of programs that controls the operation of the computer system

optical-character reader: an input device that recognizes written letters, numbers, and symbols

optical-mark reader: an input device that can sense the presence or absence of marks made in specified locations on input media

optical scanner: a scanner that sends data to the processor as it "looks at" data in printed or written form

original data: raw data

output: useful information that leaves a system

parallel: a term used to describe an interface in which the bits used to represent a character are all sent at the same time (side by side)

parameter: an indication of whether a Pascal program uses input, output, or both

parity bit: a bit added to a character code to allow parity checking

parity check: a procedure used to help ensure the accurate transmission of character codes from one device to another

Pascal: a high-level language especially well suited for structured programming

pixel: an individual point of color

planes: two-dimensional tables that appear to be stacked together

plotter: an output device that uses pens to draw on paper

PRINT: the keyword that causes output to be displayed on the screen or printer

printer: an output device that produces written characters on paper

printhead: the part of a printer that actually does the printing

print zone: an area of the screen into which each print line is divided

procedure: something that Pascal is able to perform

Procedure Division: the division of a COBOL program that contains the actual processing instructions to be carried out by the computer

processing: the steps that are set up to make sure everything that should be done to data is done

processor: the computer system unit that receives and carries out the instructions contained in a program

PROGRAM: the Pascal word used to specify what the program is about to be named

program design: the steps to be performed by a computer program, written in English instead of a particular computer language

PROGRAM-ID: a reserved word that identifies the title of a COBOL program

programmer-supplied words: any nonreserved word used in a program

programs: individual sets of instructions

PROM: programmable read-only memory

prompt: a message to the computer user indicating what kind of data should be entered

pseudocode: same as program design

punched card: a card in which data can be represented by punching holes

pure binary: the method in which a number is stored directly in binary, rather than coding it first in some other manner

query language: a very high-level language that allows the user to ask questions of the computer

queue: a waiting line

RAM: random-access memory

random access: a method of accessing a storage device in which data can be written and read in any order desired

random file: a file in which the records may be stored and retrieved in any desired order

raw data: data to be processed

READ: the keyword used to read data from a DATA line and assign it to variables

READLN: the procedure used to accept input from the keyboard and assign the data into previously declared variables

real number: a decimal number, also known as a floating-point number

real-time controller: a device that converts computer output to some kind of action that controls a process

real-time sensor: any input device that constantly monitors a process or event and transmits its findings to the processor without the need of human assistance

real-time system: a system in which data is processed as it is created

record: related data treated as a unit; a group of related fields

recording: the process of writing, rewriting, or reproducing data

redundant data: the same data existing in more than one file

relational data base: a data base system that stores data in the form of related tables of data

relational operator: a symbol used to indicate the relationship of one data item to another

relations: tables containing related data

relative file: a random file in which each record is stored and retrieved by referring to its record number

REM: remark; the keyword used for entering comments in a program

report spacing chart: a row and column arrangement showing what the output of a particular computer program should look like

report writer: a very high-level language that allows the user (without writing a program) to instruct the computer to produce various reports

reserved word: a word that has a specific meaning to a COBOL compiler

retrieving: making stored information available for use

revision: making changes in text, such as correcting misspellings, adding or deleting words or characters, or rearranging the text

ring network: a network without a central computer

ROM: read-only memory

RUN: the keyword that causes the statements in a program to be executed

scalar: a variable that holds one value at a time; a point on a scale

scanner: (a) a device that "reads" the Universal Product Code; (b) a device that "reads" data in printed or written form

sector: a segment of a disk

sensor: a device that can detect changes in such things as temperature, movement, or pressure

sequential access: a method of accessing a storage device in which data must be read from the medium in a one-after-the-other sequence

sequential file: a file in which the records are stored and retrieved one after the other

sequential instructions: steps that are performed one after another

serial: a term used to describe an interface in which the bits used to represent a character are sent one after the other

slide rule: a computing tool consisting of an outer rule and a central sliding rule

software: instructions the computer uses to process data

soraban: a Japanese version of the abacus

sorter: a machine used to sort punched cards into the desired order

sorting: arranging information according to a logical system

source computer: the computer that is used for translating a program

source documents: forms on which raw data may be written

source program: a program in the form written by a programmer before it is entered into the computer

SPACES: a reserved word in COBOL meaning blank space

speech recognition device: an input device that recognizes human speech, allowing voice command or voice response

speech synthesizer: an output device that imitates the human voice

spelling checker: a program that looks up words of a document in a dictionary

spindle: a vertical shaft in a hard disk drive upon which several hard disks are stacked

spreadsheet: a program that uses a row and column arrangement of data to make calculations

star network: a network in which the different terminals are attached to the central processor as if they were the points of a star

storing: saving data or text for future use

string variable: same as a character variable

structured design: the planning of a structured program

structured programming: programming according to a proven set of standards for planning and writing a program that is more error free

structured walkthrough: the process of several persons reviewing the steps to be taken by a program; the process can catch many errors before the program is coded

subscript: a number in parentheses that tells which element of a vector or table you are working with

summarizing: presenting data in concise, meaningful form

supercomputer: an incredibly fast and powerful computer

system: a group of devices and procedures for performing a task

system flowchart: a graphic representation that shows the input, processing, and output of a system

systems analyst: a person who designs company procedures for using computers

systems software: programs designed to keep the computer functioning and programs to perform many everyday tasks related to the operation of the computer system

table: a row and column arrangement of data

tabulator: a machine used to tally data from punched cards and print reports

terminal: a keyboard and screen used to access a computer

terminator: a fake item of data used to indicate the end of data items

text: one character after another stored in the computer's memory

text entry: the process of getting words from the mind of the writer into the computer system

three-dimensional: a term used to describe an object having depth as well as length and width

time-sharing system: a network in which several input devices (usually terminals) are attached to one processor

top-down design: a method of program planning whereby you define what the program is to do, then gradually place more and more detail into the plan

track: a path on which data is recorded, usually on a magnetic medium

two-dimensional: a term used to describe an object having length and width

UNIVAC I: the first commercially available computer

Universal Product Code: a series of bars of varying widths that is used to identify an item; it is especially popular for use by grocery stores

user-interface shell: a program that makes the use of the operating system commands easier

utility program: a program designed to do a routine job, such as copying data from one disk to another

VAR: a Pascal term for variable

variable: a named storage location in the computer's memory

vector: a row or line of data

video display: an output unit that uses a display such as a cathode-ray tube to display information

video display terminal: an input/output device consisting of a keyboard and a display (usually a CRT); used for interaction with computers

VLSI: very large scale integration (refers to the number of electronic components on an integrated circuit chip)

volatile memory: memory that loses its data when the power is turned off

word processing: the composition, revision, printing, and storage of text

working storage: variables that are not associated with a file

WRITE: the procedure used to display output without sending the cursor to the next line upon completion of the display

WRITELN: the Pascal procedure used to display a line of output

writing-style checker: a program that checks a document for such things as overused words or grammatical errors

Index